SO-AYQ-886

The Quotable Actor

1001 Pearls of Wisdom from Actors Talking About Acting

Damon DiMarco

SANTA
MONICA
PRESS

Copyright ©2009 by Damon DiMarco

All rights reserved.

This book may not be reproduced in whole or in part or in any form or format without the written permission of the publisher.

Published by:

Santa Monica Press LLC
P.O. Box 1076
Santa Monica, CA 90406-1076
1-800-784-9553
www.santamonicapress.com
books@santamonicapress.com

Printed in the United States

Santa Monica Press books are available at special quantity discounts when purchased in bulk by corporations, organizations, or groups. Please call our Special Sales department at 1-800-784-9553.

ISBN-13 978-1-59580-044-2

Library of Congress Cataloging-in-Publication Data

The quotable actor : 1001 pearls of wisdom from actors talking about acting / [compiled] by Damon DiMarco.
    p. cm.
Includes bibliographical references.
ISBN 978-1-59580-044-2
1. Acting—Quotations, maxims, etc. 2. Actors—Quotations. I. DiMarco, Damon.
PN6084.A25Q68 2009
792.02'8—dc22
                    2009002319

Cover and interior design and production by Future Studio

In memory of Joe Patenaude,

for Bill Esper,

and for actors.

"We're actors.
Actors speak a certain language to each other."

AL PACINO

Contents

Introduction

My first acting teacher was a font of knowledge.

One time, he wasn't satisfied with a scene my partner and I were working on. We ran the scene the way we'd rehearsed it, but my teacher kept stopping us. Each time he did, he dropped a pearl of wisdom.

"There," he'd say. "Right there. What are you doing in that moment?"

We had to admit that we didn't really know.

"Aha," my teacher said. "If you don't know what you're doing, your audience won't, either. Make a choice and try it again."

We'd start the scene all over again, but our teacher would stop us, this time at a different moment. "There," he'd say. "That moment right there. What are you doing? It isn't clear."

I told him I was trying to communicate an idea, but he shook his head.

"*How* are you trying to communicate your idea? Are you beating her over the head with it? Are you painting her a beautiful picture? Are you guilting her into seeing your point of view? General actions lead to general performances. Be specific. Always be specific."

At one point, I asked my teacher, "What do you do when you're working on a scene and everything's going great, but a moment comes up like it just did here, and you realize you don't know what to do?"

My teacher shrugged and said, "Sometimes, not having the answer is the answer. When in doubt? Discover."

At the end of that rehearsal, I picked up my notebook and wrote these three pearls down in big block letters.

IF YOU DON'T KNOW WHAT YOU'RE DOING, NEITHER WILL YOUR AUDIENCE.

ALWAYS BE SPECIFIC.

WHEN IN DOUBT: DISCOVER.

Later, I went back to my room and wrote those pearls on my wall, also in big block letters. That way I could read them often and reflect on them. More were soon to follow.

My first acting teacher made me a junkie for good quotes. The wise ones. The funny ones. The ones that summarized a lifetime's worth of experience in a few simple words.

They say a picture's worth a thousand words, but don't rule out the value of a good quote.

Quotes are windows to someone else's experience. Here and there, they've saved me months of grappling with issues I faced in my work.

I hope this book will do the same for you, my fellow actor. All the people quoted within probably love acting as much as you do. They're worth listening to. My thanks and respect to them for dropping their pearls of wisdom, and to you for picking them up.

DAMON DIMARCO

On What Acting Is

"The best definition . . . that I have ever heard about acting was given by George Burns. . . . [He said:] 'I'll tell you what's the most important thing about acting, and that's honesty. If you can fake that, you've got it made.'" **JACK LEMMON**

★   ★   ★

"Acting is living truthfully under imaginary circumstances."
SANFORD MEISNER

★   ★   ★

"Acting is a form of confession."
TALLULAH BANKHEAD

★   ★   ★

"Acting is all about listening. . . . I think I listen a lot better as an actor than I do in real life." SAM ROCKWELL

★   ★   ★

"Of all arts, I think acting must be the least concrete, the most solitary. One gains experience continually, both at rehearsals and in performance, from the presence of a large assembly of people. These people are essential to the development of one's performance—they are the living canvas upon which one hopes to paint the finished portrait which one has envisaged." SIR JOHN GIELGUD

★   ★   ★

"I saw a famous actress on *60 Minutes.* 'Cry,' they told her. And she did. Big tears rolled down her cheeks. I will never believe her sincerity again. . . . That has nothing to do with acting." LIV ULLMANN

★   ★   ★

"Acting is something that most people think they're incapable of but they do it from morning to night." MARLON BRANDO

★   ★   ★

"Acting is horrible, painful, and yet also intoxicating and emotionally liberating." JODIE FOSTER

★   ★   ★

"Acting is an intimate thing. You entrust your partner with something very private, a tremendous bond develops and that intimacy is like love." KEVIN KLINE

"Acting provides the fulfillment of never being fulfilled. You're never as good as you'd like to be. So there's always something to hope for."   **GLENDA JACKSON**

★　★　★

"Acting is simply my way of investigating human nature and having fun at the same time."   **MERYL STREEP**

★　★　★

"[Acting is] the ability to dream on cue."
SIR RALPH RICHARDSON

★　★　★

"Acting is just a matter of farting about in disguises."
PETER O'TOOLE

★　★　★

"I was a show-off. That's all acting is—showing off."
MORGAN FREEMAN

★　★　★

"[Acting is] a sad business where you crawl from hope to hope."   **WALTER SLEZAK**

★　★　★

"Acting is a form of confusion."
TALLULAH BANKHEAD

★　★　★

"Acting is the most minor of gifts and not a very high-class way to earn a living. After all, Shirley Temple could do it at the age of four."
                                                    KATHARINE HEPBURN

★   ★   ★

"Acting is a leap of faith. There has to be that moment where you go, *I give myself to . . . the spirit.*"
                                                    CHRISTOPHER WALKEN

★   ★   ★

"Thrust into my profession without any training whatsoever, I had to just flounder and just find my way. It was an agonizing experience. It's like jumping off a diving board in the Olympic contest without knowing how to swim or dive, and I just had to find my way. So one day, I said to Jimmy Cagney, 'Jimmy, what is acting?' and he said, 'I don't know.' He said, 'All I can tell you is whatever you say, mean it,' and I thought that marvelous counsel. It is key. Wonderful."
                                                    OLIVIA DE HAVILLAND

★   ★   ★

"Acting . . . is the ability to react to imaginary stimuli; and its essential elements remain the twin requisites . . . 'unusual sensitivity and extraordinary intelligence,' this latter not in the form of book learning but in the ability to comprehend the workings of the human soul. The essential problems in acting—does the actor 'feel' or does he merely imitate? Should he speak naturally or rhetorically? What is natural? etc.—are as old as acting itself. They derive not from the realistic movement but from the nature of the acting process."
                                                    LEE STRASBERG

INTERVIEWER: What's the secret to great acting?
ROBERT DE NIRO: There's no secret. Show up.
INTERVIEWER: Surely there's more to it than that.
ROBERT DE NIRO: Never indicate. People don't try to show
                 their feelings, they try to hide them.

★　★　★

"In a well-written script, what people say to each other—
the dialogue—is what a character's willing to reveal, willing
to share with *another* person. The 90 percent he or she isn't
willing to share is what I do for a living."   MARTIN LANDAU

★　★　★

"The pleasure comes from watching the performer who,
with a single movement of his head, explains everything."
                                              LIV ULLMANN

★　★　★

"Acting is a great panacea. I can turn the world to right, all
the sad and distressing things that happen in real life can be
transformed into something soothing and great."
                                          SIR DEREK JACOBI

★　★　★

"Like all actors, I really just reveal my shadow every time I
work. And the shadow is all the pain, shame, anger and rage,
the creativity and sexuality."   JOHN CUSACK

★　★　★

"Acting is a childlike thing. To act well you have to be childlike in order to free yourself. Because they're still young and being formed [children] don't have judgments about looking silly or feeling stupid."   **LAURENCE FISHBURNE**

★   ★   ★

"Acting is so pure. It's not necessarily all the mundane moments that we have in real life. It's like condensed drama. It's all the exciting moments in two hours. Your senses have to be heightened."   **SAM ROCKWELL**

★   ★   ★

"Acting isn't nice. . . . It's giving but it's also stealing."
ANNA DEAVERE SMITH

★   ★   ★

"There is something peculiar about the [dramatic] process. . . . It probably began when men first left their caves to hunt, and the women, children, and old men left behind danced and acted out stories to counteract their boredom."

MARLON BRANDO

★   ★   ★

"[Acting is] researching everything and then putting it all aside and imagining a person's life from the inside out. There's a part of me that likes little Mary Smith with her little hat, little winter overcoat, not particularly attractive, who feeds her cats at night, reaching into her box of tricks and playing Cleopatra, the greatest temptress of them all, brilliantly and convincingly. When you act, you bring out something that may not be apparent."   **RALPH FIENNES**

"I'm not prone to talk much about what I do. . . . But then I never have been. I mean, I don't think hookers rush home from work and say, 'Honey! I had the most incredible hand-job today!'" **JOHN MALKOVICH**

On What Actors Are

"The actor is Camus' ideal existential hero, because if life is absurd and the idea is to live a more vital life, the man who lives more lives is in a better position than the guy who lives just one."

JACK NICHOLSON

★   ★   ★

"There are three kinds of actors. There's the actor who acts for himself, there's the actor who acts for the audience, and the actor who acts for the other actors. The actor who acts for the other actors is the only one who's an actor. . . . The one who acts for the audience is at least doing it for someone, and the one who's doing it for himself is not an actor."

attributed to **MICHAEL CHEKHOV**

★   ★   ★

"Actors are people who were good at playing 'Let's Pretend' as kids and now we're getting money to play house."

MICHAEL J. FOX

★   ★   ★

"Artists are the only true aristocrats."

ROD STEIGER

★   ★   ★

"Actors are cattle."

SIR ALFRED HITCHCOCK

★   ★   ★

"[Actors are] rogues, vagabonds, and sturdy beggars."

ACT OF PARLIAMENT, 1597

★   ★   ★

"An actor is a guy who, if you ain't talking about him, he ain't listening."   **MARLON BRANDO**

★   ★   ★

"They say that all great actors are crazy. Life has driven them mad, but that madness gives them a well of opportunity to draw experiences from 'til they can relate to what seems obscure and far away and out of reach."

TERRENCE HOWARD

★   ★   ★

"There's one thing that exceeds all others: the eyes of the

actor. If he sees, he sees specifically. He doesn't generalize.
. . . He must learn to see the difference between different
reds—The reds of a racing car, the red of a hibiscus, and the
red of blood. They're three different reds. They mean three
different things." **STELLA ADLER**

★   ★   ★

"I am not socially acceptable. People are afraid to invite me
to their homes. . . Actors are always publicized as having a
beautiful courtesy. I haven't. I'm the most impolite person
in the world. . . . I never think to light a lady's cigarette.
Sometimes I rise when a lady leaves the room. . . . I don't
see why I should conform to Mrs. Emily Post, not because
I'm an actor and believe that being an actor gives me special
dispensations to be different, but because I'm a human being
with a pattern of my own and the right to work out my
pattern in my own way." **HUMPHREY BOGART**

★   ★   ★

"Theoretically, the actor ought to be more sound in mind and
body than other people, since he learns to understand the
psychological problems of human beings when putting his
passions, his loves, fears, and rages to work in the service
of the character he plays. He will learn to face himself, to
hide nothing from himself—and to do so takes an insatiable
curiosity about the human condition." **UTA HAGEN**

★   ★   ★

"My father used to say, 'You blankety-blank actors, it's nothing
but a mutual admiration society.' . . . I said: 'It better be. It's
like the Army—you get out there, they take a shot at you.'"
RIP TORN

"As Julia Roberts said, 'We're ordinary people with
extraordinary jobs.'"   DENZEL WASHINGTON

★   ★   ★

"Some basic truths about us, some fundamentals: married,
single, divorced, rich, broke, breaking in or holding on,
the morning after Oscar, Tony or Emmy, or struggling
along without recognition; whether we are newcomers,
superstars, an enduring light, a flash in the pan, a has-been
or a comeback king, from low self-esteem to insufferable
arrogance—we are the seesaw kids. Kids who hold on
tight and wait, wait for the call, the audition, the part, the
review—and then we do it again. Those are the ground rules.
You accept them if you are an actor."   FRANK LANGELLA

★   ★   ★

"The actor is an athlete of the heart."
ANTONIN ARTAUD

★   ★   ★

"[Actors are] as true as that which the sculptor perceives in
Michelangelo, the painter in Raphael, and the musician in
Beethoven; all of these artists having sight and sound to
guide them. I, as an actor, know that could I sit in front of
the stage and see myself at work I would condemn much
that has been lauded; and could correct many faults which
I feel are mine, and which escape the critic's notice. But
I cannot see or hear my mistakes as can the sculptor, the
painter, the writer, and the musician. Tradition, if it be traced
through pure channels, and to the fountain head, leads on as
near to Nature as can be followed by her servant Art."
EDWIN BOOTH

"Actors are always saying that instead of going to therapy, we shoot movies—[*laughs*]—and end up understanding many more things about ourselves."   **MONICA BELLUCCI**

★   ★   ★

"Like the aristocrat, the actor lives in ideas. Ideas are what playwrights write about. If you speak ideas, they enter into you. They become yours. Accumulating ideas is what gives you power."   **STELLA ADLER**

★   ★   ★

"For is not the artist, the actor in the truest sense, a being who is endowed with the ability to see and experience things which are obscure to the average person? And is not his real mission, his joyous instinct, to convey to the spectator, as a kind of revelation, *his* very own impressions of things as he sees and feels them?"   **MICHAEL CHEKHOV**

★   ★   ★

"Someone asked me why I said that Spencer Tracy was like a baked potato. I think it is because I think that he was very basic as an actor. He was there skins and all—in his performances. He was cooked and ready to eat."

KATHARINE HEPBURN

★   ★   ★

"Many people think that actors are airheads and that once they finish spouting lines written by someone else, they have nothing original to say. I've found that all good actors are intelligent and multifaceted. I'm amazed at all the different talents displayed by entertainers."   **KIRK DOUGLAS**

"Actors are the best people in the movie business. They're the ones willing to put the most on the line. I feel this more when I'm directing. It's the toughest job in the business. You have to create a world inside your own experience and hold onto it while they're putting up lights and fluffing pillows and all that stuff. I think there's a real generous spirit at the heart of that."

SEAN PENN

★   ★   ★

"I believe that an actor must be interested in one thing—the part. If the part excites me, I'll play it anywhere—in films, television, radio, or on the stage—because I'm an actor. That's my job."

ROD STEIGER

★   ★   ★

"The actor is merely a crude empiricist, a practitioner guided by vague instinct."

ANTONIN ARTAUD

★   ★   ★

"Actors are migrant workers; we go where the work is."

KARL MALDEN

On Actors and Society

"Ronald Reagan once said he couldn't imagine being
president without having been an actor." **CHARLES GRODIN**

★   ★   ★

OSSIE DAVIS: "When Ruby and I came into the professional
theater in 1946 and 1947, World War II was
just over and America was saying, 'We're
going to do something about racism and
get rid of it, because look at that Hitler
over there.' But Black soldiers were coming
back and getting killed in Macon, Georgia,
and four more down in Monroe, Georgia.
Another Black soldier, Isaac Woodard, was
coming through the South on a bus when he
was dragged off and his eyes were gouged out.
Two more out on Long Island were killed.

And the theater was responding. Every night somebody would have a party to raise money for somebody about to be lynched. We raised money for Rosalie Ingram, whose two sons came to her defense after she was attacked by a White man on a farm down in Florida. The state was going to execute all three of them. We in the theater had a sense of purpose. It wasn't about money. It wasn't about your name on the marquee."

RUBY DEE: "It was how, as artists, we could respond."

★   ★   ★

When pressed to consider the social implications of violent movies he's made, such as the Dirty Harry *movies:*

"I consider the social implications. But you mention violence as a means of resolving conflict. Well, conflict is the basis of drama. I guess that goes back as long as time has existed as far as mankind is concerned, dating back to the Greek tragedies or the Old Testament. And violence is a form of conflict, so whether that's catharsis or whether that has some socially damaging effect on audiences—I suppose that would just depend. I tend to believe that audiences are relatively well-balanced people. You're making the film for the average person. You are not making it for the one guy out there who is going to take it seriously and go, 'Yeah, gee, that's crazy, I might jump off a building or what have you.'"

CLINT EASTWOOD

★   ★   ★

On being a political activist:

"There's baggage attached to coming out publicly on stuff, but there's baggage—in my view, more damaging baggage—to goin' and jerkin' off on Jay Leno's show, philosophizing about *Uncle Buck* or whatever you're hawkin'."   **SEAN PENN**

★   ★   ★

"My agent called and said excitedly . . . she had lined up a cigarette commercial that would pay me exactly fifty thousand dollars.

"'No. Thanks,' I said. 'I'm not interested.'

"She was shocked. Why would I turn down fifty thousand dollars?

"'Well,' I said, 'because I don't want to take money so people can get cancer.'

"She thought that was a strange line of reasoning. . . . This was a time when cigarettes were advertised on television and the surgeon general's warning was not yet on the package. If you wanted, you could tell yourself you were simply in step with everyone else. But in reality, we all knew cigarettes were killers. I said no again and hung up."

ALAN ALDA

★   ★   ★

"Change . . . is very hard to effect. In America particularly, change only comes out of money. People don't wake up and say, 'Our country embraces so many cultures!' Instead, it's corporations who go 'Hey, look at that market out there!' . . . But that's OK. . . . You just take that and you use it. It's a ripe time to implement change. And I'm in there trying; that's all I can say."   **JIMMY SMITS**

When asked if he'd ever watched a horrible bit of news on TV and gone back to eating his dinner as if nothing had happened:

"I'm an artist so I'm already predisposed to be kind of
   sensitized to stuff like that for my own selfish reasons
   of wanting to feel it and wanting to understand it and
   wanting to know about it, and become more interested in
   it. I understand somebody who works eight hours a day
   in a job that they may or may not like and just trying to
   put food on the table and going A) [the situation is] way
   over there, B) it's too overwhelming for me to know what
   to do with, and C) what can I do anyway? So I understand
   that sort of apathy that can happen. But I do think it's what
   allows things like that to continue to happen."

DON CHEADLE

★   ★   ★

"I hate, hate, hate it when famous people say they're not
   political, because everyone is political. What they're really
   saying is that they're stupid."   **ALAN CUMMING**

★   ★   ★

"I'm sick to *death* of celebrity spokesmen for causes. Critical
   issues are being decided on the basis of who you like the
   best. It's who has the prettiest team? Vote for your favorite
   star. It's complete bull. Drives me nuts."   **HARRISON FORD**

★   ★   ★

"Remember when Jonathan Pryce was almost barred from
   doing *Miss Saigon* in New York, when Equity said they
   had to use a Eurasian actor instead? I called up the head of
   our union and said, 'Listen, do what you want. But unless
   you rethink that decision, I'll happily withdraw from the

union.' . . . There's always valid social and racial and regional stuff to consider. But I'm rather sick of the so-called black experience, the so-called Asian experience, the so-called Indian experience. To me, acting is an act of imagination. I'd venture to say, in all humility, that I could play Malcolm X as well as anyone else. . . . People will say, 'What makes you think you could do that?' And the answer is: nothing. Probably, I would have more in common playing a big, fat, retarded guy. But, you know—so what?"

JOHN MALKOVICH

★   ★   ★

"As an actor you have to be willing to play good and evil. Evil does exist and you have to be able to show it. . . . I don't believe people are born evil. I believe evil takes over a person's soul because there are events in childhood or circumstances in life that can rob people of their dignity, rob people of hope, and turn them onto the wrong things in life."

DENZEL WASHINGTON

★   ★   ★

"I'm committed to the idea—and I always have been—that the audience doesn't always know when they're being lied to. And the lies do have damage that they leave behind. But there's always hope that they know when they're being told the truth."   SEAN PENN

★   ★   ★

"If I wanted to contribute in some tiny way to make the world better for my children and their children, I knew that I had to work."   VANESSA REDGRAVE

"I wanted to go into politics and work as a civil servant. . . .
When I went off to college, I felt the world was in such a
bad way that everyone should devote themselves to ending
the arms race and preventing nuclear war and solving the
problems of global poverty. . . . I have come to a somewhat
more complex analysis . . . in that I no longer think that
it's enough for a few well-meaning Harvard graduates
to sit in offices and carry out some bureaucratic tasks
conscientiously. I realize that the problems of the world are
caused largely by things that are inside people's heads, and
it's entirely possible that by altering people's consciousness
a writer or a musician might do something that would
improve the world situation. . . . So I've come to believe . . .
that artistic works may have their place in saving the world."

WALLACE SHAWN

★   ★   ★

On his choice to involve himself in so many projects like The
Tuskegee Airmen *and* Miss Evers' Boys, *which highlight little-
known aspects of African-American history:*

"It's not as if I'd laid out a master plan to do [such films]. . . .
It's just that there's this—and I hate to use 'role model' in
relation to this—but there is a responsibility that comes
with my success. And for me it's always been important to
represent my culture in positive ways. So when I have the
opportunity to do these things, I do them."

LAURENCE FISHBURNE

★   ★   ★

"I think there are a number of individuals in Hollywood who
are trying to make things happen in their own ways. And I

do think that film is an incredibly powerful medium, when it comes to moving people. You can probably change more hearts and minds with one good film than with thousands of e-mail pamphlets or whatever. So I'm very conscious of the power of this thing—not that you have to be pushing an agenda. . . . I remember driving around one day in Chicago, I don't remember how old I was at the time, when Scorsese's *Last Temptation of Christ* had just opened at the Biograph Theater. And I saw all these protesters out on the streets, and the debate over the movie was all over the papers, all these people wrestling with the issues raised by the movie. And I remember just being in awe of what Scorsese did. I loved the film, I thought it was one of his best. But I was also invigorated by the debate and the controversy."

JOHN CUSACK

★   ★   ★

"There are these Uriah Heep-type people who are always knocking actors for being political. Why don't they criticize people who aren't political? I've always been political. I was political before I was famous. I'll probably be political after I'm famous. 'Political' only means that you are interested in being a good citizen." **RICHARD DREYFUSS**

★   ★   ★

"[There're] quotas [in Hollywood]. There continues to be a problem of underrepresentation and lingering racism. I hear weird stuff, and I don't know whose fault it is. One studio head said, 'Latin people don't want to see Latin people on screen; they want to see white people. And white people don't want to see Latin people either.' I've also heard comments like, 'This isn't a Latin movie; there isn't enough dancing.' It's absurd, but there is the idea that [Latinos] have to dance. . . . I like to dance, and it is part of our culture, but it's not a necessity in every story we tell. So there's still work to be done."   **JOHN LEGUIZAMO**

On Why We Act

"Everybody says, 'You impress me as a guy who never wanted to be a movie star.' I say, 'Everybody in the world wants to be a movie star.'"   **RIP TORN**

★　★　★

"At 18, I was a movie usher . . . for six months. The first film was Al Pacino's *Dog Day Afternoon*. I tried to watch it through as much as I could. I constantly caught bits of it. I watched it uninterruptedly over 40 times. But my memory is so bad that I never memorized the dialogue. Now, whenever it comes on TV, I look to catch it because that film is what got me into acting."   **STEVE BUSCEMI**

★　★　★

"An acting teacher told me when I was about 16—he said,
'Why do you want to be an actor?' I said, 'I'm not sure.'
He said, 'To express yourself.' So I said, 'Well, that's good . . .
that's an apt response.'"   **ROBERT DE NIRO**

★ ★ ★

"I want to come out of the theater feeling that someone
has touched me. The whole point is to have a revelatory
experience, to be carried to the heights."   **KATHY BATES**

★ ★ ★

"Loving the theatre is not enough. Who does not love it? To
consecrate oneself to the theatre, to devote one's entire life
to it, give it all one's thought, all one's emotions! For the sake
of the theatre to give up everything, to suffer everything!
And more important than all, to be ready to give the theatre
everything—your entire being expecting the theatre to give
you nothing in return, not the least grain of what seemed to
you so beautiful and so alluring."   **RICHARD BOLESLAVSKY**

★ ★ ★

"Acting was the first thing [for me] that made the work and
the commitment effortless."   **MICHELLE PFEIFFER**

★ ★ ★

"Every time a new script is opened there is a feeling of
excitement that the outcome of the reading could possibly
be momentous, with life gallivanting off in a totally
unpredictable direction."   **MICHAEL YORK**

★ ★ ★

"When you're a little kid and play in the sandbox, or pretend
to be someone else, you're doing it for the fun and not
for any ulterior motive. That's why people get into show
business, to continue having fun. I always told our cast that
we were there to have fun, then to entertain the 300 people
in the live audience, and transport it out to the audience at
home. It was about the f-word: fun."   **CAROL BURNETT**

★   ★   ★

"I would arrive early in the morning, feeling at home in
this half-darkness; the dusty air, the cramped dressing
rooms, the stage with its worn slanted boards—the place
in the world where I most wanted to be. Rehearsals and
discussions without anyone watching the clock. The buzz in
the auditorium before the curtain went up. The arc lights.
The excitement. The audience. The tension. The part that
was to live its own life. Weep with a role. Laughter and
yearning and fury borrowed from an imaginary person.
Emotions I had scarcely known. The eyes and expressions
and movements of my colleagues. Sometimes we were so
close it seemed unreal there existed other relationships
outside the theatre. Surely no love, no hatred could be
stronger than the passions that quivered on the stage
between eight and half-past ten each evening.

"For most, this complete absorption by one's
profession belongs only to the first years.

"But some very few never find their way back to life
outside the stage. They grow old, and they take your hand,
and they recite a speech they spoke in 1930. Hamlet or King
Lear sits in front of you and you feel slightly embarrassed
because you are afraid some thoughtless remark might wake
somebody from a lovely dream which has lasted a whole
professional life.

"And even longer."   **LIV ULLMANN**

"When I was starting out, we were led to believe quite clearly that our futures, if we were lucky enough to work, were going to be in the theater. And if we did OK at that, if we were really lucky, we might get to do the classic roles. And that was the rite of passage. That was like the fiery hoop through which you had to leap if you were going to be taken seriously. But I had a guilty secret. Because I'd seen *A Place in the Sun*. I'd seen *From Here to Eternity. On the Waterfront. Streetcar . . . Night of the Hunter.* And I'd seen *French Connection, Mean Streets, Taxi Driver, Raging Bull, The Godfather.* And my secret hope, my great hope, which—and at that time, from where I came from, there weren't many actors getting a chance to do this—but I wanted, if possible, to make a contribution to this tradition. And I'm so grateful that I've been allowed the chance to do that."

DANIEL DAY-LEWIS

★   ★   ★

"I found that acting was like a virus, growing stronger and consuming me. My true calling came out. And it came with great force."   ANDY GARCIA

★   ★   ★

"We play other people, basically because we loathe ourselves, right?"   RICHARD GERE

★   ★   ★

"All of us seem to be playing roles in real-life dramas that we are not only starring in but have been scripting, too. We are each the author and the leading player in the entertainment called, 'my life.'"   SHIRLEY MacLAINE

"When I went to pick up my first check as an actor in a film, I was afraid that the studio would see the truth, which was that I was so happy to be acting that if I'd had the money and they'd asked me, I would have paid them for the privilege."

SIDNEY POITIER

★   ★   ★

"[For my first audition] I didn't get the role, but suddenly I knew that what was going on in that room was where I wanted to be. I began to go to acting classes four or five nights a week. I just couldn't get enough."   **KEVIN COSTNER**

★   ★   ★

"I like the challenge of conveying an emotion or idea that isn't right there in the dialogue. I like to be able to say, 'I think I'll have a drink,' and let the audience know that what I mean is, 'I love you.'"   **MEL GIBSON**

★   ★   ★

"All of us have two barrels inside us. The first barrel is the one that contains all of the juices which are exuded by our troubles. That's the neurotic barrel. But right next to it stands the second barrel, and by a process of seepage like osmosis, some of the troubles in the first barrel get into the second, and by a miracle that nobody fully understands, those juices have been transformed into the ability to paint, to compose, to write, to play music and the ability to act. So essentially our talent is made up out of our transformed troubles."

SANFORD MEISNER

★   ★   ★

"The great gift of human beings is that we have empathy. We can all cry for each other and sense a mysterious connection to each other. If there's hope for the future of us all, it lies in that. And it happens that actors can evoke that event between hearts. They can make us feel enhanced. In the audience, I can be drawn out of myself into someone else's life and yet suddenly I myself feel more alive! I'm pulled out of what I do every day into something larger and more lasting, into humanity. That's what an actor can do."

MERYL STREEP

★ ★ ★

"All of the great stories in literature deal with loneliness. Sometimes it's by way of heartbreak, sometimes it's by way of injustice, sometimes it's by way of fate. There's an infinite number of ways to examine it. And if there's a reason it always seems to be there with me, it's because it's so palpable to all of us. You can turn everything into an aspect of that battle against quiet despair, because we all fight it at some point in order to feel we're part of humanity. And sure, the work gives me a chance to re-examine that from the places I've been as a human being. But the battles against loneliness that I fought when I was 16 are very different from those I fought when I was 27, and those are very different from the ones I fight at 44."

TOM HANKS

★ ★ ★

"Everything else in my life receded once I discovered theatre."

BETTE MIDLER

★ ★ ★

"Acting saved my life. It taught me to be in the moment, not get caught up in what happened yesterday, or what will happen tomorrow. It taught me to acknowledge my feelings and embrace them, rather than be ashamed of them and try to cover them up. Acting validated my desire to define myself. It challenged me to be honest about who I am and what I feel. It forced me to be my authentic self. Acting was the conduit for the unfolding of my spirit. Acting has allowed me to go on."   **OLYMPIA DUKAKIS**

★   ★   ★

"Theater has an inner connection with the human condition. You learn things about yourself through plays. Your character's circumstances and emotions cause you to examine what is going on inside yourself."   **NICK NOLTE**

★   ★   ★

"I'm not a performer. I don't want to hop up on a stage and go, 'Look at me! I'm Renée! What do you think?' That's not me. What I do is very different. If I want to express something, it's through the filter [of a character]. So I never feel exposed."   **RENÉE ZELLWEGER**

★   ★   ★

On how she moved 23 times and attended 9 schools across America and Europe before the age of 18 because of her father's career in the military:

"Travelling childhoods are a common theme among actors. Army kids, embassy kids, travelling salesmen, clergy. Thing is, you learn about behavior, that different places are separated by behaviors which are culturally driven. Most kids will have a different experience because they think behavior is what it is—unchanging." **JULIANNE MOORE**

★ ★ ★

"I first knew I wanted to be an actor when I was about six years old and watching the television. There were people moving around inside that thing and I thought, 'Wow, how do they do that—how do they get to be inside?' When I was eight or thereabouts I was bullied on the school bus by a boy who kept stealing my Twinkies. So I got dressed up as my bigger brother, slicked back my hair and put on his shades and boots, along with a lot of attitude and swagger, and tried to pass myself off as Nicky Coppola's brother Richard, and told him I was going to kick him right up his ass. Nobody stole my Twinkies again." **NICOLAS CAGE**

★ ★ ★

"Peter Brooks said it once: there is nothing more exciting or more barbaric or more basic than one person walking onto an empty stage." **CHRISTOPHER PLUMMER**

★ ★ ★

"I most enjoy the loss of self that can be achieved only through detailed understanding of another life."

DANIEL DAY-LEWIS

★ ★ ★

"[The childhood event that had the most impact on my world attitude] would probably be the early films my mother took me to when I was just a baby. When my mother got home from work, she would take me to the movies. It was her way of getting out, and she would take me with her. I'd go home and act all the parts. It had a tremendous influence on my becoming an actor."   **AL PACINO**

★   ★   ★

"I remember as a young man seeing *Death of a Salesman*, with Lee J. Cobb. When the play was over, nobody in the audience moved. All you could hear was a little sniffling. The silence was just overwhelming. It was a remarkable demonstration of the power of the theater. I'll never forget that. Never."   **LESLIE NIELSEN**

★   ★   ★

Describing how he once fell head over heels for a young woman headed for drama school, and this led him to be an actor:

"She could have said astronaut, and I would've given it a stab. This is how deeply pathetic I was. I didn't know what audition meant. I thought it was a grant or something."   **BILL NIGHY**

★   ★   ★

"At the age of eight or nine, I'd create scenes for myself and I'd act out all the parts—usually as people I knew."   **JESSICA LANGE**

★   ★   ★

"I gradually created someone I wanted to be and finally I became that person."   **CARY GRANT**

"I come from a tight knit, conservative Catholic family. What kind of girl would go for that? They were looking for the exotic, hot-blooded Cuban boys with skintight pants and forbidden, dark-eyed lust. I presented myself as the wrong kind of guy. I was acting, even at that age."   **ANDY GARCIA**

★   ★   ★

"People who start out as actors are actors because they're glory hounds. They're not satisfied with who they are. And you cannot turn that off. No matter how humble you act, you cannot turn that off—that you love it when that camera goes flash, flash, flash."   **TERRENCE HOWARD**

★   ★   ★

"Being an actor is a hell of thing. . . . It's up and down, it's just—it's great. But I found the best thing about it is hanging around the craft service table . . . with other actors . . . and crew people . . . eating doughnuts. And I hang around a lot there. . . . So I'd like to take this opportunity to say thanks to all the actors and the crew people who have spent time with me at the craft service table, shooting the shit, and eating doughnuts, and having a hell of a good time, because they're weird, interesting people in our business. And I'm proud to be numbered among them."

PAUL GIAMATTI,
accepting the SAG Award for Outstanding Performance by a Male Actor in a Supporting Role

★   ★   ★

"I love acting because when it's time to speak everyone else has to shut up before your cue."   **FRED WILLARD**

"I [started acting because I] had my dad hangin' out with the coolest, smartest, maverick fuckin weirdos of the twentieth century in New York. I useta [sic] fall asleep listenin' to my dad's poker games, and they were only playin' poker so that they could riff on lines and put-downs. So I heard this rhythm—it'd be quiet and then someone would hit it and they'd all fuckin' lose it, and it was like winnin' the pot wasn't about the chips. That, to me, used to be the most comforting feeling goin' to sleep at night, just hearing that. This is what men are supposed to do—this two-layered thing—and it's about wit and repartee and a lot of sarcasm."

ROBERT DOWNEY, JR.

★   ★   ★

"I had a horrible stutter when I was a kid, from the time I was 9 until the time I was about 17. And a miraculous thing happened when I was in high school. I was doing this goofy play. It wasn't a goofy play, we just did it in a goofy way. *Connecticut Yankee in King Arthur's Court.* And when I got onstage, I stopped stuttering. When I stepped off the stage, I started stuttering again. And I went, 'This is a miracle. I got to investigate this more.'"   BRUCE WILLIS

★   ★   ★

"I used to sit in the phone booth of the Optima Cigar Store on Broadway and 42nd Street looking out the window at people walking by. I saw them for perhaps two or three seconds before they disappeared. . . . In that flick of time I studied their faces, the way they carried their heads and swung their arms. I tried to absorb who they were—their history, their job, whether they were married, troubled or in love. . . . These are matters I have been interested in since

I was a child. I was determined to know, to guess and to assess quirks that people did not know about themselves."

MARLON BRANDO

★   ★   ★

"I had always felt a freedom and a sense of assuredness when I was on stage that I never felt as a human being."

KARL MALDEN

★   ★   ★

"This is what is interesting about acting—you prepare your character; you know where you're going; you know what you want to do; but then a part of your character takes over. . . . What happens to my character in [a] film has never happened to me—I've never experienced it, but I did play it. How? I don't know."

MONICA BELLUCCI

★   ★   ★

"You get a good script or a good opportunity and that's what dictates the choice of what you do. I saw early on that there's no real way to exhaust the possibilities of what you can explore. It's what I like about acting. There's no past or future about it. You don't get credit for your last performance. It doesn't necessarily help you getting your next job. You can't really exhaust the varieties of human behavior. And that's what I find the most fun about doing the job. When you study acting it's really life study."

JACK NICHOLSON

★   ★   ★

"As a child, I was neither seen nor heard. I was not taken

seriously. Everything I attempted to articulate was diminished, distorted or interrupted. It's a miracle that I got out of that: affluent, middle-class, horrible. That is why I honour that child and voice in me by saying: 'They're going to hear me, and see me, and I'm not going to be interrupted. I'll put them in a place where they can't interrupt me.'"

SIR BEN KINGSLEY

★   ★   ★

"I look for a role that hopefully I feel empathy with and that I can understand and love, but also that has that challenge for me to play—a different kind of role, a different type of character, a different time period. But in general, if I get the same kind of visceral reaction with a script like you do when you see a finished movie, that kind of thing of knowing what its possibilities are and you get excited and you think, 'Yeah, I need to do this. I want to do that.' It's a very kind of primitive visceral response that's hard to be more specific about."

KATHY BATES

★   ★   ★

"While my father had opera in his background, my mother was, and continues to be, the really dramatic, theatrical character in our family. She's way larger than life. Her kind of Irish . . . I don't know what it is—she's nuts! I think I learned comedy watching my father react to her, because you had to have a sense of humor because, well, she's formidable! We'd have nightly gatherings around the dinner table that usually ended in a harangue by my mother, in truly Wagnerian volume. She'd rail against whomever was the Republican President at the time, blaming him for this or that social injustice. An opera-singing father and a mother who could really make herself heard when she got up on her soapbox—I guess that's how I learned to project my voice onstage." **KEVIN KLINE**

★　★　★

"[Acting] was just my way. I was always playing characters and pretending I was somebody else. A painter starts painting from infancy. They rub some spit on the ground or the wall and see something in it. I was always rubbing my spirit on the people that I met by trying to entertain them." **TERRENCE HOWARD**

★　★　★

"I was going through this dark night of the soul when I was 37 [and] I thought, 'What did I ever do that thrilled me, that made me happy?' And it was acting. I thought, 'I've got to do it again.'" **JOHN MAHONEY**

★　★　★

"When I was a little kid, my older brothers took me to see my first R-rated film, which was David Lean's *Ryan's Daughter*. It was the first naked woman's breast I ever saw, and that completely changed my life." **STEVE CARELL**

★　★　★

"At school I was no longer Alfredo, the gangly, overweight son of a disappointed father and a mother whose emotional and creative horizons had dwindled to an obsession with food and daily assessments of how quickly she was aging. At school, I was Fred, and, more important, I could pretend and lie that I came from a stable family home where both parents lived in the bosom of each other's love."   **ALFRED MOLINA**

★   ★   ★

"There was something about being in front of audiences when I was in elementary school plays that gave me a thrill. It was like the rush you get from a fast downhill skiing slope or a roller coaster drop."   **MIRA SORVINO**

★   ★   ★

"I have such a fear of embarrassing myself that I will do anything not to embarrass myself. That's it.
    "That's the key to my success."
    MICHELLE PFEIFFER

★   ★   ★

When asked why some people just know that they need to be onstage:

"I'm not sure. . . . I was just attracted to it by the time I was eight years old when I did a school play and the kids liked what I did. It had nothing to do with talent but everything to do with being accepted, because the kids kept saying, 'That was terrific, tell us more funny stuff.' I had to start making things up between classes and they'd all come over and gather around my desk and I'd tell them a lot of b.s. I guess it was when I was into my teens that it suddenly stopped, and that was when I realized that I really loved acting."
    JACK LEMMON

★   ★   ★

"To completely become an artist is to expose yourself. You can't say 'Don't look at me, I'm exposing myself.' If you're going to do it, you have to do it all the way. Nobody's going to take notice unless you step out of your own way and go, 'Look at me!' It's kind of a horrible trait, but we can trace it back to childhood, when the child who is the most noticeable gets the most attention."   **DANIEL CRAIG**

★　★　★

"I was so affected by movies as a kid—they gave me direction to think about things. I had this idea, and it may be idealistic, that putting films out there might do the same for someone else sitting in a little theater in Oklahoma, and that's going to surprise and entertain them. And you know, there's something for everybody—that's something I respect and believe in."   **BRAD PITT**

★　★　★

"It may be the lost kingdom of childhood I am in constant search for."   **LIV ULLMANN**

★　★　★

"What I know now about myself as an actor, and about why I continue to act is this: If I could paint, I would do that. If I could sculpt, or do any other artistic form to express myself, I would do that. In acting, I am trying to get something out of myself. I'm trying to express myself creatively. I'm still learning how to act. I'm still learning how to be an actor. I'm still learning how to find moments, and how to make something, how to keep it honest, keep it real. I learn from every film, and I've learned from my mistakes in films."   **BRUCE WILLIS**

"No notices, however good, can ever quite satisfy an actor. No applause is ever quite long enough. At the end of a reception, no matter how tumultuous, one part of an actor's vanity must ask, 'Yes, but why have you stopped?'"

SIR MICHAEL REDGRAVE

★   ★   ★

"I found that the only way I could cope with life was to remove myself from social mores and routine and run my own track. So I became an actor." **JEREMY IRONS**

On Conquering Stage Fright and Developing Confidence in Your Talent

"I always forced myself to do crazy things in public. In college I would push an overhead projector across campus with my pants just low enough to show my butt. Then my friend would incite the crowd to be, like, 'Look at that idiot!' That's how I got over being shy." **WILL FERRELL**

★ ★ ★

"I've worked hard as a person, and as an actor, to fight my way through shyness. It's our responsibility as human beings to share with others. Being shy and withdrawn is selfish." **MICHAEL DOUGLAS**

★ ★ ★

"We must overcome the notion that we must be regular. . . . It robs you of the chance to be extraordinary and leads you to the mediocre." **UTA HAGEN**

"I knew a fisherman once who, during a storm, did not leave his rudder for 48 hours, concentrating to the last minute on his work of steering his schooner. Only when he had brought the schooner safely back into harbor did he allow his body to faint. This strength, this certainty of power over yourself, is the fundamental quality of every creative artist."

RICHARD BOLESLAVSKY

★　★　★

"I'm always afraid I'm going to mess something up. It's not like, 'Oh, yeah, I've got this one down, I can do this.' I never, ever feel that. . . . I love my job, but my job is scary to me."

HILARY SWANK

★　★　★

"I think I'm basically an introvert. It's always been hard for me to do things in front of people. And it's not like riding a bicycle, it just doesn't come back [on its own]. Even with a lovely script, fine actors and directors, you're always alone."

AUDREY HEPBURN

★　★　★

"Don't hide. Come out. Just as you are. That's what we want to see. Offer us your most hidden, tender part. We receive it gladly."

ELLEN BURSTYN

★　★　★

"Gee, maybe not being perfect is what perfect really means."

GOLDIE HAWN

★　★　★

"Have confidence in yourself. Don't feel it's your destiny to be more refuse: Free yourself! You must feel you're worthy of bigger-than-life ideas. . . . You wear a crown, not a baseball cap. No one ever disposes of a crown."   **STELLA ADLER**

★   ★   ★

"In my theater training I showed no aptitude at all. Funny enough, four nights ago I had dinner with three other colleagues who were at theater school with me, and [one of them said] he had always thought I would give up very quickly, like in a year or two years after leaving drama school. He said, 'You had no talent.'"   **JEREMY IRONS**

★   ★   ★

"I still, when I'm getting ready to do a scene, I have a kind of opening night jitters or whatever, but I like that. That's part of the reason that I'm still in the business. There's something at stake; you're not just showing up, you're not a day player, [and] you're not just trying to make a living. The thrill of that is that there's nothing like it, absolutely nothing like it."   **GENE HACKMAN**

★   ★   ★

"I'm really no good without a script, and I get incredibly nervous. I get very red, and I sweat profusely."   **LIEV SCHREIBER**

"At some point in our lives . . . we've all lessened ourselves— in any way, in a relationship or in a situation—to kind of blend in or to make people comfortable. But I don't think it's a good thing to do. I think we should all absolutely be everything we can be and encourage that from others."

ANGELINA JOLIE

★   ★   ★

"I've made peace with insecurity. You have to. Because there is no certainty of any kind. Once you let go, it's really freeing."

DICK VAN DYKE

★   ★   ★

"I consider myself one of the leading actors of my country. I believe it. I have to. The belief gives my ego the strength it needs to go forward."

ROD STEIGER

★   ★   ★

"If you fail the first time, try try try try try try try again."

PETER O'TOOLE,
upon being nominated for his eighth Best Actor Oscar in 2007 at the age of 74

★   ★   ★

"If this is what you want, you have to be passionate otherwise you will never reach anything. Because it's a very hard road to go on. But when you get there, it's the most beautiful thing in the world."

SOPHIA LOREN

★   ★   ★

"To be a success in the screen trade, I think you've got to . . .

either have a lot of talent and a little bit of ability or a lot of ability, a little bit of talent."

CLINT EASTWOOD,
accepting the SAG Life Achievement Award

★ ★ ★

"When I was a kid they had a painting contest and it was at my local dairy where I went and bought my ice cream, and when you bought you voted. And as an idealistic child I didn't vote for my own painting, and lost this thing by one vote. At my own dairy. And at that moment I vowed I would never vote for anyone else but myself in any contest I was in!"

JACK NICHOLSON

★ ★ ★

"Desire is almost probably more important than talent. I've seen it, where people have this real need to do something, and then they do a thing. Maybe they're not as gifted as somebody else . . . but they have this need. And they get it done."

AL PACINO

★ ★ ★

"I was looking at a video that someone sent me recently of an after-school theater program that I was in when I was about 14. It was such a shock to see myself at that age. It was really amazing how fast this sensation shot through my body of all the tension you feel at that age, the struggle to be cool. It was almost painful, looking at how hard I was trying and what a little dweeb I was."

EDWARD NORTON

★ ★ ★

"I think it's that early training, if anything, in vaudeville for me that gave me any kind of gumption. Touring endlessly around England, doing the second show on a Saturday night in places like Glasgow or Newcastle or Liverpool or Swansea or Cardiff, that's pretty dicey. I was very, very young. There were days when they would have to turn all the house lights on in the theater because people were hurling beer bottles and things like that. And there was this determination to get through. My mum . . . would say, 'Don't you dare complain. Don't you dare say you can't sing in cigarette smoke,' because in those days you could see it spiraling down the great arcs onto the spotlights onto the stage. . . . She would say, 'Don't you dare get a swollen head. . . . Get up and do it. What are you complaining about? You're so much luckier than most other people.' Absolutely true."   **JULIE ANDREWS**

★   ★   ★

"[To be an actor,] I think you have to have a very responsive nature. Think about anyone who reads a book. You visualize the characters. You become one with each of the characters. For a moment, through reading a book, you have the life experience of the character you are reading about. I fancy that reading gives you all of these extraordinary experiences that are helpful in understanding people. And that's true for a person without an acting talent. For an acting talent, it is a very developing thing. . . . It takes empathy. If you are going to do a good job, you have to empathize with a character, either instinctively and through feeling, or intellectually. Preferably in both ways."   **OLIVIA DE HAVILLAND**

★   ★   ★

When asked about booking one of his first jobs at an out-of-town dinner theater:

"It was in Ohio, and me, a friend, and my girlfriend at the time all went. She waited tables, while I performed. The next summer I couldn't get arrested, so I went and waited tables at the same dinner theatre. My girlfriend was hired as an actress; I got hired as a waiter. . . . But I saw guys that were worse than me doing real good . . . so I figured, 'What the hell, man. If they can make it, I can!'"   **JOHN GOODMAN**

★   ★   ★

Jack Lemmon's father was an executive for a bakery company. When asked if his father would've preferred him to go into the family business, Lemmon replied:

"One of the greatest lines he ever said to me was when I borrowed a few hundred dollars from him so I could go down to New York . . . to see if I could get an agent or get into the theater somehow or another. . . . He gave me the money and he said to me, 'You really want to give this a shot, huh?' And I said, 'Yeah, I've got to find out. Otherwise, I'll never really know whether I could have done it or not.' And he said, 'You've done similar stuff, and you've done enough to know that you love it?' And I said, 'I love it,' and he said, 'Great. Because the day I don't find romance in a loaf of bread, I'm going to quit.'"   **JACK LEMMON**

★   ★   ★

"The feedback I received [when I went to] L.A. was, 'You're a wonderful actress. But we're looking for someone attractive.' I don't think the aesthetic has changed out there. And I don't think my being persistent would have changed anything either. I was as aggressive as anyone. There's nothing you can do about your genetics. You are who you are."

BETSY AIDEM

★   ★   ★

"I've always been something of a pleaser: I want to make other people happy. That's not the worst thing. I mean, the fact that you like people and want them to like you is great—as long as you're not sacrificing who you are. I'm not someone who has a lot of regrets, but last year I did something that I wasn't comfortable with, and I'm really sorry I didn't listen to my intuition. There was a scene in a movie that felt inappropriate to me, but I didn't want to make waves. So I let myself get talked into it, even though it shook me up. From now on, I'm going to trust my gut more. Sometimes the most powerful thing you can do is say, 'no.'"

NATALIE PORTMAN

★   ★   ★

"Mom was always pretty supportive. She saw me do plays and she'd always act out the parts I did. My aunt, who played a big part in my life, was a little bit more reserved, because if they don't see you on TV every week they think you must be starving. They're in North Carolina and they watch a lot of television. But as the years have gone by, she's come to understand how it works. She didn't want me to major in theatre at Yale, she wanted me to be a molecular biologist or something."

ANGELA BASSETT

★   ★   ★

"You're the only person who can tell whether you have talent or not, and there's a certain point where you've got to be really honest with yourself and say, 'Yeah, I do, and I'm going on,' or 'No, I don't.' And your parents can't do it for you, and critics can't do it for you. Once you've determined that, then there should be no room for doubt, you know. There is room that, 'Well, maybe this isn't the right role for me.' That's always going on, you know. You're told every day you're not right for this role. And they might [say], 'It's 'cause you're too tall.' They usually don't know why you're not right for it. It's just, you didn't ring a bell for them, that's all. And that's okay. You've got to accept the fact that you don't ring a bell for everybody."   **JAMES EARL JONES**

★   ★   ★

"It's not easy to become a star. You have to have a very determined character. You have to work and to do so much. You really have to be stubborn; to know what you want and to think about it every day, every hour of the day: 'I want to be a star.'"   **SOPHIA LOREN**

★   ★   ★

"I had a gig one night at a club called Flamingo East. It was one of my favorite places to perform. Before the gig, however, I was in a bathroom scrubbing a woman's toilet. It was my job.

"I thought, 'This sucks. . . . Am I going to do this my whole life?'

"I had this incredible moment of self-pity.

"Then I had an epiphany. 'If you really want to be good a being a performer, then you had better scrub this toilet really good.' That was what the voice said . . . 'Clean this toilet with as much tenacity as you would turn out a song.'

"It was so real to me. . . . The voice said, 'Do everything with incredible love and incredible caring.' It was about being in the present."

DAPHNE RUBIN-VEGA

★   ★   ★

"When the shooting begins on a picture, it becomes a matter of health and weather and whether you have picked a good cast and crew. And whether, of course, the script makes any sense. And your own worth is also involved. Can you do it? I think most of the people involved in any art always secretly wonder whether they are really there because they're good or there because they're lucky."   KATHARINE HEPBURN

★   ★   ★

"When I was 19, I was proposed to by a student at Yale with the proviso that I give up my desire to have a career as an actress. He put the ring on my finger. I wore it for four or five days, then returned it, telling him it would be impossible for me to comply with his request. Thank God even at that age I was wise enough to do what I did. Had I agreed to give up my desire for an acting career, all through the years I would have wondered if I could have been a success as an actress."   BETTE DAVIS

★   ★   ★

"I had a certain fear of exposing myself too much in my work for a long time. . . . A lot of what performing to me had been was elaborate, and at times quite clever, concealment. Someone once said of acting that it is 'telling beautiful lies,' and well, it became just no longer satisfactory to work that way."   **PATRICK STEWART**

★   ★   ★

"When someone is successful, there's always a feeling that they were lucky. Luck plays a part, sure, but to be successful, you must have iron discipline. You must have energy and hunger and desire and honesty."   **FAYE DUNAWAY**

★   ★   ★

"Fail in private. When you announce, 'This is what's going to happen,' it's like God says, 'Hold on a second. I don't want that guy to work out.' It's like the Billy Bob Thornton-Angelina Jolie marriage. This guy was making his moves public and telling everybody. One thing I've learned is don't do that."   **ALBERT BROOKS**

★   ★   ★

"I always shake my head when I hear that a person must be willing to take criticism. Of course you must take criticism from the people in charge. The problem is, people everywhere are always ready to offer criticism. . . . I have found much of the criticism (with obvious notable exceptions from extremely bright, sensitive people) to be not constructive but destructive."   **CHARLES GRODIN**

★   ★   ★

"I never realized I had talent. I just feel that I'm a jobbing actor."   **DAME JUDI DENCH**

"We lived in a rat-infested tenement on the Lower East Side for several years . . . and ate spaghetti, and I loved every minute of it. I loved it when it was happening [because] . . . I knew success would be coming.

"I remember getting evicted . . . thrown out into the street with my wife and child—baby, 17 months old. And I bummed a ride to Ohio to see my father, who had never met my wife or seen my baby, and to visit my brother, who was in jail, and try to help him out of jail. It was one of the worst times and the best times.

"And I remember one of my brothers saying, 'You're a burden to our family.' And I got angry and I said, 'There is going to come a day, as surely as the sun rises tomorrow, when I will make more money in an hour than you'll make in a year.' And I knew it was true. Despair, yes, but I always believed in myself. Absolutely."   **Martin Sheen**

★   ★   ★

"The worries and fears about personal lacks are immobilizing and make me dream the dream too long. But the dreams stay in my head, they haunt me, they push me and become a kick to my consciousness, making me act. The Divine Impulse—it's always safe to follow it. We've got to trust it and go wherever it takes us."   **Ruby Dee**

★   ★   ★

"If I had a prayer that I would pray every single night for myself, as an actor, it would be: 'Please, give me more and more every day, courage, courage, courage, to enter into and display the truth.'"   **David Suchet**

★   ★   ★

On his conversion from vaudevillian performer to serious actor:

"If you open up too much to people, they have power over
   you and make you do things for them. Better [I assumed] to
   . . . keep them on the other side of the footlights. . . . Keep
   them as an audience where you can be in control. Keep the
   curtain up, keep the play going. It holds off judgment. *See
   me up here? You love me, right? I'm the best right?* But if I
   wanted to really act, I was going to have to find the doorway
   to compassion."   **ALAN ALDA**

★   ★   ★

*On his time as a member of Columbia Pictures' New Talent
program, a system designed to turn young unknowns into
movie stars:*

"They sent me to the studio barber with a photograph of
   Elvis Presley and instructions that I come back with my hair
   styled like his. . . . They had this perception of you being
   some green Elvis or green Cary Grant, but I didn't want
   to be those people. I thought imitating other actors was
   a recipe for disaster. I wanted to develop my own way of
   expression."   **HARRISON FORD**

★   ★   ★

"I developed an iron will that has enabled me to travel the
   peaks and valleys of my career—periods of exciting work
   alternating with others of no work at all, parts you loved to
   play and those you had to play simply to work or to support
   yourself and your family."   **BEN GAZZARA**

★   ★   ★

"When they talk about intelligence as being a barrier to good acting, that makes me cringe. Those people want puppets."
WILLIAM HURT

★   ★   ★

"There are many born actors who have never faced an audience, as there are many true poets who have never written a verse, and painters who have never taken a palette in hand. To some only is given the power of expression as well as of feeling, and they become artists in the sight of the world as the others are in the sight of our semi-divine mistress, the Art universal."   **TOMMASO SALVINI**

★   ★   ★

"The thing about acting in the theater for me is if you're not dangerous, if you're not courageous, if you don't think you have the right to be up there, get the hell off the stage."
FRANK LANGELLA

★   ★   ★

"The way you get to be a very good actor, in my book, is by playing as many roles as you can in as many great plays as you can with as many great actors and directors as you can. Probably in that order. If you can do *Glass Menagerie* on Broadway with Laurette Taylor, good for you. If you can do *Glass Menagerie* with Laurette Taylor in Delaware, good for you. But the key first and foremost, is to do *Glass Menagerie*. I don't care where."   **ROBERT SEAN LEONARD**

★   ★   ★

"I wasn't a bad looking guy. . . . I wasn't one of those guys in the corner with my hair hanging across my face going 'I'm ugly.' . . . I know I wasn't as handsome as some other guys, but I was OK with that. Good work is the only thing that would make me feel jealous or envious. Vanity is something that will only get in the way of doing your best work, and ultimately if you're truly vain you care more about your work than how you look in your work. I actually consider myself a pretty vain guy when it comes to that."

PHILIP SEYMOUR HOFFMAN

★   ★   ★

"Some people are natural performers. Not me. I used to have certain rituals that got me through. I would have to drink chamomile tea. I tapped for a while, knocking a certain number of times before I could play a scene. I had pet doves that I brought to the set. On *Boys Don't Cry,* I would swear loudly before each take. . . . Now I'm more confident, and I'm looking for that feeling of insecurity. A part has to be important enough to be worried again. When I care, I get nervous. And I like being nervous."   **PETER SARSGAARD**

★   ★   ★

"The most important job, to me, is the one I haven't done yet. . . . I view my strongest competition as myself. You're always trying to top yourself, rather than worrying about what other people are doing."   **JOHN C. REILLY**

On the Actor's Life

"Some of my best friends are actors."
KIRK DOUGLAS

★   ★   ★

"You wait eight months for a movie to come out, and all that keeps you going is the unemployment."   **ROBERT DE NIRO**

★   ★   ★

"Everything I've done in my career as a professional actor, it's like, I got the gig way after I've got the experience enough to do the gig."   **RUSSELL CROWE**

★   ★   ★

"For actors, the difference between L.A. and New York is, in California, you never know when you're unemployed."

COLLEEN DEWHURST

★　★　★

"What makes me more nervous than anything is knowing exactly what's gonna happen. Being with people who are all very polite and have planned lives and do things on schedule and life is going just perfectly for them—man, I can't deal with that."

CHRISTIAN BALE

★　★　★

"The stage is a lonely place. You can't lead a big social life. I'm not very social anyway. It's crossword puzzles."

ANGELA LANSBURY

★　★　★

"Every time someone comes up to me and says something [nice], it still surprises me that they've seen [one of my movies]. To me, these are little projects that I have to believe are private experiences or I couldn't do them. I couldn't do them knowing that potentially I'm going to disappoint people."

RENÉE ZELLWEGER

★　★　★

"You're never in a nice location. I'm always in the middle of some field, or on a glacier, or in a copper mine, in some ugly, horrible location. . . . [Then] you get the one night a year at a premiere or something where its kind of glamorous, and you're still doing interviews most of the time."

MARK WAHLBERG

"It's one of the tragic ironies of the theatre that only one man in it can count on steady work—the night watchman."

TALLULAH BANKHEAD

★ ★ ★

"I don't believe in fate, but it's very hard not to."

GENE WILDER

★ ★ ★

"So much of our profession is taken up with pretending, with the interpretation of never-never roles, that an actor must spend at least half his waking hours in fantasy, in rehearsal or shooting."

RONALD REAGAN

★ ★ ★

"Childbirth is easy compared to giving birth to a role in a play."

HELEN HAYES

★ ★ ★

"The greatest compliment I can pay anybody is by being with them and by allowing myself to feel what I feel in their company. I could, after all, walk out of there."

WILLIAM HURT

★ ★ ★

"[After a show] you'd go to Charlie's or Barrymore's, and you have four, five, ten drinks and then roll into bed at five in the morning. There was Jimmy Ray's, a rat hole on 46th and Eighth, that was famous because it had everybody's bounced checks on display. The men's room was in the basement.

Barney Hughes once said: 'We gotta find a new bar, Brian, because I can't fall down this f—in' stairs every night.'

BRIAN DENNEHY

★   ★   ★

"One big night [while filming the movie *Romper Stomper,* in which I played a Nazi skinhead gang leader], nine of us got arrested. And we're not doing anything particular, we're not hanging out in skinhead hangouts, we're just going to regular pubs. However, we don't have any hair, and we've got serious 16-hole fucking Doc Martens with white laces, which signify to the police 'White Supremacy.' In an odd way, I was kind of weirdly comforted that these nine or ten blokes walking around together in Melbourne would immediately attract attention from the police . . . Two constables came out and grabbed me and said, 'Who do you think you are?' and all that sort of stuff. And I said, 'Mate, I'll tell you exactly who we are—we're a group of actors, and we're doing a movie where we're playing neo-Nazi skinheads.' And this sergeant of police in South Melbourne says, 'Is that right? Right. Well, I hope you're a Method Actor, son, because you're really going to enjoy this. Put him in the fucking cell.'"

RUSSELL CROWE

★   ★   ★

"Richard Harris—I worked with him. Great storyteller. One time he was onstage, and he was drunk. And someone in the audience yells out, 'He's drunk, he's stunk-up!' And he yells back, 'You think I'm drunk, wait till *O'Toole* comes on!'"

ROBERT DUVALL

★   ★   ★

"One of the greatest moments in my life, at least as an actor, came one day outside the Winter Garden Theater in Manhattan, where I was playing Cassio in *Othello*. It was a just after a matinee, and I was on my way to lunch when a young man came up to me and said, 'Mr. Grammer, I saw you do *Macbeth* last year, and I wanted you to know that I've been reading Shakespeare ever since.

"It was one of the most beautiful things I had ever heard . . . and I actually fought back tears. I had never been so proud, or so thankful." **KELSEY GRAMMER**

★   ★   ★

"Only a few of us will admit it, but actors will sometimes read a script like this: *bullshit . . . bullshit . . . my part . . . blah, blah, blah . . . my part . . . bullshit . . .*" **MICHAEL J. FOX**

★   ★   ★

"No matter how good things get, there's always that little voice in your head whispering this might be the last job. When you realize everybody hears the same whispers, it gets easier to live with." **PHILIP SEYMOUR HOFFMAN**

★   ★   ★

"The only thing you owe the public is a good performance." **HUMPHREY BOGART**

★   ★   ★

"Some time ago, I visited several psychiatrists over a five-year period. . . . All I learned is that everybody has problems and that my shrinks had more problems than I did." **KIRK DOUGLAS**

"Here's one last tip with a moral for film actors. It's something
I noticed after going to Hollywood parties with big-name
actors, big-name producers. Every time I went to an actor's
house, the walls were covered with pictures of himself.
Every time I went to a producer's house, the walls were
covered with Lautrecs, Van Goghs, and Picassos. Just bear
that in mind."
                                         SIR MICHAEL CAINE

★　★　★

"I've got a few scripts I'm reading, and they're all absolute
rubbish. . . . But if you wait for a good script, you might wait
forever. You finally have to say: 'Well, how much money will
I get for this one, Charley?' One has to live, you know, and
live *well!*"
                                         CHRISTOPHER PLUMMER

★　★　★

"During school break from Juilliard, I went back home to
California. One day, when I was talking to my father in a
shopping mall, a little boy walked up behind me with two
cap pistols. I didn't see him. He shot me and I jumped about
10 feet in the air. It scared me so bad. My father said, 'So,
you live in New York City, do you?'"
                                         BOYD GAINES

★　★　★

"Usually, life in the theater took one of two paths: being
cast in a play that would flop after a short amount of time
or settling down to a long, successful run, which offered
the actor financial security but came with a Faustian
punishment: boredom."
                                         ELI WALLACH

★　★　★

"I constantly experience failure in that my work is never as good as I want it to be. So I live with failure. What buoys you up? The people who you have deceived who think you are great and congratulate you on things."   **Jeremy Irons**

★   ★   ★

"If you read Shakespeare, you realize it was ever thus."
Rip Torn

★   ★   ★

"As a lot we . . . moan about not working; and if we get a job, we moan about the director, the script, and the reviews. If the play's a hit, we then moan about the long run ahead of us. Then we moan because the play closes and we're out of work."   **Sir Derek Jacobi**

★   ★   ★

"*Beyond Therapy* was my first professional job, and it could not have been a more complete experience. . . . I was working with John Lithgow, Dianne Wiest—all these amazing people—Peter Michael Goetz and Kate McGregor-Stewart and Jack Gilpin. So I was sitting a lot in rehearsals just watching and absorbing and seeing these people put the thing together. And going into the Brooks Atkinson and seeing my dressing room, which I now know is just a pit—but at the time I thought I'd gone to heaven. The magic of the tech and the preview audiences going nuts and elderly women in the matinees banging their heads on the seats ahead of them, they were laughing so hard. And opening night with my mom and dad in the audience and going to Sardi's with them for dinner afterward. . . . Then *The*

New York Times review came out and [former *Times* critic]
Frank Rich hated it, and we closed in two weeks. . . . I saw
how great [this business] could be and also what a difficult,
treacherous business it is and how it is a business. I think it
was the best thing possible because even though it had such
a sad ending, I just thought, 'Wow, this is what it's like when
it fails. How incredible!' For me, it was the perfect prep for
coming to New York and learning about what can and can't
happen."   **DAVID HYDE PIERCE**

★   ★   ★

"It's unlikely I'll ever submit to a psychiatrist's couch. I
don't want some stranger prowling around in my psyche,
monkeying with my Id. I don't need an analyst to tell me
that I have never had any sense of security. Who has?"
                                            TALLULAH BANKHEAD

★   ★   ★

"George Frederick Cooke, when playing *Othello*, was
hissed by an audience probably more versed in the ways
of melodrama than in Shakespeare, though it is also
possible that in Cooke's production there was not so great
a distinction between the two. He stopped in mid-sentence
and turned on them in a fury, saying, 'So ye hiss George
Frederick Cooke, do ye? Let me tell you that every stone of
your damned city was cemented by the blood of a Negro.'
One would dearly love to have seen the audience's reaction
to that."   **SIR MICHAEL REDGRAVE**

★   ★   ★

"As an actress I feel that my identity is for rent. Not for sale.
But for rent."   **ANNA DEAVERE SMITH**

"It's a very odd relationship acting with someone. You are of course thrown into a most intimate relationship with a person. Then the picture ends. You may never see the person again. But people—and especially ones writing articles or books—say, 'What was he [or she] like?' And I don't know. I don't really know them or anything about them. I wonder if this is true of most actors."

KATHARINE HEPBURN

★   ★   ★

On feeling competitive toward other actors:

"There is still this part of me that says, 'Hey, I'm fucking better than that guy. I should be playing that role.'"

ADAM GOLDBERG

★   ★   ★

"The very first day [on a movie called *I Could Never Be Your Woman*], I had this scene where I was supposed to be making out with Michelle Pfeiffer. I told my wife, 'Look. I want you to know that I'm going to be making out with Michelle Pfeiffer today, and I will be thinking about . . . Michelle Pfeiffer.' My wife's response was that when she makes out with me she also thinks of Michelle Pfeiffer."

PAUL RUDD

★   ★   ★

"When you first walk onto a film set, it's the most wonderful thing, like running away to the circus. You feel like you've gone to a special place because everybody works very intensely and parties very hard and gets on with each other because they have to. On the whole, people are genuinely nice, and you end up with a million phone numbers—a million phone numbers that you don't call. It's kind of sad."

DANIEL CRAIG

★   ★   ★

"There's the two kinds of lives you have. The one is where you're working because it's good to work. You like working, it's a way of life, you'll meet people and learn things. And the other one is where you feel this need to do this thing because it's something you want to express. And then, sometimes, you do nothing, right? And that's very good sometimes. I mean, I went four years without working. So I know what it's like to do it and not to."   AL PACINO

★   ★   ★

"I believe an artist dies twice. The first time, it's just terrible—I've been there when the phone isn't ringing for years. . . . But the most important thing is not to implode. People go from the mountain into the valley and click into that dark, reptilian part of their brain and self-destruct. I see it all the time."

SYLVESTER STALLONE

★   ★   ★

"A doctor becomes a doctor because he or she is formally given an MD. A scholar in a university is formally given a PhD, a counselor an LLD, a hairstylist a license, and so forth. [Artists] are on the fringe, and we don't get such licenses. There are prizes and rewards, popularity and good or bad press. But you have to be your own judge."

ANNA DEAVERE SMITH

★   ★   ★

"The theater can be the most unhealthy life. You don't eat before the show, and afterward you want to go out and have a good time. So you have a big meal—and 10 drinks—at midnight. I don't want to end up like Orson Welles. When he died, I had a friend who said, 'You know what happened to Orson? His heart just said: F—k you! I'm outta here! We're closed for business!'"   **BRIAN DENNEHY**

★   ★   ★

"I've been a zombie, a vampire, and a squid. It's quite nice to play someone in a normal pair of trousers."   **BILL NIGHY**

★   ★   ★

"It's like holding sand in your hands when you have [upcoming] projects in this business because they just don't happen. 'I thought that we were going to be doing so and so in June.' Well, they didn't get the money or the script is not ready or the producer or the studio changed heads. . . . There's all kind of stuff shifts and it's constantly in flux. Hopefully you've always got a lot of projects ahead of you. Hopefully one or two of them will pan out."

MORGAN FREEMAN

★   ★   ★

"I've made good pictures, I've made bad ones that weren't even released—they escaped! [*Laughs*] I say, 'Forget 'em— on to the next one!'"   **MICKEY ROONEY**

★   ★   ★

"Never be tired. I'm always suspicious of actors that say, 'I'm tired,' all the time. You've got to have incredible energy."

DAME JUDI DENCH

★   ★   ★

"I think that most actors have a self-destructive power in them, a capacity to tear themselves to pieces—even the best ones, Olivier, Brando, and Burton. . . . When a marriage breaks up or something, this naturally affects their work and then the critics have a go and a terrible thing starts, and it takes over inside. [The actor] then says, 'Right, let's do shit, let's wallow in garbage so they can't get me. You want to see how bad I can get? Ok, just watch.'"

SIR ANTHONY HOPKINS

★   ★   ★

"If there was a mirror behind the camera so I could look at myself, then I'd be happy."   **TERRENCE HOWARD**

★   ★   ★

"The oddest bad behavior I ever witnessed came from [an actor] I had worked with whom I raved about in print. This guy was deeply offended that I didn't say even more about him."   **CHARLES GRODIN**

★   ★   ★

"I love actors, I married one. . . . But even more than acting, I love the community of actors. I love the green room, I love the hair and makeup trailer, and I am so grateful that I am acting, and I am so grateful that I can make a living at it, because I was never very good at math."

FELICITY HUFFMAN,
*accepting the SAG Award for Outstanding Performance
by a Female Actor in a Comedy Series*

★   ★   ★

"Let's be blunt: The worst thing about being an actor is
waiting on other people to give you a shot at a good part."

EDWARD NORTON

★   ★   ★

"Quite frequently, I've been talking to somebody, telling
a story, and then I realize halfway through, 'This didn't
happen.' . . . After a few years, you can't differentiate between
the clarity of something you've played and a real event.
I find that funny. I have some friends who find it sad and
disturbing."

CHRISTIAN BALE

★   ★   ★

"I've been called difficult. I'm glad that Meryl Streep once
told someone that it's because I was good. I don't think you
come in order to be complacent, you come to be challenged.
And not just by the administrative difficulty of making a
movie but by the material itself. I cannot come to a film set
and let myself be overwhelmed by the complexity of a film
set. I have to remember that I am there to be overwhelmed
by the challenge of solving this scene today and what it
means about life, not what it means about whether or not
we're making a movie."

WILLIAM HURT

★   ★   ★

"The birth of a child, the growth of a tree, the creation of an artistic image are all manifestations of a kindred order."

CONSTANTIN STANISLAVSKI

★   ★   ★

"We can talk about a cello having a soul . . . but when an actor talks about his soul people think, 'What a pretentious wanker.' A cello's soul is the resonance that makes it unique: how it was made, when it was made, who's played it. Mine may be who my parents were, what I know about life, who I love and have loved. All that makes my bones resonate. If a director is fortunate enough to tap into that, it's an endless well of information."

SIR BEN KINGSLEY

★   ★   ★

"If I don't think I'm doing well [in a role], I'm unpleasant. That's my neurosis, you know what I mean? If I don't feel like I'm doing the job well, and I don't know how to get there, or I'm too scared, or whatever, I'm not a happy guy and I'm not pleasant. I'm not pleasant to be around."

PHILIP SEYMOUR HOFFMAN

★   ★   ★

"All actors have a fantastic sense of mortality. Particularly stage actors, because to choose a way of life where you give your life's blood to concentrating and perfecting events that pass in a second, and only live in the memories of those people who are watching it, is an incredible throw-away relationship to eternity."

FIONA SHAW

★   ★   ★

"The vast majority of people wouldn't even have the slightest idea who I am. Why should they? I'm an actor. So what? The people who do [care] are just star-struck. To most autograph collectors, it doesn't matter. It could be me, or it could be Joan Collins or it could be an amalgam of the two. Maybe I already am an amalgam of the two. It doesn't matter who you are, it's just that you are known."   **JOHN MALKOVICH**

★   ★   ★

"It all happened one day while I was walking up Tenth Avenue in New York. I was starving, along with everybody else, and I'm saying to myself, 'Dummy. Why did you ever get into this business? Why? I know I can act just as good as Charlton Heston, if not better.' But he was getting all the parts and I was getting nothing. It just didn't seem right to me. . . . And suddenly I smelt hot chestnuts. There was a vendor . . . and it remind[ed] me of my mother when she used to cut the chestnuts and put them on the stove and the whole house would be permeated with that wonderful smell of chestnuts. . . . I went closer to the vendor—not to buy any because I didn't have any money to even buy a chestnut. Just to smell. And I saw a sign on this vendor's cart that became my philosophy of life . . . And it read, 'I don't want to set the world on fire, I just want to keep my nuts warm.'"

ERNEST BORGNINE

★   ★   ★

"It was difficult for vaudevillians not to drink in those days [the late 19th century], for alcohol was sold in all theatres, and after a performer's act he was expected to go to the theatre bar and drink with the customers. Some theatres made more profit from the bar than from the box office, and a number of stars were paid large salaries not alone for their talent but because they spent most of their money at the theatre bar. Thus many an artist was ruined by drink—my father was one of them. He died of alcoholic excess at the age of 37."   **CHARLIE CHAPLIN**

★   ★   ★

"The only thing you have as an actor is the legacy you leave behind. I can spend my 15 minutes of fame trying to draw attention to myself, or I can reflect the light of some of the greatest human beings on this planet."   **TERRENCE HOWARD**

★   ★   ★

"O Thespis, my muse, my blessing, my curse! Like you I have been graced by the gods with a vivid and abundant gift for the performing arts. A born talent with heroic lineaments, the aquiline profile of a Barrymore, and the corybantic suppleness of a strutter and fretter in the Kabuki, I was not content to settle merely for the bounteous hand dealt me by providence but immersed myself in the dramatic arts of the classical theater, of dance and mime. It has been said that I can do more with the raising of an eyebrow than most actors can do with their entire bodies. To this day, denizens of the Neighborhood Playhouse recount in hushed tones the psychological detail with which I imbued Parson Manders during a summer workshop. The downside of a histrionic life is that beneath a certain minimum figure, the number of calories required each day to postpone starvation demands that I bus the tables at Taco-Pox, a burrito palace that languishes before the unsuspecting on La Cienega Boulevard like a Venus flytrap."   **WOODY ALLEN**

★   ★   ★

"One of the greatest regrets of my life [is that my father never lived to see my success]. I was completely down and out, unemployed, and destitute when my father died. It's a funny thing, because my father was a great horse-race gambler. And I eventually bought a house which was right next door to Windsor racetrack. And I shared a small fence with the racetrack, and in it was a gate. The deed to the house said that I had the right to take people through that gate into the racetrack for free. It would have been my father's idea of paradise."   **SIR MICHAEL CAINE**

★   ★   ★

"Two and a half percent [of actors] work, ninety-seven and a half percent do not. The profession has always been overcrowded; you might well expect this to have been realized by now, but it possesses a fatal fascination for too many people, and there seems to be no effective way of scaring them off."   **SIR LAURENCE OLIVIER**

★   ★   ★

"The pleasure of my life is that, however long it takes to make a movie, when it's over, I'm back to reality."

HARRISON FORD

★   ★   ★

On having her mind constantly preoccupied with work:

"Last night [I was preoccupied with] this line from *The Apple Tree*: 'The Really Real Acting Academy has shown me that all my films, alas, are naught but tinkling trivia, sugary, shoddy, shallow shadows. Schlock.' [I kept wondering] How

am I going to say that? How am I going to make that funny?
It's so frustrating because people say, 'It comes so easily to
her,' or 'She's just playing herself.' Well, I work my butt off [to
make it look easy]. These ideas don't come from nowhere.
You have to think them up. Sometimes I think until I think
my head might explode."   KRISTIN CHENOWETH

★   ★   ★

"You're in the part and you're like, I gotta be true, honest,
never lie, never lie, never lie, and then you see it and you're
like, I'm such a liar. Don't they all know I'm a phony, I'm
faking? That's not the case, really, but maybe I'm seeing the
character I've created and it's a shock, because it was such
a real experience to me. Then I sort of kick myself; I go,
God, how could you deign to say that you actually had that
experience? It was a movie, get over it. I'm always surprised
that it's not me, on some level, but of course it is, because to
do anything you use your own life, your own imagination,
everything, and you give it all away. I'm never happy when I
see myself, never, but I've been happy with the 'experience'
several times, which is more than I think anyone can ask for."
                                    MARY STUART MASTERSON

★   ★   ★

"I love the theater. It's my favorite medium. I just don't love
the theater lifestyle. I've done it all my life. I'm attuned to it,
but it's no life at all. And you gain weight because you eat
candy for a sugar rush to get you through. In the old days,
we'd stuff ourselves at midnight dinners, drink all night and
sleep all day. Lucky I'm still alive."
                                    CHRISTOPHER PLUMMER

★   ★   ★

"I prepare for [my part] all day long. I sleep as late as I can. I work out if I can, if there's time. I eat correctly so that I'm not too full before I have to perform. I vocalize for about 45 minutes. I stretch. Then I come to the theater. The key for me is to not do anything during the day. I play in these fantastic cities, and I've never seen one of them. I'm in my apartment or my hotel room preparing for the evening show."

PATTI LuPONE

★   ★   ★

"I don't care much for social life with people in the theatre. I'm rather good at being with people when I want to make the effort, but I'm bad at listening to people when I know what they're going to say. It isn't very interesting, and on the whole it's very draining. The interesting thing in the theatre is the work and working with people. I usually like people in the work, but I can't go on with them outside the work as long as most actors can. And when I'm working on a part I'm thinking about it all the time, going over all the possibilities in my mind. I like to be alone when I'm working."

PAUL SCOFIELD

★   ★   ★

"The day that Stan Laurel died, the press came by my house to interview me about him. As I'm talking, a sprinkler spout that I was standing over burst. Water shot up and just drenched me. I looked up to the sky. It was obviously his last bit of comedy. If that won't give you religion, what will?"

DICK VAN DYKE

On Auditioning

"When I first got [to Los Angeles], I was in a one-room studio—you know, one room and my dreams. The Chevy commercial [I'd booked for the previous Super Bowl] had been a huge deal in Chicago, when there's less opportunities. When I came to LA, I had a swagger, and I thought I was the kid, you know: 'Here I am—let's go.' And I found out that it wasn't that easy. There were times I sat there in Los Angeles with a culture so different from where I was from, by myself, didn't have any friends. I'd have an audition for three lines on *Who's the Boss?*, and I'd say, 'What am I doing.'"

VINCE VAUGHN

★ ★ ★

"In the '70s, New York was the busiest producer of TV commercials. I frequently had three or more auditions a day, on camera and voice-overs. One morning I read for two voice-overs, one for a car, the other a cereal. I hadn't been getting many voice-overs at the time, so when my agent called to tell me I had a booking I was more than surprised.

"'The car one?' I asked, because I gave a great audition. 'No, the cereal one.' That was odd. That audition I thought I sucked, but what the hell, I took it, voice-overs were hard to get.

"At the recording session on the third take, I began to feel what I was doing was awful, I mean, awful. Unable to contain myself, I asked the producer, 'Why did you hire me, I'm terrible.'

"'I know,' he said.

"'What? Then why did you hire me?'

"'Because when you auditioned, you gave the worst reading.'

"Shocked, I said, 'But if I was so bad . . . I don't understand.'

"The producer said, 'That's what we wanted. . . . Someone who did it very badly, you were the best one.'"

LOUIS ZORICH

★   ★   ★

"You have to think of yourself as that toy that looks like a clown, with sand on the bottom, then when you punch it, it comes right back up. . . . You cannot allow yourself to be defined by rejection. The casting director and directors are not defining you as a person. On that particular audition, you weren't right for this job. . . . It's really important to keep your eye on the prize. My lawyer once said to me, 'If you sit at the table long enough, the chips will come to you.'"

HENRY WINKLER

★   ★   ★

Recounting an audition for the part of a bad guy on a TV western:

"When my name was called I went into the office, where there were four people. I kept my head down, discouraging any chatting. Quickly they asked if I was ready and I nodded. I then looked up and let out the rage. (Rage: something most actors with years of rejection can do very well.) . . . As the audition went on, they looked at me in terror with a real question of whether all this rage would be confined to the audition. When it was over they gave me the part, I think because they were so relieved that I didn't attack them."

CHARLES GRODIN

★   ★   ★

"Some of the greatest actors in the world just cannot audition well. They get nervous and self-conscious, so they act weird around people. Instead of thinking 'I hope I'm right for this role' I go in thinking 'Look, I'm right for this role.' I'll pick up the vibes in the room and go with it. Some people who aren't great actors are great auditioners. You wonder why they're getting work when they're not that exceptional, but it's a different talent."   PENELOPE ANN MILLER

★   ★   ★

"They ask you basically to make a fool of yourself, which I was very good at. I made enough of a fool of myself that they thought they could work with me."   MEL GIBSON

★   ★   ★

"I went to a wonderful party . . . and I met an actress there . . . [who] was in her own way. . . . The party was wonderful

... with free spaghetti. . . . We were drinking Black Russians. And she said, 'I have to go home because I have a reading in the morning.' I said, 'How many readings have you had in the morning and how many jobs have you gotten?' 'Not too many.' 'Why don't you stay until you're the last one to leave the party, don't worry about your hair, and go in tomorrow with a little of the party instead of the reading?' . . . See, that's the main problem. [Actors] always make an adjustment for the consequential thing of getting the job. . . . Instead of coming in like they come into the Safeway and say 'Where's your liver? Where's the dog food?' they come in, and because it's consequential, they change. [She] got the job which lasted four years—the lead in a television daytime soap."

CHARLES NELSON REILLY

★   ★   ★

"The American Negro Theatre was in need of actors for its next production. . . . 'What the hell,' I thought. 'I've tried dishwashers wanted, porters wanted, janitors wanted—why not try actors wanted?' . . . Acting didn't sound any more difficult than washing dishes and parking cars. . . . But when I went in and was auditioned on the spot, the man in charge quickly let me know—an in no uncertain terms—that I was misguided in my assumptions. . . . I could barely read! . . . So I set out on a course of self-improvement. I worked nights, and on my evening meal-breaks I sat in a quiet area of the restaurant where I was employed, near the entrance to the kitchen, reading newspapers, trying to sound out each syllable of each unfamiliar word. An old Jewish waiter, noticing my efforts, took pity and offered to help. He became my tutor, as well as my guardian angel of the moment. Each night we sat in the same booth in that quiet area of the restaurant and he helped me learn to read."

SIDNEY POITIER

"If I went in for a role and I heard back that I wasn't right for it, I would always say, 'They made a huge mistake.' If the word came back that I was nervous and didn't know what I was doing, I would think, 'Without me, that movie is going to sink like a stone.' Rarely did it ever hurt my feelings. Nothing would set me back."

TERI GARR

★ ★ ★

"I remember when I first started coming to grips with the fact that, unlike swimming, the fastest person didn't always win [in acting]. That was a tricky thing to wrap your head around. In sport, the winner is clearly the winner and in this job, in terms of getting jobs, you can be the guy that they said blew everybody away but not the one that we're going with. People are opening and closing doors and that's out of your control. That's a lesson in life. You can't do anything about it so you have to disregard it and move on."

TIMOTHY OLYPHANT

★ ★ ★

Early in her career, Betsy Aidem was an audition crasher. She'd show up at auditions without an appointment and insist that she be seen. This aggressive move got her hired for a part in John Malkovich's 1984 revival of Lanford Wilson's Balm in Gilead *and Sam Shepard's* A Lie of the Mind. *But she doubts very much that audition crashing would work today:*

"Now we live in a global community that's become dependent on the Internet. . . . Almost all information can be gotten online, including audition tapes that agents email to casting directors. There's also fear: if someone attempts to crash an audition today, there's the concern that the actor might be a psychopath."

BETSY AIDEM

"I would get on the Trailways bus from Philadelphia, where I was living at the time [to New York] . . . and make the rounds. . . . The A to M agencies on Tuesday and the N to Z agencies on Wednesday. I had a picture with four different Brucies on it and a bunch of horseshit on the back, which was my resume. It consisted of scenes that I'd done in class and *Waiting for Godot*. I would leave that picture. The girls trashed it as soon as I left."   **BRUCE DERN**

★   ★   ★

On why, at a certain point in his career, he refused to audition anymore:

"I went to an audition for a commercial because I was really unemployed for a long time. It was obnoxious, and I thought, 'I don't have to do this.' My idea was I'll lose 50 percent of the work by auditioning and I'll lose 50 percent by not auditioning, so what the fuck? [My refusal to audition] came about out of embarrassment, and I've stuck to it. And it's served me all right. When I've auditioned actors as a director, I've always thought the reading was absolutely irrelevant. It's flawed for me, because there's many, many times I've worked with an actor who showed up on the set and didn't have a clue and I'll turn to the director and he'll say, 'Well, [they gave] a really good audition.' That happens more often than I care to count."   **TIM ROTH**

★   ★   ★

"Auditions, most struggling actors will tell you, suck. . . . You want to be familiar enough with the material to look up from the page every now and then, but for God's sake don't memorize it; you'll appear arrogant, like you already have the job. Above all else, no matter how badly you need work, no matter how hungry you are, how exhausted you've become from playing duck-the-landlord, never, ever show desperation."   **MICHAEL J. FOX**

★   ★   ★

"Auditioning's a whole different beast. . . . It's actually a moment of just throwing down and trying to see what you can bring there, 'cause you haven't evolved the character [yet]."   **PHILIP SEYMOUR HOFFMAN**

★   ★   ★

"When you begin to realize that some of the biggest successes of all time . . . have initially been rejected by people who supposedly should know better, you can't take all these rejections too seriously."   **CHARLES GRODIN**

★   ★   ★

"Back in our early TV days, Harry Dean Stanton, Warren Oates, Jack Nicholson, Dick Bradford, and I had a deal. . . . We got to know all the secretaries in all the offices of all the shows. They would slip you the script for the next week's episode. You would walk around the lot or get in your car and read as fast as you could. You'd look for a part they could play. . . . When we left the studio, we'd find a gas station and call our agent . . . 'The part of Dave in the *Virginian* episode 'The Prey' starts shooting next Tuesday. Works a day or two, it doesn't matter, but Bruce is right for the part of Dave, and tell Jerry Hinshaw that he's right for it.'"   **BRUCE DERN**

★   ★   ★

"Like most actors, I worshipped Mel Brooks. If he thought you were funny, it was like the Good Comedy Seal of Approval.

"I auditioned for Mel, and he watched me without expression, then declared, 'You're not funny.'

"I was flabbergasted and not a little insulted. I almost grabbed at him over the table. 'I am too funny!' I roared.

"'No you're not.'

"'Yes I am!'

"'Not.'

"'Am.'

"'Not.'

"'Am.'

"A long silence. We stared at each other.

"'I am funny.'

"'No.'

"'Am.'

"Two kids going back and forth. Now, that was funny."

LORRAINE BRACCO

★   ★   ★

"You have to be good at what you do, and you have to work hard and take care of yourself and all that, but I think everybody has to be lucky, too. Luck is a big factor."

CHRISTOPHER WALKEN

★   ★   ★

On starting out in New York during the '50s and '60s:

"In order to audition, you needed an appointment, but I had no contacts, so I tried to crash auditions! I had no agent, no manager—I didn't even have a resume or a headshot. I must have seemed right off the farm. All I had was one good pair of shoes and a lot of drive."   OLYMPIA DUKAKIS

On Struggling and Building a Career

"Even at the beginning, when I was doing junk television,
I still had one thing—focus."   **MICHELLE PFEIFFER**

★   ★   ★

"No, I didn't have that much confidence. As you get older,
you have more confidence, obviously. In certain areas.
In others . . . still don't have much confidence."

ROBERT DE NIRO

★   ★   ★

"I made my stage debut as an altar boy, or, more aptly, a falter
boy. I used to trip over my cassock or light myself on fire."

MEL GIBSON

★   ★   ★

"I don't want to pick scripts [just] to keep me in the status-phere." **JIM CARREY**

★ ★ ★

"There is nothing like those years when you don't yet have what you're working for. There's a lot of freedom because there's so much possibility." **ANNA DEAVERE SMITH**

★ ★ ★

"I was fortunate. Even before I left school I had an agent, an Equity card, and a job working 45 weeks a year, doing five plays in repertory." **KEVIN KLINE**

★ ★ ★

"My sister Lorraine told me—I was undecided as to whether to stay East and go to school or come to California—'If you stay around here, you'll always be Jack Nicholson, and you could be a big fish in a little pond, but it's better if you go to a big pond.' That was her way of nudging me out of the nest, I think. I don't know if it's the best piece of advice [I ever received], but it has worked out the best, anyway. I'll tell you one thing: Don't ever give anybody your best advice, because they're not going to follow it." **JACK NICHOLSON**

★ ★ ★

"It was Cocteau, I think—Cocteau said advice is a great thing to listen to and disregard. [*He laughs.*] And at times it is, you know? Because nobody really knows what you're feeling, what you're really going for, what you're really trying to do. Hell, I didn't even know what I was going for [in my career]. I just knew that I didn't want to be assembly line . . . Cheez

Whiz. There were agents, upper-echelon agents over the years who said, 'Listen, here's the deal: You have to do this because you can make this much money and you can do this and you can do that, success and power and all that.' I listened to them and they were right, you know, but I was right. I couldn't go where they wanted me to go."

JOHNNY DEPP

★   ★   ★

"Did you know I started out as a stand-up comic? . . . People don't believe me when I tell them. . . . That's how I saw myself, in comedy, and I didn't know I would do this with my life. I didn't know what the hell I was going to do."

AL PACINO

★   ★   ★

"Listen, everybody was offered the part of Lawrence of Arabia: Marlon Brando, Greta Garbo, Groucho Marx. Everybody but me. They all turned it down for various reasons. And David Lean had banked his life on that picture. David's wife was seeing a guru at the time, and this guru had seen a film called *The Day They Robbed the Bank of England*, in which I played a silly English officer. And the guru told her that he had just seen the man who should play Lawrence."   **PETER O'TOOLE**

★   ★   ★

"What affects your career is the quality of [your] product."
JOHN TRAVOLTA

★   ★   ★

"I use this [story] often with the young people I work with. The first thing that my students ask when they are about to graduate is, 'How do I get an agent?' And I say, 'That's the last thing that you want. What you want to know is how to deal with the only two things that this industry guarantees. One is rejection, the other is insecurity.'"

ANDRÉ DESHIELDS

★   ★   ★

"I do believe that work breeds work, and you get to work if you have honesty, range, and a sense of humor on and off stage."

BETSY AIDEM

★   ★   ★

"[The industry] tried to kill me off with poisons, sharp sticks, and blunt objects, and I was like a fucking snake that grew a new tail."

HARRISON FORD

★   ★   ★

"When you decide to do a movie, you don't go into it saying, 'Oh, man. I'm so excited to [be] making this movie. It's really gonna suck!' You go into it thinking, 'I'm gonna rock this thing,' and only then you find out it's gonna suck. And then you'll say or do anything to try and get out of it."

JOHN LEGUIZAMO

★   ★   ★

"If you are convinced [acting] is what you want to do, don't be afraid, go forward. When immigrants came to this country, they really wanted what they sought to be a part of their lives, and they fought for it. I was raised with a really strong work ethic, which is good, but the down side was that our parents would always tell us the bad things about the field because they were trying to protect us. You have to know what you want and go for it. Don't let the money be an issue. You can always pay your bills if you're willing to work."

OLYMPIA DUKAKIS

★　★　★

When asked, "What do you look for in a role?":

"I look for the echo inside me. Maybe we're all born with our future coiled up inside us like a spring, and we just unravel this coiled spring and work it out. I'm sorry if this sounds a bit bizarre. I'm trying so hard not be pretentious because I'm always called pompous and pretentious."

SIR BEN KINGSLEY

★　★　★

"I'll never play a victim."
REESE WITHERSPOON

★　★　★

On meeting the legendary John Houseman while studying at Juilliard:

"I was shown a seat in his office. He closed the door and settled into his rocking chair. After a long pause, he intoned, 'Mr. Reeve. It is terribly important that you become a serious classical actor. (*Pause.*) Unless, of course, they offer you a shitload of money to do something else.'"

CHRISTOPHER REEVE

"Agents, business managers, etc., etc. are not the authors of your career. They make suggestions. They are part of your research team. You are the author. You are the center of your career. You run the show."   **Anna Deavere Smith**

★   ★   ★

"John Wayne became my sort of foster father in Hollywood, always giving me advice. He'd say, 'Talk low and talk slow, and don't say too much if you want to be a big movie star.' I then made four pictures in a high voice talking at great speed."   **Sir Michael Caine**

★   ★   ★

On what she learned as a young supporting player on The Sonny and Cher Show:

"Cher would always come over to my room to sneak cigarettes. . . . She taught me to do needlepoint, and we'd sit around working on our pillows between scenes. When I got stuck, I always wanted to know the by-the-book way to fix my work. Cher would simply say, 'You just do what you have to do. It's like life: You don't have to play by the rules. Just get it done.'"   **Teri Garr**

★   ★   ★

"I never believed in my 'God-given talent.' I adored my work and I did my best. But that was all."   **Audrey Hepburn**

★   ★   ★

"To be young, out of work, and an actor is to say yes to everything. Can you ride a horse? *Certainly.* Can you play the trumpet? *Oh, yes.* How tall are you? *How tall do you need?*

"You take any acting job you can get—not just to be able to live, but also to learn how to act."   **ALAN ALDA**

★   ★   ★

"Actors that I've liked over the years, not all of them would play a lot of diverse roles. But they'd have diverse interests in the roles that they played and liked literate things. Like Burt Lancaster wasn't really a chameleon, but he played serious movies, comedies, acrobatic movies. I loved him as a performer. But if you look at Brando he really was a character actor because he played all different kinds of parts and he was a real actor. To me I've played leads, done cameos and supporting roles. It doesn't matter to me. I'm happy; I wouldn't want to be a lead in everything. It's not the most creative way to live to always have to carry something. For years Bob [De Niro] just did little parts, he was always doing supporting roles. What's the big deal I don't get it. To me it's kind of fun, like *The Big Lebowski.* . . . I don't understand what that word [character] means, it's strange to me. The actors I've always liked play many different characters. Sometimes it gets boring watching the same guy do the same lead role."   **JOHN TURTURRO**

★   ★   ★

"There were times when I was going to *have* to get a real job, but I've been very fortunate to always get either a job or a residual check when I most needed them—residuals checks can be so important to the struggling artist! But sure there were those times, and it wasn't just that I felt like it's not going to happen, but also feeling like my best wasn't enough and not really knowing what else to do."   **AMY ADAMS**

On his first job acting in a touring children's theater:

"Some real sleazy guy in Scottsdale, Arizona, was running
seven companies, doing *Little Lord Fauntleroy* with real
cheesy sets, removable mustaches and all that terrible stuff.
You'd drive around in this little van, do three shows a day,
sometimes a hundred miles apart, sometimes in big junior-
college theaters and other times in the library of some rich
day-care center. It was only six months, but I look back on it
fondly. It really was like vaudeville because you were always
flying by the seat of your pants."   **WILLEM DAFOE**

★   ★   ★

"He also acts who stands and waits."
SANFORD MEISNER

★   ★   ★

"I got my Equity card playing a duck."
KATHY BATES

★   ★   ★

"I don't miss the days of struggle. I've had enough of that.
That's like saying, 'Do you miss the time in which you used
to soil your diapers?'"   **TERRENCE HOWARD**

★   ★   ★

"I really was an actor from the streets, a gypsy, homeless and
penniless. My education comes from the sixties. I lived in
dives and dumps, in rooming houses and crappy hotels.
To me, anything that had running water and a bathroom in
the room was paradise."   **AL PACINO**

"It took longer than I thought it would take to get recognition. . . . I had to work my buns off. Sometimes I look at my shelf with all those astonishing awards and remember where I came from—this humble house in Humacao, Puerto Rico, with no running water."

RITA MORENO,
Oscar, Grammy, Emmy, and Tony Award winner

★　★　★

On a not-too-terrific production of Troilus and Cressida *he once did at McCarter Theater with John Lithgow, Tom Tarpey, Jim LaFerla, and John Braden:*

"During one Sunday matinee we were all down in the greenroom watching the NBA play-offs. A real cliffhanger was in progress: the Knicks against the Celtics in double overtime. We were listening to the play on the monitor, but we couldn't drag ourselves away from the game. We all missed our entrance. I think it was a council scene or a camp meeting where the Greeks are making plans against the Trojans. Unfortunately, the scene just didn't happen. The lights came up, and gradually six actors wandered on. Only the fact that so many of us were involved made it look like it might have been done on purpose."

CHRISTOPHER REEVE

★　★　★

"The worst thing [about starting out in the theatre] was understudying, because you had to fit in with the rhythms and do the precise same thing [the actor you were replacing] did, otherwise you upset everything else. It really was an odd feeling, a hideous thing, because you possessed no autonomy then."

SIR ANTHONY HOPKINS

"I was working for the Budget Director of the State of Connecticut. . . . [I] announced to the world I was an actor, and moved to New York City, Greenwich Village. . . . For the next four years I kicked around doing off-Broadway plays, $10.00 a week rehearsal, $30.00 a week when the show opened."

PETER FALK

★　★　★

"My first film of [my] new Fox contract was going to be a science fiction thriller called *The Day the Earth Stood Still.* I was not encouraged in the least, but I did not want to begin my career at Fox by going on suspension. . . . I do think it's the best science fiction film ever made, although I admit that I sometimes had a difficult time keeping a straight face. Michael Rennie [my co-star] would patiently watch me bite my lips to avoid giggling and ask, with true British reserve, 'Is that the way you intend to play it?'"

PATRICIA NEAL

★　★　★

"I eventually left home at 23, got a job tending bar. But the day I was supposed to start, I got another play, *Short Eyes.* Then I got a job in a movie, *Quicksilver,* with Kevin Bacon. That's when I figured out how to get a job when you still have a job: All I had to do was [keep one] coming down the pike; that's how you can make a living as an actor. At that point, after having been confronted with the business side of things—I was 24—I realized it wasn't so much about being a great actor; it was much more about doing something that will make people sit up and go, 'Hmmm. That guy's good.' You had to take what you could get and make something of it."

LAURENCE FISHBURNE

"The strange thing is . . . I never thought I'd do films. I was studying theatre, and my dreams were about riding my bike to the theatre on Sunday afternoons to do a play, and they still are."   **PHILIP SEYMOUR HOFFMAN**

★ ★ ★

"Struggling to be a genius is endemic to young artists who are starting their careers, but after being bloodied a few times, they just hope that they won't be ridiculed by the press or on television by those few who have the power to coronate them or tear them down."   **GENE WILDER**

★ ★ ★

"Keep working."
SANFORD MEISNER

★ ★ ★

"Keep working. Never be 'available' . . . Keep playing in theater or TV, anywhere, as often as you can. Eventually, if you're any good, somebody will see you."
                                              HUMPHREY BOGART

★ ★ ★

"The three things I said when I came out of school were I want to work consistently, I want to do good work and I want to be paid fairly, and that's happened. But I didn't become an actress for the money. I do it for other reasons."
                                                ANGELA BASSETT

★ ★ ★

While filming Hell Is for Heroes, *a film that went through several evolutions as directors, producers, et al., were changed:*

"I found myself committed to a movie that was totally different than the one I agreed to, but that alone wasn't a legitimate out for a rookie actor. There was no clause in my contract stating that I would be allowed to approve any changes, and I didn't dare protest too hard for fear of [the producer] assigning me to shoeshine duty. So I concluded that the only graceful exit was to find a way of getting [my character] killed. On a daily basis, I would pester [the director] with suggestions for my premature demise. I was aiming for just the right amount of verisimilitude. . . . 'In this particular scene I see that a tank is coming over the hill. . . . Maybe—and I'm just offering this up because it could be funny—but maybe I could roll under the tank and get killed.' [He'd] reply: 'Bob, you're on the movie until the end.'"

BOB NEWHART

★   ★   ★

On why he dropped out of college to pursue acting:

"I got a job in an off-Broadway musical called *Best Foot Forward*, which was Liza Minnelli's debut. She was 16 years old, I was 18. I had auditioned and I got the job and it was just about the end of the school year, and that was it. I was never keen on school, to tell you the truth. I was probably not qualified for advanced education."

CHRISTOPHER WALKEN

★   ★   ★

The best piece of advice he heard while starting out:

"'Get out of show business.' It's the best advice I ever got, because I'm so stubborn that if someone would tell me that, I would stay in it to the bitter end."   **WALTER MATTHAU**

★   ★   ★

"Right before I went and did the first workshop for *Angels in America*, I was seriously thinking about going to law school. It had just taken way too long, and I didn't think anything was going to happen. I was tired of waiting on tables. Then we did *Angels* out there, and I was talking to Rosemarie Tichler, who was the casting director at the Public Theater, and she said, 'Just ride that out. See what happens.' And you know, it ended well."   **STEPHEN SPINELLA**

★   ★   ★

"If necessity is the author of invention, she is the foster-mother of art, for the greatest actors that ever lived have drawn their early nourishment from her breast. We learn our profession by the mortifications we are compelled to go through in order to get a living."   **JOSEPH JEFFERSON**

★   ★   ★

"Right from the beginning, I believed that staying on course was what counted. The sheer process of attrition would wear others down. Them that stuck it out was them that won. That was my belief then. Still is."   **HARRISON FORD**

★   ★   ★

"The [career] choices I've made have come in large part from my unconscious. That goes for when I read a script and even when I hear about one—though there have definitely been

times when I heard about a script and immediately thought, 'No way.'"
JAKE GYLLENHAAL

★   ★   ★

"Don't go to parties to meet people."
HUMPHREY BOGART

★   ★   ★

"It seems to me that in this business of acting, it's not about doing good work so much as it is about being given the chance to do good work."
HUGH LAURIE,
accepting the SAG award for Outstanding Performance by a Male Actor in a Drama Series.

★   ★   ★

"I've gone through periods of depression during lengthy hiatuses [from work]. Everybody wants a sense of purpose, and when your mind's set on doing one thing and it's not happening, you just feel useless."
CHRISTIAN BALE

★   ★   ★

"At 17, I attended my first Oscars and sat in the balcony with 20 Spaniards. Then I could only speak two English words— 'Johnny Depp.'"
PENELOPE CRUZ

★   ★   ★

"I resisted the Hollywood dream. . . . My dream was to work with foreigners—not only from America, but from Europe, from the world."
JULIETTE BINOCHE

"It's tough, because you're always looking at the big contracts and the people making twenty million dollars, and you think, wow, I wish I could have that. Then you look at the other side of it, the Oscars and stuff like that, which has a little more weight to it. What you try to do is you try to marry them as best you can. I know one thing, when you do shoot for the big money, it's high risk, high return. Most of the time with the big money there's not a lot of substance there, but you cross your fingers and you try to find those projects that can give you both." **JAMIE FOXX**

★   ★   ★

"Choosy is not really a word that's in my vocabulary, in relation to my career. I can't be choosy. Scripts aren't, you know, flying in. I'm lucky to have any kind of job in the movies, and that's the truth." **DIANE KEATON**

★   ★   ★

"I got in the Screen Actors Guild back in the early '50s. And Walter Pidgeon was the president then. . . . I remember calling my parents and saying that I'm in the same union with Walter Pidgeon, Cagney and Cooper and Barbara Stanwyck and Bette Davis—all these fabulous [actors] that I grew up [watching]. And I thought I was . . . hot stuff, until I started knocking on doors and getting the turndowns. So I appreciate everything that all [actors in the Guild] have had to go through at some time in your life."

CLINT EASTWOOD,
accepting the SAG Life Achievement Award

★   ★   ★

"[My career] just kind of worked out that way. . . . I did a play called *A Soldier's Play,* which won a Pulitzer Prize and became a film. As a result of that, a director by the name of Richard Attenborough saw me and said he wanted me to play Steven Biko in his film *Cry Freedom.* I'm like, 'When do we start,' you know.

"As a result of that, Spike Lee had seen me do a play about Malcolm X and wanted to make a film about Malcolm X. 'Do you want to be in it?' I'm like, 'When do we start,' you know. So it wasn't a plan; it never has been and it still isn't."   **DENZEL WASHINGTON**

★   ★   ★

"If you're true to yourself, you'll turn someone on."
                                    JIM CARREY

★   ★   ★

"If you want to be an actor be honest with yourself. Don't let them push you around. When you believe in something, you fight for it even though you may suffer for it. . . . Just remember to put some dough aside for the times you're suspended."   **HUMPHREY BOGART**

★   ★   ★

On why he takes so much time deciding on which project to do next:

"I've got to believe in what I'm doing and most films are just junk."   **WILLIAM HURT**

★   ★   ★

"Much to the distress of my agents at the time . . . I actually started turning down [projects] very early on. I turned down things that my agents didn't understand. Movie opportunities. I was just like, 'I just don't wanna do that.' It's not that I knew what I wanted to do—because very often you can't know what you want to do until it's presented to you—but I knew what I didn't want to do."   **KEVIN SPACEY**

★　★　★

"A casting director suggested that it might be easier for me to get work if I changed my name, made it less Italian, more American. . . . I thought of names—Anthony Dane, John Allenby, James Farnsworth, Charles Butler . . . but then my father and my Uncle Jack, who was still alive, came to mind. How could I insult them by giving up their name? 'Fuck 'em all,' I thought, 'I'm keeping it.'"   **BEN GAZZARA**

★　★　★

"At the beginning of my career, somebody told me: 'You will never play anything other than like a soubrette.' I looked up what that means—it means playing a support part. And then, I wanted to make sure that this would not be true."

DAME JUDI DENCH

★　★　★

"Success as an actor, or getting on and getting parts that you really want to play, is not something you can easily manipulate yourself. You can have agents, you can have managers, you can have people scouting around on your behalf but in the end it probably comes down to the luck and the chance of knowing the person who makes the decisions. . . . Yep, chance and luck. It just means you have to try with each job, be as good as you can so directors will want to employ you next time round." **SIR IAN MCKELLEN**

★   ★   ★

"Any art or any job of work that's any good at all sells. If it's worth selling, it's worth buying. I have no sentimentality about such matters. If someone offers me five dollars a year more than I'm getting I take it." **HUMPHREY BOGART**

★   ★   ★

"I'm hoping to start [my film career] with comedies, move toward dramas and eventually go into pornography. I'm frankly happy to be employed right now." **STEVE CARELL**

★   ★   ★

"When you first start out as an actor in this business, you're just a hired gun—'You have the job, show up Tuesday.' [Producing] became a way I saw of being able to control your fate out here, which we are so in need of doing as actors, because we're really the low man on the totem pole."
DON CHEADLE

★   ★   ★

"I did not expect [success]. No one asked me to be an actor, so no one owed me. There was no entitlement. Still is not. . . . I think the arts in general, no one asks you. They might ask you to fly an airplane; they might ask you to raise wheat. But they don't ask you to sing a song. That is still considered, in this society, one of those elitist or luxury endeavors. . . . And so actors have to accept that, you know. No one asked us.

So the idea of not getting work, that's part of the territory."

JAMES EARL JONES

★   ★   ★

"I'm always willing to learn. There used to be a critic in Sydney—he used to review theatre—and his name was Harry Kippax. Old Harry, kind of a curmudgeon, he could be pretty tough, and early in my career I was getting big parts on stage and boy I remember Harry landing on me a few times. But I started looking at it, and I bumped into Harry in New York in the Algonquin Club; he was having a scotch and soda and I sat down and talked to him and it was a really valuable experience. Because I was a very young man then and Harry was old and knew theatre, and he was more experienced and more traveled, and knew more about theatre than I did. It was interesting to sit down and sort of talk to him—and he was real honest. I never begrudged him any of the stuff that was negative because I used to look at that and think, that man's being honest. He has no personal axe to grind, there's no agenda; it's really what he believes and he saw. I wanted to know more about that, and I learned a great deal from him."

MEL GIBSON

★   ★   ★

"I've never really had a [career] plan, you know? I'm the guy sitting at the U-Haul place: 'If you need help moving, I'll move it.' Lately, I've done one comedy, one western, one war story. [I don't feel like] 'I'm so serious, but now I want to play a cross-dresser just to prove I'm versatile.' I still love the goofball parts. . . . I'm like a drummer in a band. I just love free crap."

STEVE ZAHN

★   ★   ★

"I had a kind of meandering little career, and then I was given a chance to play one of the bottom six in *The Dirty Dozen*. I originally had one line in the whole film—'Number two, sir!' Then one day we were all around this big table. Telly Savalas, Clint Walker, John Cassavetes, Robert Ryan, Charles Bronson, Ernest Borgnine and Lee Marvin, really extraordinary guys. And Clint Walker got up and said, 'I don't think it's appropriate for me, as a star in Hollywood, and a representative of the Native American people, to play this stupid scene where I pretend to be a general.' And the director Robert Aldrich, who had a huge authoritarian streak, turned to me—we'd all had our heads shaved—and said, 'You! With the big ears! You do it!' He didn't even know my name!"   DONALD SUTHERLAND

★   ★   ★

On starting out in repertory theater:

"We opened a play on a Monday evening, on Tuesday morning we read the next week's play, on Wednesday morning we went through Act One and Thursday, Act Two. I don't know, but we fitted it all in somehow. But there were times when I had a lot to do, you would sit and after supper everyone would go to bed and you would sit up with a candle learning lines. If you sort of knew it by the time you went to bed, it sank in. The next morning you'd know it, more or less."   PETER BARTLETT

★   ★   ★

"When I first started out, I didn't know what kind of actor I was. Well, I was a bad actor. . . . I thought I was [a] character actor, but I also thought I was not very good at it, because

I hadn't figured out how to do it. I learned on the job and by experience." **HARRISON FORD**

★ ★ ★

"There have been plenty of times when it seems like you have a burst of [career] momentum and you think this [project] is going to change things, and it does for that instant and then that's it." **ADAM GOLDBERG**

★ ★ ★

When asked what advice he'd give to struggling young actors:

"Learn to type. Find something you can fall back on without selling out your honor. Keep your head in the ball game. Stay reasonably sober. And keep your body in shape and your mind will follow." **JOHN GOODMAN**

★ ★ ★

"[I thought of quitting the business] many times. I've left it many, many times. I left it and went back to college. I left it and went back to law school. I've probably spent more years out of it than in. What keeps me coming back? There is nothing like a live audience. To me it's like great sex. They let you know when it's working and when it's not." **TONYA PINKINS**

★ ★ ★

"I'll never forget my original name: Issur Danielovitch. . . . During one college vacation, I worked at a summer stock playhouse with Karl Malden (after he'd changed his name).

He and the rest of the players debated what my name should be. I suggested Ivan Daniels . . . they disagreed; they thought it should be a simple last name and an unusual first name. The director of our group blurted out, 'Kirk Douglas.' We all liked that name. Ivan Daniels was kicked out and Kirk Douglas stayed."   **KIRK DOUGLAS**

★   ★   ★

On being an actor Off Off Broadway in the mid-'50s and early '60s:

"It was a very fertile period to be an actor in New York City, in the Village, because you could actually live and be an actor. We would do 16 shows a week in the cafes, and you'd pass the hat around after each show, and that's how we ate. . . . It was a livelihood literally. But without any idea that it was going to be successful or not successful. It was about a way of life."   **AL PACINO**

★   ★   ★

"As a rule it usually takes three or four readings for me to be interested in a script, and if I'm interested I'll read it three or four times before I make a strong decision."   **CHRIS COOPER**

★   ★   ★

"I'd say that the responsibility I feel is to know enough when to say no [to a project]. And that's hard to do sometimes, because you know it's going to be a big movie and it's actually going to get made and it's going to be the Big Thing that everyone is talking about. But I read the script and, for whatever reason, I just don't get it. So I have to be responsible to my own aesthetic reasonings. I have to be

able to say to whoever is offering it: thank you very much, I'd like to help, but I just don't understand what's going on in this movie."
                                                              TOM HANKS

★   ★   ★

"I've seen really talented people just kind of disappear from where they were headed.

"I've seen people of notable ability who really don't even think that much about doing as well as they can. Then there are people who, in principle, would like to do really well, but don't seem to have a good idea of what it takes. Then there are those who understand the effort it takes but lack the will to do it. Then there are people who want to do well, understand what it takes, and have the will to do it."
                                                        CHARLES GRODIN

On the Importance of Technique and Training

"Create your own method. Don't depend slavishly on mine. Make up something that will work for you! But keep breaking traditions, I beg you."

CONSTANTIN STANISLAVSKI

★   ★   ★

"To act is the final result of a long procedure. Practice everything which precedes and leads toward this result. For when you act, it is too late."   **RICHARD BOLESLAVSKY**

★   ★   ★

"The most difficult thing to learn is the art of simplicity."

SANFORD MEISNER

★   ★   ★

"I used to have a lot of philosophies about acting; they fell apart over the years."   **ALAN ARKIN**

★   ★   ★

"The methods by which actors arrive at great effects vary according to their own natures; this renders the teaching of the art by any strictly defined lines a difficult matter."   **JOSEPH JEFFERSON**

★   ★   ★

"Mostly what I like about acting is that it's almost impossible to achieve perfection in it. No matter how good you are, you can always be better. That's the challenge."   **KELLY McGILLIS**

★   ★   ★

"I can't understand actors who learn their lines *approximately*. If it's a good script, the writer has sweated over every part of it and a single word can throw everything. If it's a bad script, you shouldn't be doing it."   **KATHARINE HEPBURN**

★   ★   ★

"The more you do comedy, the better you can do drama."
GLENN CLOSE

★   ★   ★

"Comedy is really hard. It's so subjective, and everybody has their own sense of humor. I'm honestly amazed whenever you can get more than a few people to laugh at one thing."
BEN STILLER

"I had to make my acting look simple, like nonacting, like anybody could do it. . . . Sometimes you watch an athlete and you think, 'I could do that.' All the training has to disappear and the effort must be invisible in that one moment—the dive, the free throw, or the scene—when everything comes together."   **KARL MALDEN**

★　★　★

"When our teeth ache we visit a dentist; when the plumbing breaks we call a plumber. When acting and the teaching and learning of it are to be considered, the views of a veteran teacher of acting—who, as it happens, also is an old actor . . .—certainly are pertinent and admissible, and should be of interest and value. The notion that instruction in acting cannot be given, or rather that it cannot be received, is a mistaken one."   **DAVID BELASCO**

★　★　★

"Being bone-real is not the big problem in acting in the theatre. The problem is to express what you are expressing at close distance, 50 yards *away*—that is the problem."
                    SIR LAURENCE OLIVIER

★　★　★

"I'm a Methodist, but not in acting."
JAMES GARNER

★　★　★

"I often say to young actors the chances are that at some point [you're] going to get a break and be very lucky. You had better have done your homework and be ready. Never stop thinking, learning, watching, listening."

JULIE ANDREWS

★   ★   ★

"Every actor has his own way of working, and whether they know it or not, every actor uses some part of the Method."

RICHARD WIDMARK

★   ★   ★

"You play tennis, and you take your second lesson and a Pro says to you, 'You always start your serve on the wrong foot.' What do you have to do? . . . Fix it. And after a few years it becomes a habit. And when your way of acting is an organic habit you have a technique. That takes time."

SANFORD MEISNER

★   ★   ★

"Jerzy Grotowski taught me to discourage actors, because then, only the best will stay and work and train."

JOSEPH CHAIKIN

★   ★   ★

"People who are serious about being the best actor they can be are the ones who really work at it. At the [Actors] Studio, young actors who are in their 30s can work on Lear. Now, they're not going to play that for a while, but it sure is a challenge, because the inherent problems in it are enormous—the rage, the anger, the pentameter, the size of it—and if they meet those challenges when they're 35 years

old, my God, it's like when I was a kid playing stickball in Brooklyn. I'd been hitting with a broomstick. The first time I picked up a bat, it felt like a tennis racket, I couldn't miss the ball."
                                                        MARTIN LANDAU

★ ★ ★

"Nine-tenths of every profession is very, very boring. Unless someone wishes to go through that boredom, he will never become a professional. To achieve the skill that makes for a Heifetz or a Stern, you stand for four hours every day, very bored, but you keep going up and down that fiddle, up and down that fiddle, doing a lot of boring things. . . . Therefore, I want you to be bored on the stage. I want you to learn to bore us and enjoy it. Until you can do that, acting will always be a strange challenge and a fear. You will never be able to take enough ease and time to do on stage what you have to do, because you will be scared that either you will be bored or—even worse—that we will be bored."
                                                        LEE STRASBERG

★ ★ ★

"I never left the wings of the Old Vic, ever. I was there from 1957 to the end of 1961, and I never, ever went to my dressing room. I used to stand at the stage and watch, all the time, because only from that, you know, do you learn."
                                                        DAME JUDI DENCH

★ ★ ★

"The English technique [for acting]—ultimately the same technique as the American—is about having the internal works going 100 percent. The whole English lifestyle is about reading between the lines. It's all about what you haven't said. They have a beautiful way of playing that. There's so much going on underneath the surface and in the pauses and when they're listening and it's very still."

HUGH JACKMAN

★　★　★

On the training she received at Yale University's famed drama program:

"They told me I had no talent. They took themselves so seriously. It was fun to argue about Chekhov but the teachers had too much power."   **SIGOURNEY WEAVER**

★　★　★

"I think before any actor enters into a scene, it should be necessary to pass under a sign in the wings that reads, 'You are not allowed on this stage unless you want something with all your heart and soul—and have a way of getting it.'"

ALAN ALDA

★　★　★

"I need an actor who knows the world's literature and can see the difference between German and French Romanticism. I need an actor who knows the history of painting, of sculpture and of music, who can always carry in his mind, at least approximately, the style of every period, and the individuality of every great painter. I need an actor who has a fairly clear idea of the psychology of motion, of psychoanalysis, of the expression of emotion, and the logic of feeling. I need an actor who knows something of the anatomy of the human body, as well as all the great works of sculpture. . . . This intellectual training would make an actor who can play a variety of parts."   **RICHARD BOLESLAVSKY**

★   ★   ★

"I have discovered that the only position from which one can learn is the position of not knowing. From there you say, 'Teach me.' Then the teacher can teach."   **ELLEN BURSTYN**

★   ★   ★

"I might be one of the last generation of actors who really did receive a brand of training and heritage in the theatre. And these younger actors don't have that. By and large, they got their Screen Actors Guild card making a Hot Wheels commercial."   **TOM HANKS**

★   ★   ★

"You learn that there's a technique to [acting] and a craft and you go study with a teacher and you realize that there's an art form to it. It's a very serious thing, but you don't know that at first when you're just relying on instinct."   **SAM ROCKWELL**

★   ★   ★

"It's funny: The more I learn about being an actor, the more there seems to be to learn about it."   **PAUL DANO**

★   ★   ★

"People misunderstand it or they simply go, 'Oh, yeah, that Sanford Meisner technique, that's that, blue shirt, blue shirt, blue shirt, blue shirt, ad infinitum blue shirt.' . . . Well, this is what it means. I counteract the natural trap of wanting to be witnessed and interesting in the theatrical situation, by being interested in something out of myself. . . . I first notice something that really exists in you before I get to more refined things. So first I say you're wearing a blue outfit and you've got trainers. Just like Sherlock Holmes. Part of this is actually being present enough and interested enough [to notice these things]—then, if something about you triggers something visceral . . . what it is I'm noticing and expressing, one way or another, in word or deed [becomes] how I feel about it."   **JEFF GOLDBLUM**

★　　★　　★

"I've always been more comfortable [with comedy] because I was scared of drama. I didn't really know how to access my emotional side without wounding my own person. Once I learned how to do that it opened up all these doors to me and I realized, 'You know what? Real life contains moments of laughter followed by uncontrollable sobbing.'"   **AMY ADAMS**

★　　★　　★

"When I was a student of Bobby Lewis, a great teacher, he looked at us one day and said, 'I feel very sorry for you, because the better you get, the more it's gonna look like walking and talking. The seams will become invisible, and all your lives, strangers will say to you, 'You know something? I could do that.' It is so incredibly difficult to master a craft that, once mastered, looks as if you were born doing it."   **JAMES LIPTON**

★　　★　　★

"If you want to be able to express the maximum variety of things, then the more technical mastery you can achieve, the more fun you're going to have!"   **GERALDINE PAGE**

★   ★   ★

"Technique is something that you use if you need it. Otherwise, to hell with it."   **SANFORD MEISNER**

★   ★   ★

"In many classes, workshops, groups, whatever . . . [you might observe] an experienced talent struggling for agonizing, tedious, and hysterical periods of time to break through and become expressive. If you're interested in this sort of thing, it can be an inspiring process. It's not for everyone. It's not 'entertaining,' though it can be. . . . It can be deeply satisfying to acquire and be part of another's acquisition of the tool which allows them to enjoy and express their talent."   **JACK NICHOLSON**

★   ★   ★

On why she sought actors' training:

"My natural talent was there. The work could be fantastic. . . . But I had no control over it. I couldn't summon it. I had no technique. Talent cannot be taught. But technique can."   **ELLEN BURSTYN**

★   ★   ★

"An awful lot of actors who are considered very good actors are not very good actors. There are people who just strike gold, they have intrinsic talent, but the point is that if they did train, it would not inhibit them. If they were with a good teacher, it would only broaden them more."

MARTIN LANDAU

★　★　★

"The two most important things I learned at The Actors Studio were: don't use any technique if the situation and the author's words are working for you, by themselves; and, try to stay *in the moment*."

GENE WILDER

★　★　★

"If I'm watching an actor emote and I feel nothing, it's got to be the actor's fault. . . . You can't let yourself get trapped in technique. Technique is only where it begins. You have to trust that all the information you have about a role will seep into the performance."

LAURA LINNEY

★　★　★

"Sometimes it's more powerful for the actor to hold back so that the audience produces the emotion themselves."

KEIRA KNIGHTLEY

★　★　★

"Duse played in a play called *Magda*. There's a scene in the last act. When she's a young girl she has an affair with a guy from the same village, and she has a child with him. Twenty-five years later, or thereabouts, she comes back to visit her family who live in this town, and her ex-lover comes to call on her. She accepts his flowers . . . and they sit and talk. All of a sudden she realizes that she's blushing, and it gets so bad that she drops her head and hides her face in embarrassment. Now that's a piece of realistic acting! . . . That blush is the epitome of living truthfully under imaginary circumstances, which is my definition of good acting."   **SANFORD MEISNER**

★   ★   ★

"I don't believe in letting an actor run wild, in letting his lack of discipline destroy another actor's performance so he can make himself look better through some improvised little trick. This is one of the worst artistic crimes an actor can commit. Any actor who goes in for this sort of thing should be told to get out of the profession."   **ROD STEIGER**

★   ★   ★

"You can't improvise your way out of Shakespeare."
          JOHN LEGUIZAMO

★   ★   ★

"[*Sighs.*] They talk about acting school today but, I mean . . . Clark Gable once said to me, 'Acting school? [If you go,] I'll kill ya!"   **MICKEY ROONEY**

★   ★   ★

"I don't go through an Actors Studio process of finding a character. In the Actors Studio they teach what's known as Method acting. They instruct you to build a history of your character going back to childhood. Someone took his rubber ducky away from him in the bathtub when he was five, therefore he's homicidal. Or if you are going to play a

garbage collector, you volunteer to ride around with your
local waste management crew. If a script is given to me . . .
I find where the joke is and I figure out how to get there."

BOB NEWHART

★   ★   ★

"I'm not an actor. It's my day job, and I learned how to hustle
it really good, and I have a love for it, and I *get* it, but I don't
know what I'm doing."   ROBERT DOWNEY, JR.

★   ★   ★

"I started studying [acting] seriously when I was six. . . . Not
with anybody else, but I used to watch the world . . . analyze,
even at that age . . . why I was moved by certain things
they did. . . . I remember particularly . . . my mother was
talking to a friend of hers who had just been through some
kind of tragedy. . . . This woman was crying and sobbing
and bemoaning her fate, and I found myself saying 'I'm not
moved' by what she's doing. 'Why am I not moved?' Then I
said, 'It's because she's complaining too much. She's crying
too much. If she would do it less, then I would be moved
more.' And I just put that in the hopper for my work."

ALAN ARKIN

★   ★   ★

"When I first got to New York, everyone said, 'Just learn a
really good technique.' I didn't know what that meant; it's a
misleading word. Everyone's got a technique; they just have
to figure out what the truth is about themselves. It's taking
pieces of all good things. James Mason was interviewed
about his method, and he said, 'If I have a method, it's [a]

combination of a lot of things and finding your own truth.'
That's what I believe."   **WILLIAM FICHTNER**

★   ★   ★

"The theories of acting that I was presented with when I was
young were not useful to me."   **HARRISON FORD**

★   ★   ★

On studying at Chicago's St. Nicholas Theater:

"I just figured you'd go in, you'd learn some lines, you'd do
some scenes and get criticized for them. And then you'd
get better the next time. I didn't expect these . . . repeating
games and [games] to get you closer to the character and
break down any artifice that was there."   **JOHN MAHONEY**

★   ★   ★

"Only bad actors try to cry, good actors try not to cry. . . .
Only bad actors try to laugh, good actors try not to. . . .
Only a bad actor tries to be drunk, a good actor tries not
to be. A drunk does not want to be drunk, a drunk wants
another drink."   **MARTIN LANDAU**

★   ★   ★

"The reality is no one can tell you how to act. My own
feelings and observations tell me it requires deep personal
commitment to allow any individual to move from that
vague desirous state of 'I'm gonna be an actress (or actor)'
to a point where the actor has some vague sense that every
part in which he is cast is not some incredible piece of luck

. . . but the result of some solidly acquired skills which, in there, where the truth is, he can call his own."

JACK NICHOLSON

★　★　★

"I took a class at HB Studios when I was 16 or 17. Once you're in a class, you can't leave to work; you have to stay. They want you to really study. And I auditioned for *The Beach House* with Swoosie Kurtz and George Grizzard, and I got it, which was a problem. I didn't mean to get it; I was just practicing auditioning. So I had to say no. And George Grizzard called me on my phone. He said, 'Is this Robert Leonard? This is George Grizzard. What the hell are you thinking, turning down my play?' I said, 'I'm in a class.' And he said something to the effect of 'Let me tell you something. You will learn more about acting in one fucking night with me than a year in that shithole.' Typical George pleasantries. And I thought, 'He has a point.'"

ROBERT SEAN LEONARD

★　★　★

"When you have worked out a technique such as has been developed in me through long training, then . . . inner creative life beyond the range of your consciousness will stir in you of its own accord. Your subconscious, your intuition, your experiences from life, your habit of manifesting human qualities on the stage will all go to work for you, in body and soul, and create for you.

"Then your playing will always be fresh, you will have a minimum of clichés in your acting, and a maximum of truth."

CONSTANTIN STANISLAVSKI

★　★　★

"The first acting teacher I had taught me the worst sin was to be boring."   JOHN MALKOVICH

★   ★   ★

On the old studio system:

"You were doing tiny little parts in big pictures with stars. Then you would get a big part in a tiny little picture. . . . In the meantime you were learning your craft by acting, which I've always thought was the only way you can learn it."
                                                    JIMMY STEWART

★   ★   ★

"I was once doing a scene for Lee Strasberg, and somebody backstage dropped a big box of dishes. I kept going. After, Strasberg said, 'Somebody dropped a big box of dishes in the middle of your scene and you kept going.' I said, 'Yeah, I was concentrating.' He said, 'You're the only one in the room that didn't jump—that's not concentrating!' That was a big moment for me. I realized that concentration isn't about 'focusing.' It's about having 360-degree vision, eyes and ears open, not missing a thing."   CHRISTOPHER WALKEN

★   ★   ★

"I don't have a fixed method, because here in this country we have so many different cultural influences, and people come to cinema from so many different places and sources, with so many different intentions and so many different destinations they aspire to. . . . You have to invent a method for every movie."   TOMMY LEE JONES

★   ★   ★

"The Method is, 'If it works, use it.'"
JACK NICHOLSON

★　★　★

"Without craft, or discipline, I'd be at the mercy of my
history and my emotions. . . . The contradiction coiled
at the heart of acting is this: the only way to portray
uncontrolled feelings is to control them. You learn how to
do that through craft." **OLYMPIA DUKAKIS**

★　★　★

"It's weird, because I always feel like such a bad girl when I've
talked about technique. It's stuff I care a great deal about. It's
something I know about, but it's also stuff I'm just beginning
to try to understand, and every time I act in another part
it's a complete learning experience. I have no idea how I'm
going to get where I need to get. I know I have certain tools,
and I just have to rummage through the toolbox and go,
'Gee, I think I need a hammer for this scene.'"
MARY STUART MASTERSON

★　★　★

"When the [actor's] technique shows, it is purely the lack of
technique or it wouldn't show." **JACK LEMMON**

★　★　★

A quick note on comedy technique:

"If the physical thing you're doing is funny, you don't have
to act funny while doing it. . . . Just be real, and it will be
funnier." **GENE WILDER**

"I was in an acting class with Peggy Feury years ago on La Brea, and I thought I'd do my preparation on the street. I went down on La Brea by myself, and I was running through the scene and pounding myself in the chest and talking to myself and singing and stuff, and a police car pulls up. This was a while ago, and the cop says 'What are you doing, young fella?' They did the whole 'Look at my eyes, follow my finger.' I said, 'No, no. I'm taking an acting class. I'm just acting.' They said, 'Well, where is this supposed acting class?' I said, 'Right upstairs, but no, no please.' They say, 'Come with us,' and they interrupt another scene in the middle of class. I said, 'I'm so sorry, Peggy, please forgive me.' These couple of cops say, 'Is this guy in your class?' 'Yes,' she says. 'he is.' It was terrible."   **JEFF GOLDBLUM**

On the Importance of Maintaining a Healthy and Expressive Instrument

"Do you admire the physique of a circus strong man? For my part I know nothing more repellent than a man with shoulders that more rightly belong on a bull, with muscles that form great Gordian knots all over him. . . . We need strong, powerful bodies developed in good proportions, well set up, but without any unnatural excess."

CONSTANTIN STANISLAVSKI

★   ★   ★

"When you are a pianist you have an outside instrument that you learn to master through your finger work and arduous exercises and with it, you as a creative artist can perform and express your art. As an actor, you the artist have to perform on the most difficult instrument to master, that is, your own self—your physical being and your own emotional being."

YUL BRYNNER

"I'm extremely physical. I run four miles a day. I work out every day. It gives me a sense of resiliency and protection. As an actor, your body is your tool."   **AARON ECKHART**

★   ★   ★

"The actor's instrument is only himself, and the more interesting your instrument is, not only are you going to be remembered, but the more use you can be put to."   **RICHARD DREYFUSS**

★   ★   ★

"You can't separate your performance from your body—they work together when you've taken care of yourself. And when you haven't your body can work against what you want to express in a scene."   **KRISTIN DAVIS**

★   ★   ★

Regarding her return to Broadway in Terrence McNally's Deuce after a 23-year hiatus from the Great White Way:

"I'm sort of putting myself in training. I take care of my body. Careful about what I eat. Don't smoke. No booze except maybe a glass of wine. Sleep is important. Y'know, we who've been around know what to do. For instance, it's baby oil to remove makeup and Kiehl's moisturizer. And I prefer to do my own makeup."   **ANGELA LANSBURY**

★   ★   ★

"I do believe that the quality of the voice affects an audience, so if you want the audience to feel at ease with you, it's important that the voice achieves that. If you want to scare the wits out of them, you can do that with your voice too. If you want to communicate big emotions and feelings, the voice is really all you've got." **PATRICK STEWART**

★　★　★

"We [actors] use our body like a screen through which pass the will and the relaxation of will." **ANTONIN ARTAUD**

★　★　★

"The object onstage is to get the adrenaline coursing through the veins and yet be utterly relaxed . . . so that the mind works more and more quickly." **SIR DEREK JACOBI**

★　★　★

"I had a lot of trouble working with my co-star, who was from 'the Cocaine School of Acting.'" **SHIRLEY MACLAINE**

★　★　★

On whether or not he smoked pot to play a stoner while filming the Cohen brothers' film, The Big Lebowski:

"I didn't smoke [pot] while I was on the set. It would have been a great excuse to get high. But that's a lesson I've learned. Working in an inebriated state is fine for a couple of takes but you've got to sustain that all day and that really doesn't do you a whole lot of good. So for [the character of] The Dude I did some sense memory work. I was a bit of a pothead in my youth so I had a lot of experience to draw on." **JEFF BRIDGES**

"The actor may and sometimes does give of his best on those evenings when he feels ill, or tired, or even slightly bored."

SIR MICHAEL REDGRAVE

★   ★   ★

"If you want to be a classical actor, as Laurence Olivier said, you have to be fit as an athlete. You can't go around with a big belly hanging out, drinking late at night."

PATRICK STEWART

★   ★   ★

"It is certain that since breathing accompanies effort, the mechanical production of breath will engender in the working organism a quality corresponding to effort. . . . An actor can arrive by means of breath at a feeling which he does not have."

ANTONIN ARTAUD

★   ★   ★

On performing nude onstage:

"It's the least arousing process. . . . To be honest, when you get naked in front of 900 people, quite the opposite happens. . . . I'd be lying if I said I was completely fine. I was nervous and I was a little bit worried. But not meaning to drop a name, I talked to Gary Oldman about it, because we get on well and I know he's been naked onstage. And so I said to him, 'What's it like?' and he said, 'On the first night you'll be terrified and on the second night you'll be terrified and after that you won't care.' And that's absolutely true. When you've done it twice, it doesn't matter anymore."

DANIEL RADCLIFFE

"Let the body go into action when it can no longer be held back, when it feels the deep inner essence of experienced emotions, inner objectives which it has prompted. Then of its own volition there will emerge an instinctive, natural urge to carry out the aspirations of creative will in the form of physical action."   **CONSTANTIN STANISLAVSKI**

★ ★ ★

"Too few actresses follow their instinct. I think instinct is the direct connection with the truth."   **LAURETTE TAYLOR**

★ ★ ★

On how he realized he had a drinking problem:

"When [drinking] replaced work. Drinking became more attractive than working. . . . I like what Norman Mailer said about alcohol: 'Drink has killed a lot of my brain cells and I think I would have been a better writer without it, but it would be one less way to relax.'"   **AL PACINO**

★ ★ ★

"You just have to keep yourself very free, very loose so that something can happen, even if it's not what happened the night before, even if it's not what you thought would happen. Something must remain alive and flexible."   **SIR ALAN BATES**

★ ★ ★

"The big thing is how do you combine at the same time 100 percent concentration with 100 percent relaxation? The two

things seem to go against each other. I will always work on this until the day I die. . . . I think it's probably the secret of any art."
                                             SCOTT GLENN

★   ★   ★

On his decision to quit smoking and drinking, two pastimes for which actors are somewhat notorious:

"It's boring to say, but I feel great. I don't feel that I've lost any quality of life. I still enjoy restaurants and bars. It's not like I'm sitting at home and—I don't know what people do when they sit [at] home. I still feel like I'm out there doing things, and I'm still creatively dangerous. When people hear about me, they think, 'Oh, you're creatively dead. You should go work for Walt Disney. You have no edge.' That's not true. Other avenues open up. I didn't want to do romantic comedies before [I quit]. Now that I changed my life, I feel like I want to do romantic comedies. I want to make people laugh. I want to get the girl. I want people to come out of the movie feeling good, whereas before, when I was doing the other stuff, I turned down all these romantic comedies. I thought they weren't worthy to see. Now my whole outlook has changed."
                                             AARON ECKHART

★   ★   ★

"For the first time I looked in the glass and thought, 'I know how this man would speak and move and behave,' and to my great surprise I found I was able to keep that picture in my mind throughout the action, without my imagination deserting me for a moment, and to lose myself completely as my appearance and the circumstances of the play seemed to demand. I suppose the truth of the matter was that I was relaxed for the first time. The finest producers I have worked with since have told me that this relaxation is the secret of all good acting. But we were never taught it at the dramatic schools. One's instinct in trying to work oneself into an emotional state is to tighten up. When one is young and nervous one tightens the moment one attempts to act at all, and this violent, nervous tension, if it is passionately sincere, can sometimes be effective on the stage. But it is utterly exhausting to the actor and only impresses the audience for a very short space of time."   **SIR JOHN GIELGUD**

★   ★   ★

"The gifted actor finds by instinct how to tap and radiate certain powers."   **ANTONIN ARTAUD**

★   ★   ★

"There's nothing like getting arrested or winding up in the emergency room at Cedars to make you think you might not be a 'social' drinker."   **ED BEGLEY, JR.**

★   ★   ★

"In the theater, you're . . . a long-distance runner with a few moments of sprinting. The starting gun is going to go off at curtain time whether you like it or not. Your day is aimed at going out of the gate at your most alert. You've got to exercise. . . . You've got to eat the right food at the right time, and stop talking at a certain time of the day so your voice is fresh."   **LYNN REDGRAVE**

On the Importance of Imagination, Inspiration, Fantasy, and Storytelling

"There is no such thing as actuality on stage. Art is a product of the imagination, as the work of the dramatist should be. The aim of the actor should be to use his technique to turn the play into a theatrical reality. In this process imagination plays by far the greatest part."   **CONSTANTIN STANISLAVSKI**

★   ★   ★

"I think all good actors use the Magic If."
JANE ALEXANDER

★   ★   ★

"Life feeds you reality. Play feeds you imaginatively."
STELLA ADLER

★   ★   ★

"What you believe isn't important. What's important is that
you believe."   **GOLDIE HAWN**

★   ★   ★

"I grew up loving *The Wizard of Oz*. To tell you the truth,
I longed to see the movie again and again because I wanted
to go to Oz. I wanted to have a tornado sweep me up and
take me away from the life I was living as a teenager.
I wished that Auntie Em was my aunt."   **JOHNNY DEPP**

★   ★   ★

"I [recently panicked because I] haven't lived out every
fantasy that ever came into my empty, er, echoing head,
but enough of them that I'm relaxed about it. The only
thing lately is, I got to the point where I couldn't in any way
conjure up a fantasy. It was like, 'Ohhh, I'd love to . . .' but
there was, like, nothing in that department in my head.
And as a man who has been attracted to Eleanor Roosevelt,
it really panicked me out."   **JACK NICHOLSON**

★   ★   ★

"Uppermost in my mind was always the cultivation of
my art; and as the aim and object of all true art is the
skillful blending of the real and the ideal, it becomes the
student's duty to store his mind abundantly with facts, at
the same time that he gives free scope to the exercise of his
imagination."   **WILLIAM CHARLES MACREADY**

★   ★   ★

"I started painting watercolors . . . but I found I can't paint
and act. I [also] can't act and write [or] write and paint.

The artistic reservoir is the same, it's coming from the same source, but you're putting it in three different places."

GENE WILDER

★   ★   ★

"[Actors] are storytellers. And ours is an ancient tradition. . . . We should all be very proud of our place in society. On any given night, millions of people across the world buy a ticket for adventures that only we, as storytellers, can provide. We release burdens, we galvanize emotions, we make people laugh, we make people talk over breakfast. This is a great job, and I want to encourage every [actor] to give everything you've got to the story. God bless narrative. God bless originality."

RUSSELL CROWE,
accepting the SAG Award for Outstanding Performance by a Male Actor in a Leading Role

★   ★   ★

"I don't think there's any one of us who can't relate to the desire to poison our loved ones. [*Laughs.*] . . . Maybe [acting is] a way of venting off things inside you. I don't know. I sound high falutin', but I always gravitated myself to Stella Adler, who's one of the really great thinkers about acting. She was always saying that, fundamentally, she considered [acting] an imaginative process, and I kind of agree with that. Other people, I'm sure, have completely different attitudes toward it. I'm just saying that, for me, personally, I enjoy the imaginative part of it."

EDWARD NORTON

★   ★   ★

"The most interesting movies are those when, even though you know the outcome, you still fully believe there'll be another outcome."   **JAKE GYLLENHAAL**

★   ★   ★

"The performances you have in your head are always much better than the performances on stage."   **DAME MAGGIE SMITH**

★   ★   ★

"I think you get addicted to telling stories. The ironic thing is quite often actors are very shy and they're not good joke tellers necessarily. There's storytelling and then there's being a character in the story and that's an interesting thing to live a life on stage or in film. There's something about the detail. I just know the movies that affected me as a kid like *The Deer Hunter* and *Sophie's Choice* and *Taxi Driver* and *Badlands* and *Midnight Cowboy*. And then movies like *Mr. Mom* or *Stripes* and *Animal House* are just as important as *One Flew Over the Cuckoo's Nest* or *Citizen Kane*."   **SAM ROCKWELL**

★   ★   ★

When asked to comment on how he handles acting against a CGI screen in films:

"In my imagination I believe I'm in the place we're supposed to be—just like when I'm on stage I believe I'm in the place where the story is told. It's all happening in the imagination and young people will understand that because young people live in their imaginations more than adults so it's a very precious thing. They should try and hold on to that."

SIR IAN MCKELLEN

★ ★ ★

"It makes me feel like a very special person, that I'm able to make my living with my imagination."   TOMMY LEE JONES

★ ★ ★

"If you can go to the theatre, and you're in a room with a bunch of other people. And what's happening in front of you is not happening. But you actually believe it is. If I can do that, I've done my job. And that's the thing—that is a drug. That's a drug. That's something you get addicted to."

PHILIP SEYMOUR HOFFMAN

★ ★ ★

"Every invention of the actor's imagination must be thoroughly worked out and solidly built on the basis of facts. It must be able to answer the questions (when, where, why, how) that he asks himself when he is driving his inventive faculties on to make a more and more definite picture of a make-believe existence."   CONSTANTIN STANISLAVSKI

★ ★ ★

"I hope that what I do has some meaning. . . . When you compare three hours of the greatest Shakespeare in the world or the greatest film in the world to saving a life if you're a doctor, or saving a psyche if you're a psychiatrist, or saving a country if you're a politician, then artistically creating something beautiful seems relatively unimportant.

It seems foolish at times. Insignificant. There are times when I despair that it's utterly absurd."   **KEVIN KLINE**

★   ★   ★

"Joseph Brodsky was giving a commencement speech in 1988. . . . He was a Nobel Laureate, a Russian poet, a brilliant, brilliant, brilliant man . . . and he said, 'This is the best day of your lives,' to the graduating class. He said, 'Everything is going to go downhill from here on in. It's going to get more boring the more goods you acquire; the more toys you have it's going to become—' And in the middle of it he said the phrase that I carry like a mantra with me. He said, 'Try to stay passionate. Leave your cool to the constellations. Passion alone is a remedy against boredom.' . . . and I love what I do. I just love it."

DONALD SUTHERLAND

★   ★   ★

"I think I like period pieces because they take me so far from my reality. They give you scope for imagination, and I really like that. . . . We have a perception that people 200 years ago didn't feel the same things that we feel today, but they did. . . . So it's not a case of trying to make a period piece modern; I think it's a case of realizing that people are people and just going from there."   **KEIRA KNIGHTLEY**

★   ★   ★

On acting on film with a green screen:

"I compare it to being on-stage and having to look at, you know, 'Moscow is burning!' But really you're just looking at the exit sign in the balcony, and going 'Ahhhh! Ohhhh!'

. . . It's the same thing. You have to pretend. You have to pretend you're looking at Mars. Or you go to the window on the back of the set. You're looking out, and you're seeing the mountains of Switzerland or something. Only, really, it's just a stagehand with a cup of coffee who's reading a magazine over there. You have to pretend." **GARY SINISE**

★ ★ ★

"I did *H.M.S. Pinafore* in grade school and that's when my father taught me how to substitute realities. I had to kiss this boy and I didn't want to. It's not that I disliked him, but I didn't have a crush on him. I said, 'How am I going to kiss him in front of all these people?' My father said, 'Who do you think's the most handsome movie star?' I thought for a second and said, 'Elvis.' And then he said, 'Imagine that's Elvis standing up there and you can go and give him a big kiss on the cheek.' And it worked! Eventually, I didn't think about Elvis—I just got excited when I went up to kiss the boy." **MIRA SORVINO**

★ ★ ★

"We certainly don't trumpet the art of storytelling [in this country]. We've lost a little of the grace of it. For me, a film is at its best when you can start filling in the story with your own life experience." **BRAD PITT**

★ ★ ★

"Every movement you make on the stage, every word you speak, is the result of the right life of your imagination." **CONSTANTIN STANISLAVSKI**

★ ★ ★

"[To an actor] personality is more important than beauty, but imagination is more important than both of them."

LAURETTE TAYLOR

★   ★   ★

"The theatre is replete with emotional legends. . . . Those playing *Romeo and Juliet* are supposed to present a more stirring partnership if they develop the same passion between themselves as that which they are emulating; some believe that Shakespeare's magic depends on it. After long reflection, I must point out that this is a dangerous notion. It would imply that actual death is necessary to the feigning of it, or at least that physical pain is necessary to give a successful impression of it. Such an idea robs the work of its artfulness as well as its artistry. It is a tempting belief, but bad in principle."

SIR LAURENCE OLIVIER

★   ★   ★

"Actors don't lie, because to be effective as an actor, you have to tell the truth. Truth is the only thing the audience can recognize, the only thing that helps them accept the fantasy of what they're watching. For a play or a film or a television show to be believable, it has to be authentic. Authenticity is truth."

KELSEY GRAMMER

★   ★   ★

"A writer, a composer, a painter, a sculptor are not pressed for time. They can work when and where they find it convenient to do so. . . . This is not the case with an actor. He has to be ready to produce at a fixed hour as advertised. How can he order himself to be inspired at any given time? . . . He needs order, discipline, a code of ethics not only for the general circumstances of his work, but also and especially for his artistic and creative purposes.

"The first condition toward the bringing about of this preliminary state is to follow the principle I have aimed at: Love art in yourself and not yourself in art."

CONSTANTIN STANISLAVSKI

★   ★   ★

"I had fantasies about living in the wrong time or wishing that I were, I don't know, Louis XIV. . . . But this is not what's happening. You try to build your imagination and deal with that, while staying in the here and now."   WILLIAM HURT

★   ★   ★

"There's absolutely no point in doing a so-called period piece unless it relates to a modern sensibility."   CATE BLANCHETT

★   ★   ★

"One thing an actor cannot be is ignorant. An actor has to read. He has to know paintings and music, because they help him understand his past. They provide nourishment for his imagination."   STELLA ADLER

★   ★   ★

"There's nothing I wouldn't attempt if it was within the realm of a good story."   CLINT EASTWOOD

On Building a Character

"My first successful characterization is what I devised for myself in high school. I played the blond homecoming queen for several years. I laid out my clothes for the [next] week every Sunday so that I wouldn't repeat." **Meryl Streep**

★   ★   ★

When asked whether playing a violent character is easier to play than other types of characters:

"What kind of question is this? You got to be able to play anything. Playing your own grandmother pissing on the ground should be no more difficult than carrying the groceries up the driveway before you get shot. That's acting. That's the real answer to the question." **Jack Nicholson**

★   ★   ★

"As an actor, you tend to want to show everything—but that's not true to life. What's compelling is the sense that something isn't being revealed—you just see little flashes that give you a hint as to why somebody is acting the way he is. That's what draws people to characters—that mystery or possibility. Will we know? Will we be shown?"   **GLENN CLOSE**

★   ★   ★

"Barker [the director] said to me, 'Lear should be an oak, you're an ash; now we've got to do something about that.'"
SIR JOHN GIELGUD

★   ★   ★

"I don't give a fuck what I look like during a movie or between films. I couldn't care less. I don't have a certain haircut. I don't give a shit, you know? But on behalf of the character, particularly if it's a real person [I'm playing], now that's a huge responsibility."   **RUSSELL CROWE**

★   ★   ★

"I am interested in getting out of my own way and letting the character happen."   **SHIRLEY MACLAINE**

★   ★   ★

"I don't believe in hard work. If something is hard, leave it. Let it come to you. Let it happen. Now the decision to play a role is halfway towards understanding the character, because you empathize with it and that's why you want to play it."
JEREMY IRONS

"I believe . . . that every great actor ought to be, and is, moved by the emotion he portrays; that not only must he feel this emotion once or twice, or when he is studying the part, but that he must feel it in a greater or lesser degree—and to just that degree will he move the hearts of his audiences—whenever he plays the part, be it once or a thousand times."

TOMMASO SALVINI

★   ★   ★

"Your adjustments to your character's age must, of course, also be aligned to his work, his loves, attachments and appetites, whether they be innocent, knowing, familiar, or jaded."

UTA HAGEN

★   ★   ★

"First I'll learn Polish. Then I'll forget me. Then I'll get to her. That's my plan of action."   **MERYL STREEP**

★   ★   ★

"I don't believe in Method acting, where you walk around in character all the time. I still retain a part of myself when I come home and I still talk to my dog the same way."

KELLY McGILLIS

★   ★   ★

"Look, if an actor immerses himself in a role and travels to some place that was dark and painful? Totally fuckin' irrelevant. . . . For me, it's about concentration, right? Now, I've done scenes that people are like, 'Oh, that's so heavy. Do you stay in character? Do you take it home with you?' I don't. I do it and I get it done. It's really just about concentrating very hard."   **CLIVE OWEN**

★ ★ ★

"I'm told that people find it strange that I do the work the way I do it, but then I think, 'Well, yes, but the work is inherently strange.'

"We're spending the better part of our lives pretending to be other people. Stranger from my point of view is to have the capacity to jump in and out [of a character], which some people undeniably have. I'm kind of in awe of those people."   **DANIEL DAY-LEWIS**

★ ★ ★

"Once you do your homework, build your character's biography, immerse yourself in the period—do all the conscious work—then a moment of ease and effortlessness must come. You are transcended, you lose your self-consciousness. All ego concerns go away and you're free."   **ANNETTE BENING**

★ ★ ★

"The first thing I do with a script is divide it up into beats and measures—a measure being a sequence of beats—to get at the fundamental rhythm of the part before playing it in rehearsals."   **JACK NICHOLSON**

★ ★ ★

"In my mind, even when I was playing supporting characters,

I thought I was the lead. As an actor, it boils down to essence. You listen and break down a scene. You're really just focusing on your own work. They don't teach you in acting class to be a lead or supporting character."

CHRISTOPHER MELONI

★   ★   ★

"Brecht and Joe Chaikin and everybody introduced me to [the idea] of the actor being the actor first and the character second. It's not about dissolving into the character, which we do in movies, where it's no longer Clint Eastwood, it's the Pale Rider. In theater, the most interesting thing is to sustain the actor, not get rid of him. Keep the actor moving in and out of character, or being able to separate the two. This is one of the most interesting things in theater."

SAM SHEPARD

★   ★   ★

"When you're the lead in a movie, when you're in every moment of the movie, it's hard not to live it. We shot *Sherrybaby* in 25 days. I was never in my own clothes. I would get into [my character's] clothes, be her all day, come home, fall asleep, wake up, go back to work. I do better in that kind of work. What I found [about the character] was that she was in such a rough place that she didn't have the luxury to feel any kind of self-pity or to fall apart at all, or she would not have been able to survive. So I shot all these fucked-up scenes that were really horrible, but I didn't experience them that way. Obviously, I understood that all the things that happened in the movie were painful for her, but I didn't really let that into the work. Then all the terrible things I've had to go through surfaced *after* we'd finished filming. And I got over it. I don't think I could play that part now. I don't know that I could be okay with her things that I had to be okay with in order to play her."

                                        MAGGIE GYLLENHAAL

★   ★   ★

"It's like a woman getting pregnant. This character, this person that I am to become, starts to grow inside me and I listen. If I don't listen, he will die in me."

                                        MARCELLO MASTROIANNI

★   ★   ★

"My only problem is finding a way to play my fortieth fallen female in a different way from my thirty-ninth."

                                        BARBARA STANWYCK

★   ★   ★

"It's not important that the [character] actor commit some stunt . . . Ultimately, you don't want [the voice] to be the only thing people are talking about. [The character's] emotional and psychological life are of utmost importance. If that doesn't play, nothing will play."

                                        PHILIP SEYMOUR HOFFMAN

★   ★   ★

"When you are protected by your character, you feel that you can do all the things you can't do in real life."

                                        MONICA BELLUCCI

★   ★   ★

"Some actors prefer to start with characterization. It is more difficult . . . and the result is not so subtle, the choice of elements not so wise as it might be if you followed the inward thread of the part first. It is like buying a dress without being measured."   **RICHARD BOLESLAVSKY**

★   ★   ★

"Whoever I play, whoever I become, I must have a starting-off point. I must be sure of who I am, so sure it doesn't worry me, before I become someone else."   **BOB HOSKINS**

★   ★   ★

"If an actor can find the personal rhythm of a character, he's home free. And one of the best ways to do that is to follow a person down the street, unbeknownst to him. Pick up his walk, imitate it and continue it, even after he's out of sight. As you're doing it, observe what's happening to you. By zeroing in on a guy's personal rhythm, you'll find that you've become a different person."   **DUSTIN HOFFMAN**

★   ★   ★

"I'm not interested in transmitting my pain to someone. I'm interested in transmitting the *character's* pain or joy. That's my job."   **GEORGE C. SCOTT**

★   ★   ★

"I usually collect a lot of details or characteristics, and then I find a creature swimming about in the middle of them."   **SIR LAURENCE OLIVIER**

★   ★   ★

"One begins with the text because it's the text that leads you to the character."　　**PEGGY ASHCROFT**

★　★　★

"I think [my process for movie roles is] a continuation from years of stage work, before I did a film, when I was studying with different acting coaches, in particular Stella Adler. I took her class called Script Analysis. . . . You jot down ideas, memories, whatever, concerning your real life that somehow parallels the character you're playing, and you incorporate that in your scene work. What was made very clear early on in my studies was that often the words, though they're important, are not the most important thing. And where I have so much fun creating a character is when I'm doing the homework—imagining, going on little head trips. I love to fill my head with whatever I can concerning the scene and the character."　　**CHRIS COOPER**

★　★　★

"The basic components of the characters we play are somewhere within ourselves."　　**UTA HAGEN**

★　★　★

"When a character's written with that kind of precision by these terrific writers, they leap off the page and you want to do them. They're filled with contradictions. I remember the last time I was at a bar, I saw a bar fight. Some guy made some racial epithet and all of a sudden it went bad. Then it broke out in this very animalistic way, how fights sometimes do. All of a sudden everybody gets triggered. I saw this guy go and punch this other guy. He could've been like

Schwarzenegger from some movie. He was just pure animal, and he did it. And as soon as he finished it, you could see regret, shame, all these things wash across his face, just for a minute. And they're totally contradictory things. One was absolutely animal and macho alpha-male predator. The next minute he looked like a little baby about to cry. What we really see of a character is what's so interesting."

JOHN CUSACK

★　★　★

"There are great lessons in playing opposites. If you've got an unsympathetic role, try playing him like the hero. The script won't let you succeed, but you'll find something worth keeping."　JEFF DANIELS

★　★　★

"I just leave [the character] at work. . . . Years ago, I read a book by James Cagney called *Cagney by Cagney*, and he just talked about it. He essentially said, 'Hey, it's no big deal. It's just your job.' You know this is my job. . . . You know when I was younger, I carried the role around and, you know, agonized for months or whatever, but basically, by the time I finish a film, I'm tired of that character anyway. You know so it's not too hard to just walk away from it."

DENZEL WASHINGTON

★　★　★

"A lot of people may say you shy away from this and that. I don't even look at things that way. I don't look at them aesthetically, I look at them on an emotional level. And to me, every character I've played is emotionally beautiful.

So when I read these roles, and get to the heart of who the person is, emotionally, that's where my passion lies."

HILARY SWANK

★   ★   ★

"You can't play a character that you don't love."
RICHARD DREYFUSS

★   ★   ★

"You become very intimate with your character because you're in his skin for 15 hours a day."

CHRISTOPHER MELONI

★   ★   ★

"I think regardless of what any of us say, I think we've all had pretty interesting, if not to say rough, childhoods. So to me . . . [I see] this struggle to try and present something, this struggle as an actor to go, 'This is what I'm feeling right now.' I think you see that in performances a lot. [Whereas lately I've worked] like, 'I'm going to show up and what baggage I carry with me I'm bringing with me. I'm not going to try and create new baggage to somehow play a character. I'm showing up every day and this is what I bring with me.'"

JAKE GYLLENHAAL

★   ★   ★

"I always try to find in these bad guys [I play], something that's human that makes them even more diabolical. If you see someone that's all bad, you kind of just put them in the monster category. But if you see someone who is really bad

but is also a father and a grandfather and all of that, that's
even worse, I think."   **GENE HACKMAN**

★   ★   ★

"A dog attacked me while I was playing Tony Montana [in
Scarface], and I tapped it on the snout, I could believe I
did that. I love dogs too—but it jumped at me. Normally,
I would run for the hills, but I was fearless, and I like that
whole idea of being fearless in [a] character."   **AL PACINO**

★   ★   ★

On the challenge of playing a real-life character:

"[Do] as much as you can without trying to stick things on.
The less you do to make yourself look like the person, the
better, really. Otherwise the audience just sits there and
thinks how much you do or don't look like that person."
                                                    MICHAEL SHEEN

★   ★   ★

"It's much easier to play a character written with a lot of
emotional indicators. It's much harder to do procedural
[dramas]. Reading off credit-card numbers [for instance],
you continually have to dig deep. . . . I've been known to do
[my character's] grocery list while interrogating someone.
I'll do anything to keep that internal life going. Did she go
to the gym? Has she seen her son?"
                                          MARIANNE JEAN-BAPTISTE,
                            about her character, FBI agent Vivian Johnson,
                                       on television's Without a Trace.

★   ★   ★

"I don't feel like I'm really able to start inventing any character until I have the voice down. I'm actually not a natural with accents . . . so it's essential to me to maintain an accent throughout working. The most important thing is trying it out in your everyday life. You start with strangers in shops, restaurants. You might feel like a fool, but they don't know that you're speaking in a different voice. And then eventually with your friends and family until everyone just knows, 'All right, this is what he's doing for the next few weeks.' And that way you don't feel like an idiot every time you hear, 'Action!'"   **CHRISTIAN BALE**

★   ★   ★

"I despise those prick actors who say, 'I was in character,' and 'I became the character,' and all that stuff. . . . It's hideous. It's just masturbation at the highest level."   **JOHNNY DEPP**

★   ★   ★

"When [my character] came in, he was very green and extremely cocky. But over the years, he's learned that you get more with candy than with vinegar, and so he's learned not to bounce off the walls all the time. He's learned to do his work and keep it positive, almost the reverse of what he started with."

JESSE L. MARTIN,
commenting on the evolution of his character, Detective Green, on television's long-running series, Law & Order.

★   ★   ★

"I never look at movies so much in terms of the character. I read the movie and I say this is a movie I want to see and I kind of screen the movie in my mind in its entirety then say to myself, 'Is this a movie that I want to be in?' I've been offered roles that were dynamic and flashy . . . in movies that I thought were very mediocre, then I've played roles that weren't as dynamic in great films. I'm much more interested in being a modest component in a great film than being a dynamic component in a film that's not that worthy."

ALEC BALDWIN

★   ★   ★

"Everybody says the bad guy is the most interesting part. It's total bullshit. The bad guy might be doing bad things deliciously, but the good guy's got the dilemma, he's got the girl."   **AARON ECKHART**

★   ★   ★

"I'm quite convinced that if I do something that's a big film and I don't believe in it, I'm going to suck. Sometimes I've needed a job, and I've read it, and it's just a straight-out bad guy. And I can't find one redeeming thing, and I don't know what the guy cares about, and I'm not doing it. What am I going to do? Try and find out how to make the next line more mean and Snidely Whiplash than the last? Do I need to twirl a moustache? If I can't find a way to make this guy real, I'm quite sure I'm going to be really bad. And I don't want to be bad."   **WILLIAM FICHTNER**

★   ★   ★

When it was pointed out to him that, in the 40 or so movies he'd done, he's played "happy or positive characters maybe five times," he responded:

"Well, I think if you look at any actor who isn't just playing heroes, that's what their résumé looks like. There are characters in movies who I call 'film characters.' They don't exist in real life. They exist to play out a scenario. They can be in fantastic films, but they are not real characters; what happens to them is not lifelike. But ultimately if you're not the actor playing that hero, that 'film character,' then you're taking on other roles in other movies, and you're going to be playing characters with a slightly more realistic view of what life is like. Ultimately, all characters have some negative and positive energies. That's just how I see it. I didn't go out looking for negative characters; I went out looking for people who have a struggle and a fight to tackle. That's what interests me." **PHILIP SEYMOUR HOFFMAN**

★　★　★

"All the training I've had is based on finding things internally and bringing them to the surface. Then I started trusting that those things would be there. Now, I consider myself to be a hair actor. I find the hair, the clothes, the movement and the character starts to form. I'm also very influenced by writing. You can be flattened by bad writing." **SEAN PENN**

★　★　★

"My favorite kind of characters to play, and to see in movies, are not wholly likeable, as individuals. There's something my wife always says about acting—that if you can put a whole human being on screen or on stage, that's the challenge. Because so often in movies there's so much posturing, particularly with female parts, where they're supposed to play [only] this one side of a person: the supportive girlfriend, or the manipulative bitch, or whatever. Whereas most of us can be all of those things." **ETHAN HAWKE**

"I had to play this serial killer in Russia, based on a real man who ate children. I was very depressed before I left . . . the whole subject. . . . I kind of constructed [the role] completely, not using one ounce of myself. The whole look . . . it wasn't a make-up job, no false noses . . . but just a facial look, a walk, everything, speech pattern . . . was absolutely just made up because I did not want to take this horrible man home in any way. I can be doing silly walks . . . as they're saying 'turn over,' and as soon as they say 'Action' I can go on and do a great emotional scene, tears and all the rest of it, walk off and start doing silly walks again. Because that's what English actors do. It's acting."   **MALCOLM MCDOWELL**

★   ★   ★

ROBERT DUVALL: "I always try to find the contradiction, the vulnerability, in a [character I play]. I was doing research on *Lonesome Dove*, [a film I did] about the Texas Rangers. On the border at one time there, their leader was shot down—and, en masse, they just wept."

INTERVIEWER: *But Kilgore [the character you played] in* Apocalypse Now *is recklessly confident.*

ROBERT DUVALL: "But in the original version, I save a baby's life and put him in a helicopter. Francis Ford Coppola cut that out—it really pissed me off. . . . We got that story from a helicopter pilot over there who'd seen a guy save a baby. People have hobbies amidst these things—like, my character surfed. They say that during the Six-Day War in Israel, they couldn't find an officer, one of their head guys, when they wanted him. It turned out he was snorkeling."

"If [the actor] does not find himself in his part he will kill off the imaginary character because he will have deprived him of live feelings. Those live feelings can be given to the character he has created only by the actor himself. So play every part in your own right in the circumstances given you by the playwright. In this manner you will first of all feel yourself in the part. When that is once done it is not difficult to enlarge the whole role in yourself. Live, true human feelings—that is the good soil for accomplishing your purpose."
                                        CONSTANTIN STANISLAVSKI

★   ★   ★

"People have assumed that Stanislavsky's emphasis on the actor's need to experience truly is predicated on the assumption that the actor is not aware of the imaginary nature of his performance. In other words, the actor forgets he is acting. Obviously, this is impossible. If the actor really forgot that he was acting, he would naturally drop his cues, his dialogue, and all of the scenic directions. What mattered, Stanislavsky felt, was the truth of the actor; it is what the actor feels and experiences internally that expresses itself in what the character says and how he reacts externally."
                                        LEE STRASBERG

★   ★   ★

"I was supposed to play Yelena in [*Uncle*] *Vanya*, who'd been described as the most beautiful woman in the world. I was having a hard time with this, but my agent said: 'You just have to be the most beautiful woman in the room, and there are only four women in the play. One is a young girl, one is an elderly nurse and one is the older mother.'"
                                        JULIANNE MOORE

"I did a movie where I had to smoke, *Heaven Help Us*. I wanted to know why people smoked, why my character smoked. I decided she did because she really wanted to blow people away. Besides, I don't drink, I don't do drugs. I needed a vice."   **MARY STUART MASTERSON**

★   ★   ★

"What [Bob] Fosse taught me, by rekindling my performer's intention, was that when I, as an actor, was acquainted with each nuance of thought, movement, and heart in my character, I could then throw that knowledge to the winds and start afresh. But not until I'd earned the right. Not until I'd considered each creative possibility through thought, rehearsal, and much respect for the terrain that was new to me."   **SHIRLEY MACLAINE**

★   ★   ★

"I think actresses pay too much attention to the tradition of acting. That is a great mistake. It cramps creative instinct. I received a good deal of criticism for my walk in *Bird of Paradise*. Some critics said I should be taught how to walk across the stage. Of course I paid no attention to that. My walk was the walk of the barefoot Italians who carry loads on their heads, and I had learned it from them. It certainly was not the traditional stage walk, but we are living in a time when simplicity and truth are the watchwords of the theatre. The traditional stage walk would not have fitted the character I played."   **LAURETTE TAYLOR**

★   ★   ★

INTERVIEWER: How do you elicit emotions that you need in a scene when they just don't come?

CHERRY JONES: As I've gotten older it's much easier. I found what worked with *The Heiress*—where I had several tearful moments—was the thought of the loss of [my then lover] Mary.

INTERVIEWER: That worked 371 times?

CHERRY JONES: I could have used her every night. Some nights when I needed a break from killing Mary off, I'd use my family. I just need a springboard to get me to a heightened emotional state."

★   ★   ★

"I did *Sleuth* with Laurence Olivier, who was one of the greatest actors in the world. We rehearsed and he was screwing up, badly. We were very worried, because there were only two of us in the movie, but no one said anything. And then one day, Larry came in with a moustache, and he put it on, and he was fantastic. And at the end of the day, he took it off and he said to me, 'Do you know, Michael, I cannot act with my own face.' And he couldn't. You see Olivier in anything, he puts on a bloody nose, a wig, something. . . . And that's one of the greatest actors in the world."   SIR MICHAEL CAINE

★   ★   ★

"That I am chiefly guided by feeling is probably the reason that I have never been able to play with satisfaction, either to my audience or to myself, any part with which I have not full sympathy, and of late years I have not even attempted such parts. This attitude of mine towards his creations should, I conceive, be assumed in a greater or lesser degree by every actor who has a part to play, and not be confined simply to those who, like myself, have identified themselves more closely with what, for want of a better term, I may call 'heroic' roles. One may sympathize even with a villain and yet remain an honest man, so that in counseling a student first of all to put himself in sympathy with his character, I am by no means urging on him the acquirement of even the remotest obliquity of moral vision. After having satisfied myself that the character I was about to attempt was one with whom I could put myself in full sympathy, I have next set myself laboriously to study its inner nature, concerning myself not one particle with the outward characteristics of the points wherein the suppositious being might differ in his figure, bearing, or speech from the rest of his fellow-men. These are trifles . . . within the scope of any actor who has learned his trade and is skilled in the mechanics of his art."

TOMMASO SALVINI

★   ★   ★

"Saying goodbye to a part. I have been so close to a character whom I am never going to meet again. . . . Now it is time to leave.

"These tears of farewell are not mine. It is the role crying, knowing she will never exist again."

LIV ULLMANN

On Rehearsals and the Acting Process

"In English, the word for *rehearsal* derives from rehearsing. In French, rehearsal is *la repetition*, and it means what it sounds like—a repetition. My favorite meaning comes from the German, *die Probe*, which sounds like what a rehearsal ought to be: the probe! I want to probe, to test, to try . . . to adventure!"   **UTA HAGEN**

★   ★   ★

"The rehearsal merely clarifies the problems that an actor needs to work on at home."   **CONSTANTIN STANISLAVSKI**

★   ★   ★

"One must not think of the spectator while acting. Naturally this is a delicate problem. First stage, the actor structures his role; second stage, the score. At that moment he seeks a sort of purity (the elimination of the superfluous) as well as the signs necessary to expression. Then he thinks: 'Can one understand what I am doing?' and this question implies the presence of the spectator. . . . If the actor has the spectator as his point of orientation . . . in a sense, he will be offering himself for sale. . . . Yet I don't believe the actor should neglect the fact that the spectator is present and say to himself: 'There is no one there,' for that would be a lie. In a word, the actor must not have the audience as a point of orientation, but at the same time he must not neglect the fact of the public."   **JERZY GROTOWSKI**

★   ★   ★

"Live television has certain perils. One of them is the terror, which reaches almost obsessive intensity, that you are suddenly going to lose your mind, turn to the camera, and speak every obscenity you can think of."   **ELLEN BURSTYN**

★   ★   ★

"At 10 in the morning . . . I shuffled into the tiny, airless rehearsal room in the tiny, airless offices of the New York Theatre Workshop . . . for my first day of rehearsal. A dozen or so other actors milled around, not really expressing how happy they were to be there, especially when no one knew one another from previous jobs. In the center of the room a semicircle of metal folding chairs curved around a small upright piano, so I staked out one for myself on the end and sat, quietly watching everyone else. . . . A young woman approached me, her arms full of manuscripts. She handed me a thick rubber-banded libretto and a tape, and then repeated this with other actors, who by now were making their way to their seats. . . . I hoped I could hold my own with them. . . . I flipped through my libretto, happy (and intimidated) to see that there were many lines devoted to [my character].

"'Okay, everybody, let's begin,' a voice called out."

ANTHONY RAPP

★   ★   ★

"The actors must understand each other, help each other, absolutely love each other. They absolutely *must*."

SIR LAURENCE OLIVIER

★   ★   ★

"A guy once told me, quoting a philosopher—who was it, Emerson?—'Don't be a farmer. Be a man on a farm.' You have to be a human being first, and whatever you do is secondary."

ROBERT DUVALL

★   ★   ★

"The trouble with talking about acting is that it's like sex. It's enormously fun to do, but just dreadfully embarrassing when you have to talk about it. I always think it's more elegant not to."

PAUL BETTANY

★   ★   ★

"I'd learned as an actor that listening isn't just waiting for my cue. . . . Listening is letting the other person change me. I don't say [my line] because it's written in the script; I say it because this person has forced it out of me."

ALAN ALDA

★   ★   ★

In response to being called a 'scene stealer':

"That's never the goal. I do what the scene requires. I never try to steal anything, unless of course the script says, 'In this scene he steals something.'"   **DON CHEADLE**

★   ★   ★

On taking over another actor's part in a production that's already underway:

"I liked it. I jumped into a movie once before, on *Maverick*. What is nice about it is that you don't get time to think. You don't have to do the rehearsals. So many of the decisions are already made before you get on, so you can jump into it. I think I'm a good candidate for jumping into films— because I'm a director myself, so I know how movies are made and I can go the shorthand route without having to sit through endless meetings."   **JODIE FOSTER**

★   ★   ★

On the similarities that exist between acting and carpentry:

"There's a real simpleminded analogy: you have to have a logical plan. You have to perceive it from the ground up. You have to lay a firm foundation. Then every step becomes part of a logical process."   **HARRISON FORD**

★   ★   ★

"Actors get into some awful habits through their preoccupation with their faces. You have to look at your face in order to get it looking right, but you get more tired of your face than other people do. As soon as you are in rehearsal, it's necessary to start thinking about what you look like. . . . Hold back on deciding how you should look until you find what is commensurate with what the lines require. I don't think very often of how I myself look: I've got hair—brown hair with grey in it—and lines in my forehead, lines down past my mouth, and bags under my eyes, and my height is just over six feet. That is the kind of professional knowledge one has."   **PAUL SCOFIELD**

★   ★   ★

"I do not believe acting should be smaller than life. I just enjoy throwin' myself at stuff, risking too much. I'd rather have someone say, 'Tone it down, Hunter, WHOOAAH!' than not feel I'm giving enough."   **HOLLY HUNTER**

★   ★   ★

"After a couple of weeks of rehearsals . . . I suddenly found myself having heated arguments with the other actors about a particular moment in a scene, and I realized that I'd stopped being objective about the play and was only seeing it through the eyes of my character. That's a good sign. But it's interesting, because it completely takes you by surprise when you find yourself getting really worked up and angry about how these other actors are talking about a scene. You believe the scene is actually about this, and then you realize, no, the scene isn't really about that, it's just that now you're only seeing it through the eyes of the character."

MICHAEL SHEEN

★   ★   ★

"Movie fans always seem interested in knowing about [nude lovemaking] scenes. Is something going on there? First of all, 59 crew members are walking around, getting things ready, and they're taking forever, 17 hours a day with hot lights on you the whole time and you're sweating profusely before you even make the first move."   RUTGER HAUER

★　★　★

"For a lot of us coming from Missouri, it's about what's between the lines."   BRAD PITT

★　★　★

"Actually, there's something quite enjoyable about making the same mistakes [over and over]. You're never surprised; you are only disheartened—there's some comfort in that."   PAUL NEWMAN

★　★　★

"Marlon [Brando] was a very difficult person to know. One day, we were doing a scene in a film. . . . He had to really, how do you say? Pat my back. Like this. . . . And I said, 'Don't do that, because I don't like it,' before shooting. So he did [it] while we were shooting. And I said, 'Don't do that ever again, because I'm going to slap you right in your face.' So he was very upset about it, because I said . . . 'Why do you do that? I mean, do you like women? . . . Why did you do that to me?' . . . He calmed down a little bit. And then we went on with the scene, and everything was all right. . . . Great actor. But . . . a little bit confused inside of himself."   SOPHIA LOREN

★　★　★

On the process she used to run her successful variety show:

"My motto was: Let everybody shine, because that's the best
way to look good."   **CAROL BURNETT**

★   ★   ★

"My first husband, Martin Scorsese . . . knew about the power
of imperfection. He even revered it. At the time, he edited
his films at home and the film he was working on then was
Raging Bull. He showed me a scene he had just put together
and said, 'Perfect, but it shouldn't be perfect. I like it so
much, though, I can't change it.' So he took a splicer and
snipped a frame out of the perfect scene, though it's not
enough of a gap to be perceived as a 'hole' by the audience
when the film is projected: 'This way I know it's not *perfect*
so its soul can flow through it.'"   **ISABELLA ROSSELLINI**

★   ★   ★

On working with difficult actors:

"You can have integrity and not necessarily be difficult.
. . . There's a difference. [When I'm directing], I don't
like it when an actor is temperamental. The point is that
everybody has got their own, as I say, meschugga, their own
craziness. And when you do a movie, everybody should
leave their personal problems at home. It's difficult enough
to make a movie as it is; you don't need extra drama to get it
into the can."   **ROBERT DE NIRO**

★   ★   ★

"I don't need much when I work. I don't need friends, I don't
need a lover. I don't need a lot of strokes. I just need to know

what's going on. . . . I do need, of course, to be told when I'm going wrong. No one's acting can be an exact, 100% science."

MARY ELIZABETH MASTRANTONIO

★   ★   ★

"There is no right in acting. I watch actors destroy themselves by trying to get it right. There isn't any right. It's a living, breathing thing, acting. It's a movable feast. It changes, and you change. The idea that you should come into the theater every night and go out on the stage to reproduce what you did before is utterly absurd. I've always loved investigating as an actor, but now I feel very strongly that it's just death to an artist not to. But I want to be very clear—I have a lot of technique in my pocket as an actor. I don't mean you go out there every night and just say, 'Oh, well, when I came into the theater today, I was in the mood to play it with a German accent.' That's bull—. I don't mean that. Within the framework of the piece and respect to your colleagues and respect for the director's ideas, you have this wonderful human being to play with every night and to bring on in different ways."

FRANK LANGELLA

★   ★   ★

"The fight to prevent anticipation, to prevent thinking and planning ahead, to prevent setting yourself for an action already knowing what the consequences will be, and how to arrive at immediacy . . . is a struggle that seems to go on and on, for established actors as well as for those just beginning."

UTA HAGEN

★   ★   ★

"When I did *The Odd Couple*, I would do it a different way

each night. On Monday I'd be Jewish, Tuesday Italian, Wednesday Irish-German—and I would mix them up. I did that to amuse myself, and it always worked."

WALTER MATTHAU

★   ★   ★

"When Robert De Niro directed me in a film there were times I wanted to take in what just happened in the moment, and he'd say to me, 'Don't do that.'

"'But I don't know where I am,' I'd answer.

"'If that's the moment, it's okay. The next moment will come and it will lead to something.'"

JOHN TURTURRO

★   ★   ★

"I believe that when you're acting, you shouldn't be concerned with literary themes; you need to approach the work on an instinctual and emotional level. This is what allows the audience to experience the play as the unfolding of recognizable human experience and prevents the Classics from becoming museum pieces."   **CHRISTOPHER REEVE**

★   ★   ★

"I know that some [film] actors do turn up knowing their script perfectly, especially when they've got a difficult scene to do. But for me, it's very hard to get it word-perfect. I can't seem to help leaving gaps, and I'm still not sure whether that's purely the fear of sounding mechanical, or whether it's because I don't manage to make enough of a sustained effort to learn it perfectly. I feel the need to keep some . . . [space]. . . . But that approach can play tricks on you [too], it's played tricks on me, anyway."   **CATHERINE DENEUVE**

"If I over-prepare for a movie, I get very bored. It's important to stay passionate."   **JODIE FOSTER**

★   ★   ★

"No creative artist is complete without a fatal flaw. In life, as in art, he is paradoxically only at full strength when his spirit grapples with this flaw. He may not be aware of it—indeed, he must not be too aware of it. But the battle has begun."   **SIR MICHAEL REDGRAVE**

★   ★   ★

"During one performance in which I was repeating a role I had played many times, suddenly, without any apparent cause, I perceived the inner meaning of the truth long known to me that creativeness on stage demands first of all a special term, which, for want of a better term, I will call the creative mood. Of course I knew this before, but only intellectually. From that evening on this simple truth entered into all my being, and I grew to perceive it not only with my soul, but with my body also. For an actor, to perceive is to feel. For this reason I can say that it was on that evening that I 'first perceived a truth long known to me.' I understood that to the genius on stage this condition almost always comes of itself, in all its fullness and richness. Less talented people receive it less often, on Sundays only, so to say. Those who are even less talented receive it even less often, every twelfth holiday, as it were. Mediocrities are visited by it only on very rare occasions, on leap years, on the twenty-ninth of February. Nevertheless, all men of the stage, from the genius to mediocrity, are able to receive the creative mood, but it is not given them to control it with their own will. They receive it together with inspiration in the form of a heavenly gift."   **CONSTANTIN STANISLAVSKI**

"It's just much easier [working with someone you already know and like]. You hit the ground running and you hopefully get somewhere more interesting quicker. You're not worried about each other's ego so you can speak frankly."   PAUL BETTANY

★   ★   ★

"My sort of dirty secret is that I have no process. I can't do the stuff suggested in drama school—recreating the emotional state the character was in. I've tried, but I can't. I have no method."   BILL NIGHY

★   ★   ★

"I got fired [from *The Graduate*], I think, because I just didn't fulfill the director's and the writer's idea of what the part should've been. In rehearsals I do a lot of searching around. I try not to perform and I really feel confident in what I'm doing. I mean, you can go [the] first day and perform and probably won't go further than that. But the way that we were all trained in the '50s and '60s, you needed to keep searching. So I was doing that, and they decided that I was just taking too much time."   GENE HACKMAN

★   ★   ★

"Just let it be. Do the preparation and then let her rip."
                                    JACK NICHOLSON

★   ★   ★

"I don't feel I learn anything by watching [other actors]. I don't like to watch. Even in *The Godfather*, people ask, didn't you watch Brando? I said, 'No, I watch him when it's finished and on the screen.' I learn better and I learn more when I go through it and make the mistakes myself. Otherwise there's a tendency to avoid mistakes that might lead you someplace."   **AL PACINO**

★   ★   ★

"It comes down to you're doing some very simple actions that help the story. . . . I have a sense, hopefully, of what the scene's about and what I'm trying to do and, other than that, you make yourself available to what is going on around you. It's like a boxing metaphor. You have a sense of what you're trying to accomplish but, once you get in the ring, you don't want to be so stuck in that because, if the other guy does something that you weren't expecting, it might be a good idea to come up with another plan."   **TIMOTHY OLYPHANT**

★   ★   ★

"If you need to be sad, just try to be happy. And when you need a belly laugh, a hearty, unstoppable one, try to be still, reverent, and serious. You can see why I've had trouble with organized religious services all my life. It's like a setup for disaster for me."   **MERYL STREEP**

★   ★   ★

"I'm very anarchic in rehearsals. The kid who suddenly gets interested in that butterfly over there and walks away."
CHRISTOPHER WALKEN

★   ★   ★

"Actors have to have each other's backs. It's the only way to act well, is when you know the other actor has your back."

PHILIP SEYMOUR HOFFMAN,
accepting the SAG Award for Outstanding Performance
by a Male Actor in a Leading Role

★　★　★

"Whenever the actor anticipates what he will see, hear, or feel . . . it is because he has failed to include the logical expectations that condition his actions, or merely paid them lip service."
UTA HAGEN

★　★　★

"You can't show up late. It's very, very disrespectful and I think what an actor has to realize, when you show up an hour late, that 150 people have been scrambling to cover for you, and there is not an apology big enough in the world to make 150 people scramble. It's inexcusable, nothing but disrespect. . . . A lot of actors show up late as if they're God's gift to the film, and it's inexcusable and they should have their asses kicked."
WILLIAM H. MACY

★　★　★

"I act a lot better if I've had a good laugh just prior to the director's yelling 'Action.' And it makes no difference if it's a light amusing scene or a dark tragic scene. . . . I'm free and loose and *available* . . . totally open to be affected by only *one thing*—by what the other actor is doing or saying."
PETER FALK

★　★　★

On what he learned acting opposite James Stewart in Anatomy of a Murder:

"Between setups, Jimmy would disappear from the set. Rather than schmooze with the other actors, he stayed behind closed doors with his assistant, learning his lines, which he had plenty of, and working on his performance. He knew how to use his time better than most of us. When he got in front of the camera, he was letter-perfect, and always knew what he was doing. His acting was so natural that if you turned your back, you couldn't tell if it was Jimmy talking in life or Jimmy talking in the movie."

BEN GAZZARA

★　★　★

"My wife and I did [*Romeo and Juliet*] in China and . . . at one point . . . she says 'Romeo, Romeo . . .'

"I say, 'Shall I hear more, or shall I speak at this,' and I do a little jump, and my wife said, 'Are you going to do that?'

"I said, 'What?'

"She said, 'The little jump.'

"I said, 'Yes. Does it bother you?'

"She said, 'No, as long as I know. Where's the stage manager? He's going to do a little jump. Now you never did a little jump before.'

"I said, 'I'm not going to do the little jump . . .'

"And she said, 'No, no, keep doing it. . . .'

"Anyway the Chinese thought we were [really] fighting, [and] they were horrified.

"I said, 'Every time I have a creative moment, you kill it.'"

ELI WALLACH

★　★　★

"I place no confidence in actors who chatter a lot at rehearsals and do not make notes on planning their homework."

CONSTANTIN STANISLAVSKI

★ ★ ★

"Something that presented a problem [for me] early on was you'd study these scripts so much that you knew what the other actor was going to say next. To combat that, I fill my head with my own imaginings. And in the last 10 to 12 years or so, it's gotten to the point where I don't care how many times we rehearse the scene or how many takes we do—if I'm working well in the scene, I won't know what the actors I'm working with are going to say next."   **CHRIS COOPER**

★ ★ ★

"Of the many artists I saw as a child, those who impressed me the most were not always the successful ones but those with unique personalities offstage. Zarno, the comedy tramp juggler, was a disciplinarian who practiced his juggling for hours every morning as soon as the theatre opened. We could see him backstage balancing a billiard cue on his chin and throwing a billiard ball up and catching it on the tip of the cue, then throwing up another and catching that on top of the first ball . . . but the audience only applauded mildly [when he performed the trick]. . . . Said [the troupe manager] to Zarno, 'You make the trick look too easy, you don't sell it.' Zarno laughed. 'I am not expert enough to miss it yet.'"   **CHARLIE CHAPLIN**

★ ★ ★

"To a certain actor, of a certain generation, Professionalism with a capital P was the ultimate criterion . . . a stick with which to beat the young, the rowdy, and the trendy. The Method, Brecht, the RSC and the National with all their 'unnecessary' and 'wasteful' rehearsal time, were all clobbered.

"The Professional learnt his lines, jotted down his moves in the margin and remembered them the next morning, knew the trick of this author or that, and had a store of business, inherited or observed from other actors, which would serve for any occasion. He liked to share a little joke with the director, then withdraw to the other side of the room and study his script, because he knew his place. He detested actors who monopolized the director's attention (unless they were the star, to whom different rules applied). He complained bitterly about actors who didn't know their lines and who changed their moves. His question was: 'Are you doing to do that, love? Because, you see, it makes it awfully difficult for me to play my line if you're going to do yours that way.' He'd make this little speech within earshot of the director, to whom he'd appeal with his eyes. . . . He wore a tweed jacket and grey flannels and a polo-neck jumper. Sometimes, exotically, this would be varied with a safari suit, khaki from head to toe, except of course, for his hush puppies, which were invariable."   **Simon Callow**

★   ★   ★

"The great value of art when applied to the stage is that it enables the performer to reproduce the gift [of his performance] and so move his audience night after night, even though he has acted the same character a thousand times."   **Joseph Jefferson**

★   ★   ★

"One night at Stratford-on-Avon . . . when I was playing

Richard III, my dueling opponent forgot his moves. He was supposed to win, but he suddenly froze. To keep the fight going, I kept slashing away at him with my sword. It was so difficult because his hands were at his sides. He was completely numb. Under my breath I kept saying, 'Get me! Hit me! Stab me! Do anything!' I finally thought, I've got to die. I bumped into him and made it look like he had done a terrible stabbing. I died. When I looked up, I saw his whole face was covered in blood. There's nothing more dangerous than when you improvise a sword fight. It has to be meticulously choreographed. When the curtain came down, I ran to him. He was in shock. He had a terrible gash just above his eye from the sword I was wielding. It had just missed his eye." **CHRISTOPHER PLUMMER**

★   ★   ★

Recalling the celebrated 1973 revival of A Moon for the Misbegotten:

"It was a great performance. I went backstage, and Jason [Robards] could see I was really affected by it. He said, 'Ah, come on. Sometimes I do a sad face, sometimes I do a happy face. It's all bulls—t.'" **BRIAN DENNEHY**

★   ★   ★

"Look, I don't care how somebody gets at the performance, that's up to them. . . . Thank God, I was brought up in the good old tradition of theatre in England. Starting in rep and going to one of these companies and all that . . . so really my background is theatre. And theatre actors . . . if you can do a play, you can do a film, for God's sake. That's for sure. . . . I don't take it too seriously. It's only acting. It's really basically really easy. We're not curing cancer—wish to God we were—we're not. And it's not rocket science. We're just interpreting what somebody else who's much cleverer than me, has written."   **MALCOLM MCDOWELL**

★　★　★

"The first day Clark Gable and I worked together . . . John Huston said 'Action.' And I looked at Gable . . . thinking 'This man is the king of the movies.' . . . And Gable looked and thought, 'Who the hell is this guy from New York with his mysterious Method?' And we just stared at each other and Huston said, 'I said Action. Do something! What's wrong?' and I said, 'Well I . . .' and Gable said, 'Oh, er . . .' and [Huston] brought out a glass of Jack Daniels for each of us and . . . we bonded right there."   **ELI WALLACH**

★　★　★

"[I watch playbacks of my performances between takes] all the time. It helps enormously. You grade whatever you're doing to the scale of the shot, you know how much you can work the head to the frame. But I'm just sort of technically oriented as an actor. Everything I do, I'm sort of half in, half out. Part of me is in the character's head, and part of me is . . . well, not so much directing myself as shaping my performance. And calculating how to work effectively with other people."   **HARRISON FORD**

★　★　★

"There was a picture called *Who's Got the Action?* in which I play an old Italian bookie. . . . And at one point there's this young bookie who I think is taking my action, and I'm supposed to have him bumped off, but I'm gonna give him a break because he's got a mother. . . . And it was easy, because all I did was say the lines, but in saying the lines I knew who I was, and it was easy to cry. . . . But I wasn't thinking of the sadness, of my mother dying, of my child being run over by a car. I just did it! You gotta just do it, and it either comes or it doesn't. Because if you start thinking about it, it's too late."

WALTHER MATTHAU

★   ★   ★

"To wait, in acting, for inspiration to flash upon you is about as sensible as to wait until your house is in flames before looking for a fire escape. Night after night, often for many months, the same words must be spoken, the same actions be performed in the same way, in order to produce the same effects upon audiences which continually vary.

"This is the reason why long and careful preparatory rehearsals are essential to all fine acting. And, oddly enough, a spirit of rebellious opposition to adequate rehearsals is daily growing stronger among actors themselves—who are incompetent to render their services without them!"

DAVID BELASCO

★   ★   ★

"Time goes by and your process changes. . . . But I certainly still remind myself now and then to be sure I'm actually listening to the actor across that space from me, taking in what he or she is offering, and responding to it, as opposed to playing out some idea I had of the scene on the way to work that morning or assuming that it's going to be the same play that it was the night before."   EDWARD NORTON

★   ★   ★

"Acting in the movies is one of the most unnatural things you can do. You're surrounded by technicians, there's no continuity, you do little bits and pieces. . . . In films, what everyone is striving for is to produce moments—not a performance, not a characterization, not something where you get into the part—you produce moments that create a feeling of believability to what you're doing."

JIMMY STEWART

★　★　★

"To be honest, I don't usually do very much research, especially if I'm working with a director who also wrote the screenplay. They've usually done a ton of research. And they'll tell you about it from their perspective, which is better than doing your own research, because they'll present to you the information they want conveyed in the film. What you feel is important may not be what the director feels is important."

CHRISTINA RICCI

★　★　★

On what he learned while acting in his first film:

"I was so excited I was doing a movie. So excited. I was talking to anyone who would listen. After about five days the director pulled me aside and said, 'Look, fuckin' stop talking to the crew all day. Just say your lines.' . . . It was a serious lesson. Ultimately, you're not on camera for very much of the day. If you're sittin' around chattin', it will dissipate a little bit of whatever you've got for when the time comes. When everyone's ready, you've got to deliver in this little window. It's all about aiming everything toward that."

CLIVE OWEN

"Sometimes on a trail in the woods, you hold out your hand and offer it to a small bird, hoping it will sit there for a moment. And if you're lucky and artful, it does. But just for a moment, and then it flies off again. There's no formula that can capture it; it's a kind of art. And art is many things. It's work and intelligence and intuition, and sometimes it's thinking with your body as well as your brain. But it's also play—play that's at once intelligent and innocent, both controlled and abandoned." **ALAN ALDA**

★　★　★

"Never lose yourself on the stage. Always act in your own person, as an artist. You can never get away from yourself. The moment you lose yourself on the stage marks the departure from truly living your part and the beginnings of exaggerated false acting." **CONSTANTIN STANISLAVSKI**

On Collaborating with Directors, Writers, Producers, Designers, and Other Industry Professionals

"The director's job should be to open the actor up and, for God's sake, leave him alone!" **DUSTIN HOFFMAN**

★   ★   ★

"It's a little daunting when in the middle of a love scene your husband [who is also the director] says to you, 'That's fine darling, but I know you can do it better.'" **JULIE ANDREWS**

★   ★   ★

"I saw somebody taking the piss out of me on TV the other night, [*laughs*] talking about working for a director and how I give them 'a gold mine of ideas.' And I was thinking, 'Gosh, I suppose that does sound arrogant and fucking stupid . . . and maybe it is arrogant and stupid. But, you know, it's still true. [*Laughs.*]" **RUSSELL CROWE**

"As soon as I heard him say, 'Action,' I started to act. Sounds sensible, doesn't it? But Arthur [Penn]. . . gave me my first revelation of what it means to be an 'actor's director.' While the camera was rolling, he said, 'Gene, just because I say "Action," doesn't mean you have to start acting. . . . Film is cheap. Keep working on whatever you're working on and start acting when you're ready.'

"The scene went very well.

"When we took a break, the assistant director came up to me and said, 'Don't get used to what just happened—you're not going to find many directors who work like Arthur.'"
                                          GENE WILDER

★   ★   ★

"Directors are like a Port Authority of ideas. Ideas are like buses. You know, they come and they park, and the people go and get another bus and they go someplace. That would be the magic of being a director."   **WILLIAM HURT**

★   ★   ★

"Your audience gives you everything you need. . . . There is no director who can direct you like an audience."
                                          FANNY BRICE

★   ★   ★

"As an actor you're expecting [the director] to say, 'Cut!' That's your safety net. But we didn't hear 'cut' . . . and we didn't hear 'cut.' Then it gets uncomfortable. Odd things are happening. It's scary. It's just you and this person you're with."
                                      VIGGO MORTENSEN

"I heard the director . . . say, 'I need a butcher in this part.'
Someone suggested that he get a real butcher who knew
how to cut up meat authentically. [The director] answered:
'If I've got a good actor, I've got a real butcher. If I've got a
real butcher, the minute I put him in front of the camera he's
stiff and I've got a bad actor."   SIR MICHAEL CAINE

★   ★   ★

"The sound and shape of a finished work is the product of the
director's concept of the playwright's content expressed by
the life of the actor."   UTA HAGEN

★   ★   ★

"The meetings between actor and costume designer can be
very uneasy. Because they're very early on in the process.
The actor is in that very insecure period where, in fact,
just before the cell divides, there's chaos. Then all the
cells go to different, to opposite sides of the cell, and then
the cells divide. Have you ever seen cells divide? Under
a microscope? Astonishing. The choreography of those
chromosomes and bits."   SIR BEN KINGSLEY

★   ★   ★

"If an actor confines himself to merely speaking the lines
provided by the author and executing the 'business' ordered
by the director, and seeks no opportunity to improvise
independently, he makes himself a slave to the creation of
others and his profession a borrowed one. . . . This attitude,
unfortunately, prevails among too many of our actors today."
          MICHAEL CHEKHOV

★   ★   ★

"I was very disturbed at the [2007] Golden Globes when Jeremy Irons thanked the director for staying out of [the actors'] way, because it's just the opposite with me. I couldn't do anything without a director."   **JOHN MAHONEY**

★   ★   ★

"You know what [John] Ford used to do? He used to come to work in a big car with two Admiral's flags, one on each side of the car. He was a reserve Admiral in the navy because he made a lot of documentaries during the war. He'd arrive with the two flags flying, and his assistant would be there with his accordion, playing, 'Hail to the Chief.' Ford would get out, look around, someone would get him a coffee and Ford would stand there. Then he said, 'They're all waiting for me to tell 'em what to do. I don't know what the hell I'm going to do!'"   **RICHARD WIDMARK**

★   ★   ★

"The actor has to have enough ego to recognize the work he has to do for himself. He has to realize that sometimes the director does not know how the actor accomplishes that work, and therefore is not willing to give the actor time for it, even when it is being done before his very eyes. Then actors must learn to do as the director does when he fools the actor into doing what he wants: he must learn to keep the scene flexible so as to take the requisite time to make things come alive for himself on the stage."   **LEE STRASBERG**

★   ★   ★

"A musical is only as good as its director. The same can also be said for the CIA."   **MARTIN SHORT**

"What are directors if not surrogate parental figures?"
JOHN LEGUIZAMO

★   ★   ★

"You've got to be flexible. Directors do a massive amount
of planning and homework, and if after all that your
director decides to throw it all out of the window and shoot
spontaneously, then you must follow his lead."
SIR MICHAEL CAINE

★   ★   ★

"There are so many things that can go wrong with a film, so
[my decision to work on one] always has to start with the
screenplay and then the director. Those are the two things.
You can make a really bad film out of a good script, but
you're not likely to make a good film out of a bad script."
GEORGE CLOONEY

★   ★   ★

"A good director is like a good psychiatrist. He knows what
conclusion he wants you to reach, but he lets you discover it
for yourself."
ROD STEIGER

★   ★   ★

"[The writers of a certain project] said, 'You know, Chris,
when we were writing it, you're the only one we thought of.'
I still don't know what the f—k that means."
CHRISTOPHER MELONI

★   ★   ★

About working with a writer who's also the director:

"It doesn't mean anything if the writer and the director are the same person and that person sucks."

TIMOTHY OLYPHANT

★   ★   ★

"A lot of actors force themselves [toward an emotional result], believing, 'If the writer says something, I should be feeling it.' But if the words are good enough, they will take you there."

JAKE GYLLENHAAL

★   ★   ★

"A destructive director I once had on a movie said to me, 'You're coming off funereal' instead of just asking for more energy."

CHARLES GRODIN

★   ★   ★

While working on Robin and the 7 Hoods, *produced by and starring Frank Sinatra:*

PETER FALK: "I didn't like a couple of lines I had. . . . I went looking for Frank. . . . 'I want to show you something. I have it right here, page 29, my third line, it's—'"

FRANK SINATRA: (*interrupts*) "You don't like what you say? (*He rips out the whole page, throws it on the floor.*) Say whatever you want. (*And he leaves.*)"

PETER FALK: "That's what I call a producer."

★   ★   ★

About a female co-star who became despised by the crew for her difficult attitude:

"The costume person started secretly taking her clothes
  in a centimeter a day! It's such a funny, strategic f—k you
  revenge. Don't ever f—k with the crew. However the coffee
  comes, I drink it. If it's black, too bad."   **John Leguizamo**

★   ★   ★

"This director asked if I could cry. I told him 'no.' He said,
  'That's not what I want to hear.' I said, '. . . What are you
  talking about when it comes to crying? Real tears or real
  emotions? I can guarantee you real emotions all the way up
  the line. As far as the proverbial tears that come from your
  eyes,' I said, 'if you need a special effect, you can jab me with
  something.'"   **Elliott Gould**

★   ★   ★

After directing his own feature film:

"I now have a gigantic amount of sympathy for all directors
  I've ever worked with. I wish to issue a retroactive apology
  for every time I was even 30 seconds late to the set."
                                                    Ben Affleck

★   ★   ★

"[You] could have the 12 disciples in the cast and Jesus
  Christ playing the lead and still get bad reviews if the play is
  poorly written. An actor can help a play, but he can't make
  it a success."   **Marlon Brando**

★   ★   ★

"Some directors . . . come on [the set] shouting because they want to be known as the person you can't fuck with. And if someone comes with that, that's all well and good, but you cannot sustain it for four months or however long the shoot is. Actually, some people can, and it's quite incredible to watch."
                                       DANIEL CRAIG

★   ★   ★

"Special effects people are all the same. They like things that go *boom*, and they always say, 'No, don't worry. Everything's safe.' But there's always a risk. That's what I've learned—as an actor, you have to keep the special effects people away from you a little bit. Because here's the truth—everybody screws up once in a while, and so do they. The difference is, not everybody is playing with explosives when they screw up, and you don't want to be there when it happens."
                                       RUTGER HAUER

★   ★   ★

"Most directors will want to work towards an opening night, and that's the thing I want to work away from. I don't want an occasion, I want more of a happening."
                                     NIGEL HAWTHORNE

★   ★   ★

"I like to aid in the director's vision. I also like the abrasion that comes about when our visions collide. But I always ache to collaborate."   **JAKE GYLLENHAAL**

★   ★   ★

"I once sat with Al Pacino on the top of a film, shooting

Revolution. . . . We were looking down at this tableaux of British red-coated soldiers and tents and it was just wonderful. He turned to me and said, 'I've never said this before, but this is going to be really good.' And it was a disaster . . . because of the way they cut it. [Director] Hugh [Hudson] did a wonderful job, but they cut it for the clouds. Meaning that instead of cutting for the heart and the gut of the people in the thing, if a cloud passed . . . they would find a piece of film that matched for the cloud passing. . . . It has to be gut-related."   **DONALD SUTHERLAND**

★   ★   ★

"I don't think any director should indulge any actor, and I don't think actors should indulge themselves. . . . [We must work] in the way that a musician would know a piece he's playing. It's so boring hearing someone do a virtuoso solo, when really you want the piece of music to move on."
                                                        STEPHEN REA

★   ★   ★

"You can type this shit, George, but you sure can't say it."
                        HARRISON FORD,
             to George Lucas on the set of Star Wars.

★   ★   ★

"Woody [Allen]'s comments to actors could sting. 'I don't believe a word of that,' he would say quietly, but very intensely. 'Human beings don't talk that way.' 'That was pure soap opera' was one of the comments that upset Geraldine Page while they were doing *Interiors*. 'You could see that on afternoon television.' . . . 'There are directors,' he has said, 'who have affectionate relationships with actors, but I've never been able to work that way. I give as much contact as is required professionally.' But that didn't stop actors from wanting to work with him for a fraction of their usual salary."

MIA FARROW

★ ★ ★

On working with children:

"The trick is to let them do whatever they feel like doing and play off that; you're doomed if you try to manipulate a child into doing something specific you have in mind."

KARL MALDEN

★ ★ ★

"I think the directors that have made me feel the safest are the ones that have said to me, 'What do you need? Tell me if I'm confusing you; or tell me if I'm bugging you, or tell me if you'd just like me to go away.' I think when directors do have a specific idea of what they want, they're not making the best use of their actors, quite frankly, because sometimes actors will have an entirely different idea, a different understanding of the character, than the director."

KATE WINSLET

★ ★ ★

"You usually get pretty close to the director if you're in every single scene [of a movie]. I've done this a few times, and you get as exhausted as the director. But you really get to know him better because you are there every day, and he ends up using you as a sounding board for trying ideas. So I may be alone on camera, but the director is always there too."

TOM BERENGER

"If . . . you see people are becoming preoccupied with movie-making—that's not the point. That's like jumping on a small motorbike. It'll run out of gas very soon. [I'm more concerned with] the truth of this scene. I can be very short when I perceive the mentality of shot-administration is dominating the heart of scene-solution. I can be very, very intolerant of that." **William Hurt**

★   ★   ★

"[My director, Philippe] Garrel used to say to me, 'Don't think about acting. Just be in the character's thoughts, be simple. Her thoughts are enough. If you're thinking right, you'll be all right.' It sounds very simple, but in order to tell your actors something so simple, you really have to have thought things through." **Catherine Deneuve**

★   ★   ★

On what he learned on the set of Dead Man Walking *in 1995:*

"In my first scene in any movie ever . . . Sean Penn dragged me out to a swamp, threw me down in the mud, raped and killed me and my girlfriend. We did the scene, we took a shower, put on new clothes and did the scene again. All night long. And that was my big break."

[On how Penn took Sarsgaard and the actress who played his girlfriend out the night before that scene was shot:]

"It was a sort of I'm-going-to-rape-you-and-we-should-get-to-know-one-another meal. . . . I thought that was nice, and I've tried to extend the same courtesy to my co-stars, especially if I'm going to kill or rape them."

Peter Sarsgaard

"A play is material for acting. It may be more, but it must be that to begin with. The actor brings it to a technical completion. . . . It is useless to argue that actors can add nothing to and take nothing from the material the playwright gives them."   **HARLEY GRANVILLE-BARKER**

★   ★   ★

On shooting a scene for The Bourne Ultimatum *with director Paul Greengrass:*

"We were losing the light and I was walking through this tunnel. . . . [In the script, I had sustained a wound, and I tried to position my arm in a way that would help the cameraman get his shot in time.] I didn't want to hold my bloody fingers below his frame. Paul came running over and said, 'No, no, no, absolutely not! Do it as you would naturally do it! Even if we miss it, we'll know what it was.' As an actor, that's like air. That's somebody saying, 'I'm committed to capturing what you do naturally. I don't want you to make any adjustments for the camera.'"   **MATT DAMON**

★   ★   ★

"Movies are a collaboration, but the director is unquestionably the boss. He knows what he wants, the feeling and tone of things. I went to work every day for years knowing that it was his ship and that I was lucky to be a sailor on it. I always kept the Goethe quote in mind: 'It is within limits that the craftsman reveals himself.' I was a craftsman. And believe me, there were always limits. I could work within them if I had to."   **TERI GARR**

★   ★   ★

"There is a story told about Gadge Kazan: On opening night he goes backstage and tells all his actors how wonderful they are, to keep up the good work, while in his breast pocket there's an airplane ticket to some faraway land. I don't know if it's true, but it sounds as though it may be—if not of Gadge, then of others. By opening night the director has had enough, he wants to get away. But as an actor, I want him there, dammit. I have to be in that theater six days a week; I've been seeing him all day, every day, for months. I deeply resent being left. I want his support, I need it."

LAUREN BACALL

★　★　★

"All my life, I have been an ensemble actor. It's very nice to be a star and it's nice to lead the company and it's nice to be the one who stands up front, but I passionately believe that a production cannot survive—in fact, will be damaged—by one egotistical star performance. So I like to create a working atmosphere in which every actor is as important as anybody else, and the work is a community work."

PATRICK STEWART

★　★　★

"Special effects movies are hard on actors. You find yourself giving an impassioned speech to a big lobster in a flight suit."

MARK HAMILL

★　★　★

"Kazan, in my opinion, is the best actor's director there ever was. He was kind of a Svengali, he did it instinctively and never dealt with two actors in the same way. He said very little, but he was so astute and so good that he could give you the right little moment as to what to do."

RICHARD WIDMARK

★   ★   ★

On a conversation he had with Sir Alfred Hitchcock while filming I Confess:

"'Hitch, you never tell actors what to do. You set up the scene, we know our blocking, we come in, we do the scene, and you never tell us what you expect from the scene.'

"He said, 'Karl, I am a professional. And I hope that I have hired professionals. We all do our jobs and we go on from there.'"

KARL MALDEN

★   ★   ★

"The way I see it, if the actor's instincts are against the grain of the director's, then the director cast the wrong guy. The director has got to support the instincts of the actor, every time. You can compromise and fit the director's mould, but the spark of spontaneity will be gone."

SEAN PENN

★   ★   ★

"The worst experience I've ever had with a director, oddly enough, came from a man who never screamed, wasn't a bully, and, in fact, was a very sweet guy. The problem was he directed too much. 'Turn at the door and smile. Do that thing you do with your eyes, I love that.'

"'What do you mean, what thing?'

"'You know, that thing you do.' 'Turn you head on this line.' 'Reach out on this word.' 'Stress this word.' 'Say it like this.' And what felt like 67,000 other directions. This guy was reducing good actors to good puppets. Ironically, he's very successful."

CHARLES GRODIN

★   ★   ★

On whether or not he was ever asked by a director to change his distinctive line readings:

"It's very rare, and it's not a happy thing. You know, I get along very well with everybody. Always have. But occasionally somebody will say, 'Could you read that line another way?' And I just tell 'em, 'I'm sorry. I have no idea how to do that.' And the interesting thing is that the other actors, when that happens to me, they all gang up: '*What*? Leave him alone!'"

CHRISTOPHER WALKEN

★   ★   ★

"A long bathtub scene entailed [my character] sitting in an ornate marble bathtub, covered with bubbles, talking on the telephone. . . . We rehearsed for two days, with me immersed in real bubbles. Since bubbles do not last very long, the prop men had to keep adding to the water a mixture of dishwashing detergent and Lux soap flakes.

"At the end of the first day my nether regions were pink and puffy. At the end of the second day they were sore and swollen. On the third day, when we finally started to shoot . . . the misery on my face was evident. Something had to be done. The studio doctor was called to give me pain-killing injections, and the prop department evolved an ingenious contraption. . . . Here was a glamorous creature chatting cattily on the phone, luscious bubbles caressing her body. Underneath the bubbles, however, was a sheet of strong plywood with a hole cut in to fit my body, and the bubbles were on top of the plywood. Underneath the plywood I was encased in Vaseline and bandages, and on top of this an attractive pair of men's long johns from the gentlemen's wardrobe department. Over this was a large rubber sheet in case any sneaky bubbles managed to slither through the armor. I sat on several cushions, and all in all was feeling no pain."   **JOAN COLLINS**

★   ★   ★

"Using a stunt person is like going off on vacation and asking somebody else to make love to your wife while you're gone. If you can do it yourself, you certainly should."

HARRISON FORD

★   ★   ★

On a lesson he learned while working with Broderick Crawford on the TV show The Interns. *Mr. Farrell notes that Broderick Crawford liked to have a drink between takes:*

"When working in film, each scene usually requires a master shot and 'coverage,' which is breaking down the scene and doing close-ups and other shots of the people involved. Then the editor cuts them together to emphasize whatever points the director or writer wants made. When shooting coverage, the actors spend a lot of time waiting while the lights are adjusted and the set is prepared. This can be tricky. . . . When shooting a close-up of one actor, the others in the scene perform their role off-camera.

"This is where you find out who the pros are. Some actors give less of a performance when off-camera, which can create real problems for the actor being filmed. Some simply lose focus, but a few are either disinterested or so self-obsessed that nothing matters but their own camera time. Some so-called stars, particularly when it's an inconsequential scene with an 'unimportant' character, don't show up at all, leaving it up to the script supervisor to read their off-camera lines. [Broderick], however, always made it a point to be there for his off-camera work. He may have been somewhat slurry with the words at times, but he always showed up and gave it what he had to give, no matter how small the scene. It's a lesson that always stayed with me."

MIKE FARRELL

★   ★   ★

"On *M*A*S*H* they had an old-school camera guy from Disney, 65 or so, and that was a brilliant move. Altman brought him in specifically and it imposed a kind of discipline. I say 'a kind' because we never shot the same words twice. We'd do one take, and the next, and none of them were the same. The sound editor won an Oscar for figuring it all out."

DONALD SUTHERLAND

★   ★   ★

"In an ideal way, in an ideal world, myself and the director are one. And as you rightly say, in an ideal world, you can't see the horizon between sky and sea. I felt that the times with Spielberg on *Schindler's List*, we were moving as one creature. He in his vastly complicated and hugely responsible department and in a demanding, but in a sense, much cleaner, simpler department of storytelling. He's got the difficult bits; I've got the easy bit of just acting. But I often felt that we were moving through the waters as one beast, finishing each other's sentences. I felt that with Polanski when I did *Death and the Maiden*. We were as one beast."

SIR BEN KINGSLEY

On working with Steven Spielberg:

"He never censors his instincts or gets precious about what
he's doing. He sees it, he wants it, he gets it, and he gets
it as fast as he can. He's got the artistry and expertise to
make it all first-rate, so none of it is slap-dash or haphazard
unless he wants it to look that way. In the time it takes me
to set up one shot, Steven would have seven shots under his
belt and be working on the next fourteen. That speed and
momentum and clarity—and not questioning his instincts—
that's why he's who he is."   **TOM HANKS**

★   ★   ★

*It's been said that some directors—even famous ones—harass
one member of every cast they work with. Sometimes they do
it to blow off steam when a production obviously isn't working.
Sometimes the tactic is part of a larger dynamic; by ladling
harsh criticism on one actor, the director sets an example of his
or her power. During Jerome Robbins' Broadway production
of* Mother Courage, *he picked on cast member Eugene Roche
routinely. But then things changed:*

"One afternoon . . . we all had to stand there and listen to
Jerry Robbins railing and belittling—until he crossed the
line. Eugene, who was a devout Catholic with five children,
stood up and said, 'Listen, you little fuck—if you insult me
one more time, I'm going to come over there and smash the
teeth out of your fucking face.' From that time on, Eugene
Roche became Jerome Robbins' favorite actor."

                                            GENE WILDER

★   ★   ★

"A good script has its own architecture and topography.

I scribble notes all over it. I make charts. I'm not saying it happens all the time. Sometimes parts aren't so good. When they are, it's a lot like music. You can go in a flow. But the story comes first. An actor is only a storyteller."

LAURA LINNEY

On the Stage and the Screen

"I think the adjustments [from stage to film] are small. It's better to try not to be too busy on film. At least that's what I've found, especially in close-up shots."   JULIE ANDREWS

★   ★   ★

"Theatre or film? I often compare the two media to lovemaking. In theater, onstage one goes through the entire experience: curtain up, foreplay, excitement, then finally an orgasmic release, curtain down. In film, there's action, foreplay, excitement, and just before you reach the glorious moment of release, the director yells, 'Cut! Let's do this scene again.'"   ELI WALLACH

★   ★   ★

On relating to an audience in any medium:

"I don't think of the audience as someone separate from me. You have to seduce an audience. You can't beat 'em and you can't kiss their asses."   **HARRISON FORD**

★   ★   ★

"[In the theater] quiet audiences used to make me angry and hostile, and then I'd give more, really pour it out to get some kind of response from them. You can literally hurt yourself that way. And then you've wasted your voice for the evening show."   **JOHN LEGUIZAMO**

★   ★   ★

On movie ratings:

"G means the hero gets the girl. R means the villain gets the girl. And X means everybody gets the girl."   **KIRK DOUGLAS**

★   ★   ★

"Moving pictures need sound as much as Beethoven symphonies need lyrics."   **CHARLIE CHAPLIN**

★   ★   ★

"The silliest things happen in summer stock."
VICKI LAWRENCE

★   ★   ★

"What you learn in the theater, you sell to film."
SIR RALPH RICHARDSON

"When you're onstage and you know you're bombing, that's very, very scary. Because you know you gotta keep going—you're bombing, but you can't stop. And you know that half an hour from now, you're still gonna be bombing. It takes a thick skin." **CHRISTOPHER WALKEN**

★ ★ ★

On curtain calls:

"The bow never means anything for me. I'm always embarrassed to take a bow. I would rather not take a bow. My coming out and taking a bow, a curtain call—I'm Ron, and I don't want to be there as Ron." **RON RIFKIN**

★ ★ ★

"The camera is sort [of] godlike. It looks in your soul, it loves you. The director can hate your guts. The other actor could be lying to upstage you. The camera looks at you and says, 'If you are honest, Bruce, you're going to do great. We're in this together.' So, you always have a friend in the camera. If you start lying to the camera, the camera turns away. It's biblical—the camera turns away and you're left to be fucked." **BRUCE ALTMAN**

★ ★ ★

"I find that, paradoxically, black and white tends to lend old films a somehow modern look, as if they've kept their integrity, whereas films in color date much more quickly. . . . But black and white films are hardly ever made these days. . . . Today, I think that making a black and white film would be like committing professional hara-kiri." **CATHERINE DENEUVE**

"The camera is just like this adoring dog; it just looks at you all the time. It's so flattering, it's ridiculous."

KATHLEEN TURNER

★　★　★

"If you learn to be truthful first . . . it's terribly hard to learn to be heard. And if you learn to be heard first of all, it's terribly hard to speak truthfully."   **GERALDINE PAGE**

★　★　★

"[When I was young, I had a] tremendous ego. I figured that having done *Apocalypse* [*Now*] I had to be one of the baddest guys on the planet. I suffered as a result of that, because I didn't have sense enough to be nice and smile. When I got scripts, I was like, 'What do you mean you want me to read this bullshit? I'm an artist. This isn't art!' I guess that's what we do when we're young. So I wound up doing a lot of episodic television in L.A. Then I went back to New York in '84 and I did my first play in seven years, *Suspenders*. And that was another awakening, because stage acting is very different from film acting. The director would say, 'Wow, Larry, that would have been great if I had a camera.' It was time for me to learn all over again. So I did this play for $25 a week and I really enjoyed it."

LAURENCE FISHBURNE

★　★　★

"There is only one thing that can kill the movies and that is education."   **WILL ROGERS**

★　★　★

On working on his first film and what he learned about the culture of film actors:

"'You've worked in the theater, haven't you?' the property master said one day. How could he tell, I asked. 'Because at the end of every take you hand the prop back to me or return it to the prop table.' This, I found out, was unusual."

MICHAEL YORK

★　★　★

On the personal conflicts he experienced from accepting a long-running television job:

"From the earliest days . . . from perhaps the second season, when we all realized that we were not going to be a failure—as we had been advised we were—that we might actually see out the seven years of our contracts, something wasn't quite right. . . . It was thrilling to be in Hollywood, to be making a very successful television series, to be making some money for the first time in my life, [but] I couldn't stop thinking about what I was missing. . . . I stopped reading the British newspapers for a long time because I couldn't tolerate seeing the advertisements for what was happening at Stratford or in the West End. Reading reviews of productions became agony because all it meant to me was that I wasn't in them; they were missed opportunities."   **PATRICK STEWART**

★　★　★

"Film acting is really the trick of doing moments. You rarely do a take that lasts more than 20 seconds. You really earn your spurs acting onstage. I needed to do that for myself. . . . I would hate to say at the end of everything that I never did a stage play."   **SAM SHEPARD**

"[A movie is] life with the dull parts cut out."
SIR ALFRED HITCHCOCK

★　★　★

*On advice she received from her mother, film star Ingrid
Bergman:*

"Mama gave me only one piece of acting advice: 'Don't do
anything. It's better than doing it wrong or badly. There will
always be the violins to give your character the right mood.'
　　"I read somewhere in an interview about the making
of *Casablanca* that she used this trick herself for her big
close-up at the café, when she sees Rick for the first time
after many years. She didn't know if she had to play being
in love with Rick/Humphrey Bogart or with Laszlo/Paul
Henreid because the script kept being rewritten while they
were shooting the film, so she decided to go blank-faced for
that close-up, counting on the violins that would later be
edited into the soundtrack."　　**ISABELLA ROSSELLINI**

★　★　★

"Acting for the camera is like acting in your own bathroom.
It's kind of real but not real at the same time. It's very
strange. On stage, the audience feeds you; it's a totally
different energy."　　　　　　　**JOHN LEGUIZAMO**

★　★　★

"It's like a dead nerve. A whole generation—maybe two
generations now—all they know are special effects. Not just
all they know. That's all they *want*."　　**JACK NICHOLSON**

★　★　★

"I'd love to do another musical. When they're good, they're great. . . . I'd love to be on stage, to do anything. . . . I'd love to do a show in Vegas. I have a big ambition to do a really tacky Vegas show with drag queens. . . . I just love performing and I miss it especially when I go to see theatre."

Catherine Zeta-Jones

★   ★   ★

"What is great film acting? Well, I just know some people who've done it. For example, I've seen 10 films by Mastroianni, and I suddenly thought, 'I believe this man every time, every single time.' . . . Great film acting is about simplicity, absolute truth, and trusting yourself. Basically you're asking me what *fine* acting is, and I don't think it matters what medium it's in. In film, it's knowing where that camera is and then forgetting it's there."   **Sir Alan Bates**

★   ★   ★

"The author, painter, or musician, if he be dissatisfied with his work, may alter and perfect it before giving it publicity, but a [stage] actor cannot rub it out. . . . Should a picture in an art gallery be carelessly painted we can pass on to another, or if a book fail to please us we can put it down. An escape from this kind of dullness is easily made, but in the theater the auditor is imprisoned. If the acting be indifferent, he must endure it. . . . It is this helpless condition that renders careless acting so offensive."

Joseph Jefferson

★   ★   ★

"In my opinion, film acting would be about 80 percent better than it has been lately if actors did their homework,

if they didn't have egos that took the size of their talent for granted."
                                                    ROD STEIGER

★   ★   ★

"At 16, coming from television, I was impressed by the intense work ethic one must have on a movie set, having to constantly strive to put up on screen what you intend as an actor, because those moments will be burned into celluloid for years to come."
                                    LEONARDO DiCAPRIO

★   ★   ★

"Film acting is harder for me than stage work, in a way. I'm much more of an endurance athlete than I am a sprinter—and movies are all about the sprint. I love the marathon aspect of a play."
                                    JAKE GYLLENHAAL

★   ★   ★

"I think I find film acting quite easy. . . . As a film actor, I know what the situation is going to be when I do the shot. You learn this in theatre. But in theatre you make a broad line, you make a ground plan for a part in, say, *Three Sisters* or *Cherry Orchard* or *Hamlet* or whatever, and if that ground plan is wrong it's bad luck, you get bad notices and it's a bad performance and you are stuck with it for 10 weeks."
                                    SIR ANTHONY HOPKINS

★   ★   ★

"That's the beauty of being able to do movies. . . . Back when I was doing theater in New York I used to always wish that I could go and see the plays that I was in with me in them, but naturally I couldn't do that. So now that I'm in a venue

that allows me to watch myself, I try to do things that I want
to see myself in."   SAMUEL L. JACKSON

★   ★   ★

"Well, it's true that the stage is fun. But I can never justify
[taking a role onstage] completely in my head because
although I think it's really fun for the performers, my
experience as an audience member is 19 times out of 20
it's purgatory to sit and watch a play, I think. I don't know.
People keep going, I think, out of a sense of duty, sort of
churchgoing, than out of clever [plays]."   HUGH GRANT

★   ★   ★

"Our [American] audiences would make a pauper of any
actor who dedicated his career to Shakespeare. Ours is a
television and movie culture."   MARLON BRANDO

★   ★   ★

"Stage-acting and film-acting . . . call for the same ingredients
but in different proportions. The precise differences may
take some years of puzzling work to appreciate; in each case
there are many subtle variations according to the character
of the actor. It took me many years to learn to film-act. . . .
After that, it was necessary to relearn how to act on stage,
incorporating, though, the truth demanded by the cinema
and thereby reducing the measure of theatricality."
                                        SIR LAURENCE OLIVIER

★   ★   ★

"I think our desire for fear is related to the safety and security
in our lives. As human animals, our bodies are designed

to release adrenaline and cope with moments of fear and anxiety. We don't have much of that in our lives today because our stressors are very different. So extreme peril provokes those various chemicals in our body, which might be healthy for us. It's probably healthier than the stress we usually go through, and we probably feel more able to surrender ourselves to it because we have the safety of knowing we're watching a film. It's a thrill."

GRETA SCACCHI

★   ★   ★

"Have you ever been beaten up on the street? Well, working on a film set is easier."

WILLIAM HURT

★   ★   ★

"Certainly there's a difference between the theatre and film, and I love it when big fat movie stars go to the theatre. I [recall one instance where I'd] just gone backstage and a big movie star was coming out of this dressing room at the end of the show when this woman comes out and says, 'Hey, I'm your mother? Come back, hang up your costume, what's the matter with you?' Back he went and hung up his costume. You don't mess with the Broadway dressers, boy."

WILLIAM H. MACY

★   ★   ★

"I love comedy, and I've always found it fun to do. But comedy on film is difficult. First of all, you don't hear the laughs. . . . When you're on stage, you can gauge where all the laughs are, kill the little laughs, go for the big ones. You play with the audience. Without them there, it's strange."

KEVIN KLINE

"I don't see that anybody needs to earn $12 million for three months' work, quite honestly."   **HELEN MIRREN**

★ ★ ★

"It is true that there are few plays of Shakespeare that I haven't done. When I was young, I was interested in working in cinema, but a director told me back then: 'You have everything wrong with your face.' I settled with that, since I preferred theatre anyway. I have no control over a film. I don't know what will be left on the cutting floor. In contrast, the control you have in a theatre is very attractive to me."
                                        DAME JUDI DENCH

★ ★ ★

"I don't make good distinctions between being in a very, very popular movie and being in a play in the West End of London that a lot fewer people see. To me it's just work."
                                        SIR IAN McKELLEN

★ ★ ★

"What I know is acting. I'll always have the desire to act. Onstage more than in films. Movies today are like fast food. Today's names won't become legendary and lead to the next generation."   **ANGELA LANSBURY**

★ ★ ★

"Rodgers and Hammerstein wrote for actors. If you're in the right frame of mind, and you're actually acting the song, the singing of it is easy. It's exciting. American musical theater is that perfect blend of incredible technique and intelligence and craft to the point where you can get carried into another world that is totally unbelievable—the fantasy of going along with characters. A great American musical gets you involved. You laugh. You love it. And you love to get carried away."

HUGH JACKMAN

★　★　★

"In a close-up in the movies, you may show the thought going through your head just through a change in the color of your skin. . . . [But] in the theater, you have to physicalize it. You and the director have to do the focusing of the audience that the camera does in film. If it's done beautifully, the audience doesn't notice it."

LYNN REDGRAVE

★　★　★

"In some ways, working in the theater is like playing a one-on-one sport: the better your opponent, the better you perform."

FARLEY GRANGER

★　★　★

"On film, you make things smaller, more intimate. The distance you project is only the distance to the camera. That is your measuring tape. Film is like a medium that likes to know less—it likes secrecy, and the smallest gesture can be significant."

RUTGER HAUER

★　★　★

"[Let us recognize] that an expression does not have the same value twice, does not live two lives; that all words, once spoken, are dead and function only at the moment when they are uttered, that a form, once it has served, cannot be used again and asks only to be replaced by another, and that the theater is the only place in the world where a gesture, once made, can never me made the same way twice."

ANTONIN ARTAUD

★　★　★

"[The Motion Picture Association's] attitude toward sex and violence is backward: You can disembowel a woman, but you can't see her vagina. When you see people blowing each other away willy-nilly, that's tough on an adult, never mind a 16-year-old. No censorship, but let's hold Hollywood to telling the truth. If you want your hero to get the crap kicked out of him, that's okay. But don't have him making love in the next scene, because that's a lie. If you get beat up—and I know this—you don't want to make love for a long, long time. Put in as much violence as you want, but stop lying about it. What constitutes an R versus a PG-13 rating I find really disturbing, because phenomenal amounts of violence get put into films that are purportedly for kids. I would rather see more sex and less violence, because sex is good, violence is bad." WILLIAM H. MACY

★　★　★

"Stage is such a different medium from film. Stage is full figure every moment. You really have to think of the total image that you're creating. You're the immediate contact with an audience, which is exciting." JULIE ANDREWS

★　★　★

"I believe that in the theater you really can't do anything that doesn't have some political consequence. My work has been about finding my own voice and a way to express myself."

OLYMPIA DUKAKIS

"Plays are just easier for me to break down. It's not as apparent to me how to go about working on a film script, where what's important is what's not said. It's a director's medium. You shoot a scene, but you have no idea what they do in the editing room. You're talking about your dying mother and the camera may be focusing on the cat. When I get a call for a film or TV program, I always have a slight surge of dread. I'm not a snob about any of it—I like the money. But when I get a call for a play, my excitement level is elevated."   **BETSY AIDEM**

★   ★   ★

"Eventually, I realized that cinema and theater are not so different: from the gut to the heart to the head of a character is the same journey for both."   **RALPH FIENNES**

★   ★   ★

Recounting advice he learned from his teacher, Kathryn Gately:

"Emotions are your fingertips. . . . They have to be fluid. When you're working in film, and especially in television, you don't have any time to prepare. Kathryn would tell us, 'You don't need more than five or ten minutes to prepare in film work, especially since they don't give you more than five minutes.' It's true—you have to shift gears and get going."   **JAMES GANDOLFINI**

★   ★   ★

Regarding over-emoting on film:

"As you get a little experience you realize that [crying and screaming] are the things you'd be having underneath, but

what you'd really be doing in that situation is trying to hold
everything together, to stay calm, to keep things moving
forward."   **BRAD PITT**

★   ★   ★

"There's a difference between naturalism and realism. . . .
The movie director decides where he's going to cut from
me to your reaction. On the stage, you and I have to select
when they're going to look at your reaction. If, say, this
cup of coffee is poisoned, in film we see you put the poison
in, then I come and drink it, and the audience is waiting
for me because they know. But on the stage, rather than
just drinking the coffee and putting it down, I might do
something like this [*he raises an imaginary coffee cup to
his mouth very slowly*]. If I slow down the action for that
moment, the whole audience's attention focuses in on that
cup—'Omigod, what's in the coffee?' It's realistic behavior,
but it's unnatural."   **JERRY ORBACH**

★   ★   ★

"One of the greatest defects of the theatre is that what is
created in it is written in melting snow, and that only
memories remain of the experience."   **LEE STRASBERG**

★   ★   ★

"Acting onstage is like having one pal, a beautiful woman,
and just being with her. Meaning that acting in film is
unsatisfying. It's titillating for the moment, but it has no
substance or any real quality."   **WALTER MATTHAU**

★   ★   ★

"The camera is just a big black box. It's plastic and metal. It doesn't transform anything. We let it. There is nothing mysterious about it. The mystery had existed a long time, long before the camera—with people getting together and talking about things they didn't understand. It's people that make it happen. If the camera becomes strong, all human input is nullified—the camera becomes an element of intimidation."

WILLIAM HURT

★   ★   ★

"After first days of filming sometimes my driver will take me home and say, 'What kind of crazy drug are you on?' And I'll say, 'I'm just really happy because I've been acting all day.' But in the theatre there's even more of a post-performance high. If someone meets me for a drink after the show, I'm insufferable, like a dizzy teenager. Between curtain up and curtain down I'm incredibly happy."

OLIVIA WILLIAMS

★   ★   ★

"The difference between a movie star and a movie actor is a movie star gets a script—movie star Michael Caine gets a script and he says, 'Now how can I change this script. It's not quite Michael Caine. I've got to change it.' And they say things like, 'Michael Caine wouldn't wear that kind of thing. Michael Caine wouldn't say that to a girl. Michael Caine wouldn't drive that sort of car. So we'll have to edit the script.' And everyone says, 'Oh, of course, Michael, we'll change all that.' They change the script to suit them. A movie actor, he changes himself to suit the script. He wears glasses, puts on a fat belly, gains weight, loses weight, grows a beard, moustache, any bloody thing."

SIR MICHAEL CAINE

On Doing Television: Soaps, Sitcoms, Episodics, and Live Broadcasts

"My responsibility [as a leading actor] is to tell any actor who wants to do a television series that he should drop dead."

ROD STEIGER

★   ★   ★

"Soap acting requires certain skills that I have never been able to develop: the ability to be a very fast study, the ability to concentrate in the middle of complete chaos, the ability to learn material that is the same but slightly different each day, and always, the need for instant acting with little or no rehearsal or preparation time. I have nothing but admiration for the many fine actors who have mastered these skills. For young actors it is an invaluable technique to acquire for a limited period of time."

FARLEY GRANGER

"With a sitcom, all you have is a situation, and you spend all week trying to find where the funny parts are."

DICK VAN DYKE

★   ★   ★

"Ultimately, the best thing that working in a soap opera trains you for is working in a soap opera. Once you learn how to use a three-camera, two-boom television studio, you know everything you need to know, and that takes about 35 or 40 days. Then you have to find some other way to combat the pressure and the boredom."   TOMMY LEE JONES

★   ★   ★

On the attitude he took toward booking The Streets of San Francisco, *his first starring role in episodic television*:

"Once I realized that I was going to be doing 20-plus of these shows a year for at least five years, I knew I'd go crazy . . . or I could use it like a lab to try out different things, things that probably no one else would notice, but would keep my juices flowing."   KARL MALDEN

★   ★   ★

"Everybody was telling me, 'Don't do TV, it will ruin your career.' And I never understood that because I thought, 'Isn't it about what comes out of your mouth? Isn't it about the writing?' I thought that was a really well-written script."

GLENN CLOSE

★   ★   ★

When asked how far he thinks reality TV can go as a genre:

"I just read that a network is doing something where people
are going to jail. Torture—I think people would watch that.
I think it culminates with somebody getting killed on TV.
I wouldn't be surprised if some state allowed us to watch
an execution. All it would take is huge ratings. Budweiser
sponsors it. Then 16 other states are doing it. I said to
somebody the other day, 'I have some very exciting news.
I just sold a reality show to CBS called *Well Hung*, but it's not
what you think—it's a show about people being executed
beautifully.'"   **ALBERT BROOKS**

★   ★   ★

On the best perk about being on a sitcom that's lasted nine years:

"It has given me a reason to stay alive. A great actor, Paul
Muni, once said, 'An actor must act, and when an actor isn't
acting, it's like a tree that has fruit on it. If it's not picked, it
falls off the tree.'"   **JERRY STILLER**

★   ★   ★

"Television could perform a great service in mass education,
but there's no indication its sponsors have anything like this
on their minds."   **TALLULAH BANKHEAD**

★   ★   ★

On working his first TV job for Knots Landing *in 1987:*

"The makeup man surveyed my face [and said,] 'I think we
should pluck between your eyebrows.' . . .
        "'Really, why would you do that?'

"'Because you'll look more intelligent.'

"Foolishly, I let him do this, but he had other ideas and rummaged in his bag for a small container called Mellow Yellow.

"'This gets rid of all the red blotches,' he explained. 'Errol Flynn would have had no career without it. . . .'

"With that, he proceeded to cover up every wrinkle, blotch, and inconsistency on my entire face. It didn't really matter to him what type of character I was playing, he was more concerned with fulfilling the TV mantra—make everyone look perfect.

"That episode . . . was an eye-opener—the speed and clinical nature of it boggled my mind. Michele Lee, the leading lady, ran the set like a drill sergeant and laid out all the blocking. 'Isn't that the director's job,' I asked myself.

"After the first take, the director looked to his camera crew.

"'Okay with you guys?' . . .

"*One take? Are these people out of their minds?* I was used to 10, 15 or 20 takes to get a shot right. This wasn't filmmaking, this was posing in front of the camera.

"When I got home after that first day, my wife, Cris, chuckled at me.

"'You look prettier than I do.'

"I didn't have another TV job for six years."

BRUCE CAMPBELL

★   ★   ★

"I worked on a soap opera called *One Life to Live*. . . . You have a script, 20, 25 pages long. You might get 10 hours to prepare it. The size of the average audience when I was working on that show in my early twenties was 13 million people, so there was a lot of pressure. I was also working in the theater at the same time, and I'd leave the television studio and eat dinner in a taxicab on the way to a rehearsal or the performance. . . . It made for a lot of 18-hour days, but it was a very happy time in my life." **Tommy Lee Jones**

★   ★   ★

"I think television had more of an influence on my life than the movies, because with television, you came into somebody's home. People remember me from television."

Kitty Carlisle Hart

★   ★   ★

"A soap opera [can be seen as] the modern equivalent of the old-fashioned touring companies: the material isn't great, so you've got to make something of it, and you've got to work very quickly." **Christopher Reeve**

★   ★   ★

On working in live television in the 1950s:

"We rehearsed in sequence for several weeks. Then, after a dress and technical rehearsal, we performed it on air. There were no such things as TelePrompTers, tape stops, reshoots, fixes in editing. . . . When you got on that 30-, 60-, or 90-minute express train, there was no getting off until it reached its destination. If you or another actor went up (forgot the line) or didn't make the entrance, you had to keep going until, one way or another, everything got back on track. If the show was under, they could fill time with a commercial. It could not be over. It had to end on time. Some of the shows were bad, many of them were good, and some of them were superb. All of them were fun to do."

Farley Granger

On how he allegedly hated working with a dog on his hit TV show Frasier:

"The only difficulty I have is when people start believing he's an actor. Acting to me is a craft, not a reflex. It takes years to master, and though it does have its rewards, the reward is not a hot dog. Moose does tricks; I memorize lines, say words, even walk around and stuff. But I don't need a trainer standing off camera, gesticulating wildly and waving around a piece of meat, to know where I'm supposed to look."

KELSEY GRAMMER

★   ★   ★

"[When I was younger] I supplemented my [soap opera] roles with commercials. A wife rubbing Absorbine, Jr. on my husband's shoulder. A zany shopper trying on girdles in a posh shop for I Can't Believe It's a Girdle. A leggy cocktail waitress exchanging wisecracks with beefy guys for . . . gosh, what was that? Something for the beefy guy target market. Hey, it's a living. . . . Commercial producers had always told me, 'We just can't pin down your type.'

"My type? Maybe I'm the type who can be *any type*.

"I think that type is called *an actress*."

RUE MCCLANAHAN

★   ★   ★

"You think government is confusing, try figuring out why TV shows fail. No, don't—it's a waste of time."   **TERI GARR**

On Dealing with the Ups and Downs of Fame and Fortune

"Fame is fun for a minute, but it gets very boring. I think the real fun part is the actual work. There's not a feeling in the world like manipulating yourself into feeling something and knowing you were honest for that one moment."

WINONA RYDER

★   ★   ★

"The only thing money means to me is the freedom it buys me."

JOHNNY DEPP,
after purchasing his own Caribbean island

★   ★   ★

"Years ago, people advised me to have a business manager. . . . Coincidentally, a lawyer who worked at my agency, Famous Artists, was leaving to become a business manager.

I relaxed—I would have a friend handling my financial affairs. Things went well; I made lots of money. Sam, my business manager, gave me financial reports that I didn't understand and papers to sign. I signed away everything until I was broke." **KIRK DOUGLAS**

★   ★   ★

"Being a star is an agent's dream, not an actor's."
ROBERT DUVALL

★   ★   ★

"I'd heard people say, 'You'll enjoy being famous for a week, and you'll never enjoy it again.' I don't even feel like I had that week. I was so busy working that I didn't even get to notice that moment." **MATT DAMON**

★   ★   ★

"I have some friends who lately I don't call anymore. I feel badly that I'm working and they just never are. There's no difference [in ability] in my mind between us. But I went to another level and they're working in a bank. And they were just as tenacious, just as competitive as I was." **TERI GARR**

★   ★   ★

"[Paparazzi are] the dung beetles of the world. They reek of piss and I'll never change my attitude towards them."
SEAN PENN

★   ★   ★

"I have never felt compelled to share with [the public] my

bathroom habits or share with you my bedroom habits. Everyone has a right to privacy, so I have never felt—even though I am famous—that I had to share that with anybody."

JOHN TRAVOLTA

★   ★   ★

On dealing with the press:

"The phone rings every day. I say, 'No, of course it's not true,' and hang up."

ANGELINA JOLIE

★   ★   ★

"I've got to hunt them down, but I've got a few [places where no one recognizes me]. A very important part of human interaction is that your merit is measured by who you are while you're in the company of someone up until that moment when you say farewell. And nothing more. . . . I walk in, and you already know my bio. You could go, 'Sorry about Mrs. Hud that died, and how's Foxy?' I'm going, 'Whoa, you know the name of my dog that died and you're asking about my new dog.' What happened to, 'How's it going, and what did you do today?'"

MATTHEW MCCONAUGHEY

★   ★   ★

Responding to the suggestion that he's been misunderstood in previous interviews:

"I don't think about being misunderstood or not misunderstood. As Popeye said so beautifully, 'I y'am what I y'am, and that's all that I y'am.' For someone to say that they're misunderstood assumes that I think people have a perception of me, which means I assume they think about me. I don't think they think about me at all. Why would they?"   JOHN MALKOVICH

★   ★   ★

"You cannot make material possessions a symbol of your talent."   ROD STEIGER

★   ★   ★

Immediately after snapping at the paparazzi:

"There are people who blow their tops, and people who don't. I am told it's bad to bottle it all up inside you, but then if you blow you have to go around apologizing. . . . I suppose I should just let it come out of my ears."   AUDREY HEPBURN

★   ★   ★

"I'm not good at the majority of things that come [with celebrity]. I like my job. I don't mind getting up at three in the morning on the Isle of Man, working in a cowshed that smells like poo. I'm okay with 16-hour days. I'm okay with living out of my suitcase. I am not good at the commodification of me as a person—it's dehumanizing. I'm not good at it because my values are different than that, and so I'm disappointed by it."   RENÉE ZELLWEGER

★   ★   ★

"You get pulled into a place where you can think you are the center of your own universe in the business instead of focusing on the work, the work, the work. We have to keep that in mind because this country we live in and this business we work in is one seductive place."

PHILIP SEYMOUR HOFFMAN

★   ★   ★

"It is difficult, if not impossible for a star to occupy an inch of space without bursting seams, cramping everyone else's style and unbalancing a play. No matter how self-effacing a famous player may be, he makes an entrance as a casual neighbor and the audience interest shifts to the house next door."

HELEN HAYES

★   ★   ★

"People who have car collections—I never understood that. I always thought that was unnecessary. It's not beautiful, it's not creative. It's just showing how much money you've got."

DANIEL RADCLIFFE

★   ★   ★

"I've read interviews about myself that start with 'You may not recognize him.' If you read that enough, it does start to bother you."

ADAM GOLDBERG

★   ★   ★

"There is no other occupation in the world that so closely resembles enslavement as the career of a film star."

LOUISE BROOKS

★   ★   ★

"An actor's popularity is fleeting. His success has the life expectancy of a small boy who is about to look into a gas tank with a lighted match."
                                        FRED ALLEN

★   ★   ★

"[Metro-Goldwyn-Mayer] had us working days and nights on end. They'd give us pep pills to keep us on our feet long after we were exhausted. Then they'd take us to the studio hospital and knock us cold with sleeping pills. . . . Then after four hours they'd wake us up and give us the pep-up pills again so we could work another 72 hours in a row."
                                        JUDY GARLAND

★   ★   ★

"It's much harder to act in a bad film than in a good one. A terrible script makes for very difficult acting. Yet you can win an Academy Award for some of the easiest acting in your career, made possible by a brilliant script."
                                        SIR MICHAEL CAINE

★   ★   ★

"I've been rolling since I was 18. So every now and then you might have a movie that's whack and don't make some loot, but that ain't the end of the world."   **EDDIE MURPHY**

★   ★   ★

"People don't realize that [actors] pay ten percent to an agent, five percent to a business manager, a fee to a publicist, and by the time you get through with Uncle Sam, a lot of [your money] is gone."   **VICKI LAWRENCE**

"[The paparazzi are] the defining annoyance of my life.
I just think how strange it is for my kids. . . . They really
believe that every time you go outside there is a herd of
people with cameras snapping flashes in your face [who] are
going to kind of block your way when you're trying to get
somewhere."   **BRAD PITT**

★ ★ ★

"We tend to think that rich and famous go together but fame
takes more getting used to than being rich does."
                                              ALAN ALDA

★ ★ ★

"An actor's burning ambition, when you think about it, is to
spend as much time as possible pretending to be somebody
else. For those of us lucky (or unstable) enough to become
professional performers, the uncertainty about who we
really are only increases. For many actors, this self-doubt is
like a worm eating away at you and growing, incongruously,
in direct proportion to your level of success. No matter how
great the acceptance, adulation, and accumulation of wealth,
gnawing at you always is the deep-seated belief that you're
a fake, a phony. Even if you can bullshit your way through
whatever job you're working on now, you'd better prepare for
the likelihood that you're never going to get another one."
                                      MICHAEL J. FOX

★ ★ ★

*On the desperate need she sometimes felt to flee her rising
fame:*

"I could change my name. Dye my hair brown. Get fat. Move

to another state. I'll pick a spot on the map . . . rent a Hertz car, load up the encyclopedias, check into a motel, people do it all the time, and look for a sweet little dream house to buy (remember to call my business manager, find out how much money I have). Actually a whole different country might be best. Spin the globe. A bicycle repair shop in Peru! Dogs asleep on the dirt floor. I can even speak Spanish, sort of. There are countless options. What were they again? Change names. Dye hair. Get fat. Move to Peru. Fix bikes. Have I thought of everything? I wonder how long you can live on Sara Lee chocolate cake?"   **Mia Farrow**

★   ★   ★

"Now, if someone looks at me it's 'cause they recognize me . . . whereas before, it probably just meant I had food on my face or something."   **Philip Seymour Hoffman**

★   ★   ★

When Good Will Hunting, *the film he co-wrote (and won a Best Screenplay Oscar for), was set for release, Matt Damon refused to be on the cover of* Rolling Stone. *Harvey Weinstein,* Hunting's *producer, was not pleased:*

"Harvey came to the set of [the movie I was working on next] and was yelling at me, going, 'What the fuck is wrong with you? Did you ever think you'd be on the cover of *Rolling Stone*?' And I said, 'Sure, I dreamed about it when I was a kid, but I'm already on the cover of nine other fucking magazines. My own grandmother told me she's sick of seeing me. I can't do this anymore.'"   **Matt Damon**

★   ★   ★

"I can now be on the cover of certain magazines, which studios like because it promotes your film. And yes, at times it can be fun, but it's not *important*. And there are more negatives from that kind of attention. Overall I think it hurt work. It's harder for me to be taken seriously now. But I can't go back. I can't change what happened."   **SIENNA MILLER**

★   ★   ★

"The first time I had a major success . . . I thought I was . . . special . . . I had all these tales about how unique and fantastic my experience had been. I believed the hype about how great I was in a role and transferred that into thinking that I was the only person who could've done it . . . But the next time success came along . . . came after a humbling bunch of years as a has-been, [and] I [realized]: I'm just not that special. I understand that my life and my career will have ups and downs. I know that opportunities get given and taken away. And I finally understand that success isn't necessarily a reflection of my talent or ability . . . I'm a part of something bigger than me."   **TERI HATCHER**

★   ★   ★

"One time I went to the movies with my mother in Georgia and I was in the bathroom. All of a sudden this voice says, 'Excuse me? The girl in stall No. 1? Were you in *Mystic Pizza*?' I said yeah and she goes, 'Can I have your autograph?' and slides a piece of toilet paper under the stall. I just said, 'I don't think right now is the time.'"

JULIA ROBERTS

★ ★ ★

"If you survive [the ups and downs of fame], you become a legend. I'm a legend. I'm revered, rather like an old building."

KATHARINE HEPBURN

★ ★ ★

"A legend is only somebody that's been lucky."

MICKEY ROONEY

★ ★ ★

"If I told you the parts I turned down, you would laugh. They were really biggies." AL PACINO

★ ★ ★

"Remember that the higher the monkey climbs, the more he shows his ass." MARTIN SHEEN

★ ★ ★

"I've been quoted as saying if I ever wind up as a forty-somethin', remarried, marketable, big-action-movie dad of a teenager in a cul-de-sac in Brentwood, please run up behind me and pop two in my head—do me a favor."

ROBERT DOWNEY, JR.,
age 41, married to his second wife and living with his teenaged son in a cul-de-sac in Brentwood just prior to the big budget release of the comic book franchise movie Iron Man, *in which Downey stars*

★ ★ ★

"A lot of old movie stars couldn't act their way out of a box of wet tissue paper, but they were successful because they had

distinctive personalities. They were predictable brands of
breakfast cereal."   **MARLON BRANDO**

★ ★ ★

"I've seen the price you pay [when fame destroys your
privacy] and if you glibly give it up, you never get it back.
What I dislike more than anything else is constantly being
reminded of the difference between yourself and other
people; it's quite tedious after a while. And it doesn't get
any better, it builds geometrically. I can feel people turning
around on the street after I've passed them, or you hear your
name out of the corner of your ear, and I hate that, because
I can't get rid of it, I can't stop being aware. . . . You're
disadvantaged as an actor by becoming observed rather
than being an observer. If your life changes so much that
you're no longer able to have mundane experiences, then
your personality's going to undergo an inevitable shift that's
not going to be appropriate to the work you do. So you've
got to protect yourself. It makes it more necessary to have a
normal life, to invest yourself in real things."

HARRISON FORD

★ ★ ★

"The whole era when I was busy being a big movie star was
terribly disconcerting. I was cared for and cosseted, and yet
I was totally dependent. I didn't know where the cornflakes
were kept. I didn't know how to turn on my own washing
machine. That might sound very chic, but I'm telling you:
When you don't know how your own life works, you get
disconnected."   **FAYE DUNAWAY**

★ ★ ★

"As Terence Rattigan once told me, 'When you've had three good notices in a row, get ready for a bad one.' This was not by any means a cynical remark; critics will always find ample time to repent their over-enthusiasm."

SIR MICHAEL REDGRAVE

★　★　★

On following his agents' advice and turning down the lead in Love Story, *which eventually went on to phenomenal success with Ryan O'Neal:*

"The stupendous unexpected success of *Love Story* taught me a lesson. It was not to cleave to the old adage 'Never ask for a job; never refuse one,' for working on rubbish is both depressing and demeaning. Rather, to listen more astutely, not to one's advisors, but to one's own intuitions. As a result, I have subsequently tended to accept rather than refuse, and I would now much rather regret the sins of commission than those of omission."   MICHAEL YORK

★　★　★

"[Money is] important to pay the bills but not much more. What's really important is doing a job you love, doing good work. Everything else is a bonus."

PHILIP SEYMOUR HOFFMAN

★　★　★

"Keeping a low profile has to do with not going to places where the paparazzi are. It's not that hard. A lot of celebrities moan about how difficult it is, then they keep showing up at film premieres. Why do you show up?"   JOHN CUSACK

"The first purchase I made when I got a check for $100,000
was a Mercedes for $100,000. I didn't have money left over
for insurance and gas."   **MARK WAHLBERG**

★   ★   ★

"I entered this business before I had focus and purpose in
my life. I was very unhappy, very unhealthy, and when I sat
down for an interview, I didn't know why. I felt like I didn't
have anything to share. It was a very empty time."

ANGELINA JOLIE

★   ★   ★

"We stopped at a roadside cafe for Cokes. Inside, we sat at
one of the few tables and ordered. Then, an old man, who
was sitting across the room, came slowly over to us, peered
at Tallulah, and asked, 'Are you Edna St. Vincent Millay?'
Startled, Tallulah said, 'No, but I am someone terribly
famous. Here, I'll write my name on this slip of paper,
and, after we've gone, open it, and you'll see. Meanwhile,
my friend here, Colin Keith-Johnston, will recite for you.
Colin, this gentleman is thirsting for poetry—recite for
him!' And Colin did recite 'At a Month's End' by Swinburne,
beautifully and in a most matter-of-fact way, as though the
setting and the audience were not that unusual. We finished
our Cokes, Colin finished the Swinburne, we paid the check
and left. As we boarded the bus and looked back, the screen
door of the little cafe opened, and the old man, waving the
slip of paper Tallulah had given him, called, 'Good-bye!
Good-bye! Ella Wheeler Wilcox!'"   **EUGENIA RAWLS**

★   ★   ★

"Sometimes [having a famous] reputation is the problem.
It may help get the film made, and you're glad about that.
But the fact that you have to carry this goddamn reputation
around with you to help get the film made may be what
costs you the freedom of movement that you would love to
have to express yourself in a more creative way where you
don't have the preconceptions that reputations are made of."

WILLIAM HURT

★   ★   ★

"Very soon preconceptions of me, if there are any left, will
be meaningless, because I'll be moving too fast. 'Who's that
bloke in the white car? No, he's on a yellow horse.' 'Who's
that bloke on the yellow horse? No, he's holding a black
jaguar.' 'That bloke holding the black jaguar? No, he's a
clown up there on the tightrope.'"   **SIR BEN KINGSLEY**

★   ★   ★

*In response to being asked if his fame has had a weird effect
on others:*

"People certainly can be weird enough without me being
involved. But I suppose it does. You'd have to ask them.
The oddest thing with the modern world is someone passing
along your whereabouts, which I find strange. You know,
celebrity sightings—saw him at the coffee shop. They take
a picture with a portable phone and get it on the Internet.
It's that kind of thing that I don't really get."

JOHN MALKOVICH

★   ★   ★

On the paparazzi:

"As Eddie Izzard says, these people always hang out in fives, because these people have a fifth of a personality each."

DANIEL RADCLIFFE

★   ★   ★

"I live in a world where one is constantly being misled, either by the length of one's limo, or the size of one's face on the screen, or the kind remarks of people that surround you, and I know that they are constantly telling you lies about the true nature of what you do. . . . If I'm not in touch with truth, my true self, my true feelings, the true importance or nonimportance of what this skinny, six-foot one frame is about, then I'm lost."

JEREMY IRONS

★   ★   ★

"[Fame is] like this game that we all know we're playing but pretend we're not. But we all know how it works and everyone knows how you get where you get. Ultimately, you work your 10-hour day, agonize over what you've done, then go out and publicize it. All people are really interested in is who you are dating and what you're wearing."

CATE BLANCHETT

★   ★   ★

"In our business if you're not discreet and you just splash everything out, your life and your feelings and, then it's really terrible. . . . You have to be very discreet about your personal life, and you have to be closed in, in harmony and in affection and in everything."

SOPHIA LOREN

"You know, there was an article I was reading somewhere, and there were eleven things on this list that made me a motherfucker, right? The eleven points of motherfuckerdom of Russell Crowe. And nine of them were completely untrue, had never happened, but had been over time reprinted so much that they were now folkloric."   **RUSSELL CROWE**

★   ★   ★

"I've had people come up and ask me to sign their guns. Sign my name on gun handles and holsters and stuff. I've done it once or twice for law enforcement officials, but when people do that—and there have been quite a few of them lately— I always tell them no. I don't want to do that. I don't want my name on that and I hope you use this gun—whatever its purpose is, I hope it's used wisely."   **CLINT EASTWOOD**

★   ★   ★

"Jack [Nicholson] used to tell me that you can enjoy your celebrity if you stop feeling like protecting your privacy. He says if I don't like the attention, I should go live in the desert and run a gas station."   **SEAN PENN**

★   ★   ★

On his theory that the better the actor, the less you know about his or her life:

"If I asked you right now who you thought were the best actors, your favorite 10 actors at work, men and women, my guess is that the list you would give me would probably be pretty close to my list. And you wouldn't know much of *anything* about any of their personal lives. Monty Clift.

Monty Clift! Gay? Yes, no, maybe? Probably. Everyone says yeah. I don't know for sure. Never saw the pictures. I don't know. *Mystery*, right?"   **MATT DAMON**

★   ★   ★

"Being a celebrity can cause an accidental cheapening of the things one holds dear. A slip of the tongue in an interview and it's easy for me to feel I've sold out some private part of my life in exchange for publicity."   **STEVE MARTIN**

On Hollywood, Broadway, and Show Business

"It's such a cuckoo business. And it's a business you go into because you're egocentric. It's a very embarrassing profession."   KATHARINE HEPBURN

★   ★   ★

"[You can never forget that this is] a business. When you do a movie at Paramount, and you finish shooting . . . and you walk across the hallway, to go to *Entertainment Tonight*, which they own, you're doing a television show which the studio owns that they're charging commercial time for that they're earning money on to promote the movie that you just walked off the set of, so the synergistics are not lost on everyone. . . . They're taking actors now and . . . inserting them like suppositories into the cavities of the movie-going public. . . . What used to be clever marketing campaigns by studios has been replaced by actor-driven campaigns, so that when the movie fails, the marketing department can step back and say, 'Well, we ran Alec's picture up the flagpole and nobody came [to see it] so we're clean.'"

ALEC BALDWIN

★   ★   ★

"[Hollywood is] an emotional Detroit."
LILLIAN GISH

★   ★   ★

"Movies are terrifically optimistic enterprises. If you come into the makeup trailer in the morning and you say to the hair person, 'Did you go to the dailies?' I've never in my life heard anybody say, 'They weren't very good.' It's always, 'Oh, my God! It's electrifying!'"   **CHRISTOPHER WALKEN**

★   ★   ★

"It's been my whole life, dedicated to [art], toiled in the vineyards of culture [*laughs*]. At the same time I have a business. They say, 'We're a business, we're a business, not an art form,' but as a matter of fact, [acting] is an art form, also. 'Art' is a bad word in Hollywood. [*Laughs.*] You use 'art' too many times and they show you the elevator and then your name is taken off the parking lot. [In Hollywood] you have to be careful before you say the word 'art.'"

DENNIS HOPPER

★   ★   ★

"There's a lot of great fallacies in the movie business. The so-called great unproduced script: that doesn't exist. '*They* don't want to make good pictures.' *They* do. In fact, as I

imagine the head of a studio's job, there are always three or
four pictures every year that he'd like to make. And then he
has to fill out the program with the rest, which are all pretty
much hustled movies."   **JACK NICHOLSON**

★   ★   ★

"Whatever the pitfalls of the old studio system . . . they had
a stable of actors that worked together all the time so you
got the feeling when you saw the movies in the thirties and
forties you were watching people that knew each other, that
had some sense of communication even if it was hello-how
are you in the commissary, or to get drunk together, or to
go to the parties together. . . . Now, I go to the movies and I
don't feel like anybody knows each other. I feel like they've
met that morning, and that they're going to rush back to
their trailer in the middle of the afternoon."   **ALAN ARKIN**

★   ★   ★

"Broadway is one of the only places that you instantly get
surrounded by the best and learn from the best."
                                          BROOKE SHIELDS

★   ★   ★

"Hollywood is just as commercial as television, and
Broadway is just as commercial as Hollywood."
                                             ROD STEIGER

★   ★   ★

"I'm not 'Blockbuster Boy.' I never wanted to be. I wasn't
looking for that . . . I mean, it would be nice to get a whole
shitpile of money so you can throw it at your family

and friends . . . I just don't know if movies can ever be considered art, because there's so much money involved . . . It's all about commerce. I don't think art can come from that place. But I aspire to be an artist someday. Maybe I'll be 70. I don't know if it will come from being in a movie, though. Maybe I'll just whittle something." **Johnny Depp**

★   ★   ★

"I worry about these young kids—15, 18, 20 years old— who in the span of one year become millionaires and powerhouses. It's too much power for a kid that age to handle, and when these young actors are spiraling out of control, taking drugs and drinking too much I think their managers and their agents are morally bound and perhaps legally bound to do something about it, [but] so often the managers and the agents cover for them."

William H. Macy

★   ★   ★

"[Hollywood is a place] full of people that learned to write but evidently can't read." **Will Rogers**

★   ★   ★

"In England, an actor is an actor is an actor, and since most of their work is done in London, actors can do TV in the morning, a film job in the afternoon, and end with a stage role that night, but in the USA, with our most peculiar geography, we're stuck with those built-in prejudices. There are some actors who excel in all three areas, but we must repeatedly break down those prejudiced walls to prove it."

Rue McClanahan

"Hollywood is a factory. You have to realize that you are working in a factory and you're part of the mechanism. If you break down, you'll be replaced." **MEL GIBSON**

★ ★ ★

"As an actor I think you're always going to ride a fine line between doing something because you believe it's the right thing to do, and guessing what the public wants to see. . . . You have to be quite vigilant with yourself and question why you're doing certain things as well as what's behind all that. Because otherwise, you can find yourself having made choices for the wrong reasons. And suddenly you're a completely different person than the one you thought you were a year ago." **MICHAEL SHEEN**

★ ★ ★

"I'm glad I didn't run the [career] sprint. Even when I may have wanted to, that race wasn't necessarily open for me. So it's nice now that I've learned I want to be a marathon runner and look back on it in my 70s. I want to retire when I'm ready to retire, like a Michael Caine or an Anthony Hopkins." **DON CHEADLE**

★ ★ ★

"A lot of actors said they hated the studio system, but I loved it. It was like a college—it was a great place to learn; an actor had a great continuity of work and I found [my] seven years to be a great place to learn my trade." **RICHARD WIDMARK**

★ ★ ★

"When I first got out to Hollywood they were pushing me for sitcoms, and I didn't really have any interest in them. I wanted to do films and slowly worked that way. And then it became, I guess, this curse of the leading man."   **BRAD PITT**

★   ★   ★

Recalling how his manager, the legendary Bernie Brillstein, handled a major studio that dragged its feet paying out a bonus they owed on a feature film:

"When the chips were down, it was all about you. . . . [Bernie] was on the phone with the chairman of the studio, and it was not going well. Bernie finally just told him to 'fuck off' and hung up on him. There are a lot of managers and agents today who would tell you that they would do that, but they never would. . . . I heard it with my own ears . . . and I got the check."   **ROB LOWE**

★   ★   ★

"The essence of our industry [is to] hold your nose and dive in."   **SHIRLEY MACLAINE**

★   ★   ★

"I make four, five, six movies a year, maybe one of them gets seen, but that's show business."   **CHRISTOPHER WALKEN**

★   ★   ★

"A few days ago, I was present at a discussion about the theater. I saw some sort of human snakes, otherwise known as playwrights, explain how to worm a play into the good graces of a director, like certain men in history who used to insinuate poison into the ears of their rivals."

ANTONIN ARTAUD

★　　★　　★

"Even now, what I do on stage is irrelevant [in Hollywood]. It's not as if it's dismissed, it's not even part of the equation. It's not in the mix. It never makes it to the table. So you begin to feel disorientated. I'm used to it now. But it used to fill me with a strange malaise, because there, youth, fashion and money are what identify you as relevant."

OLYMPIA DUKAKIS

★　　★　　★

"I think [longevity in the film business] has a lot to do with being involved with people who are talented. And luck has a lot to do with it. A certain kind of ambition has something to do with it, too—that is to say the ambition to do good work, to find good projects. And I think a lot of it probably has to do simply with the fact that that's what you want to do, and so you do whatever is necessary to make it happen."

HARRISON FORD

★　　★　　★

"The truth is I don't think actors should have to do anything but come in and act. . . . I feel the film companies should pay for proper advertising to see that the movie will sell instead of putting it on our backs. I've tried to narrow the contractual language, which requires a 'fair and reasonable' amount of publicity. I've said in negotiations: 'How much will you pay me not to have to promote? I only want to charge you for my acting. And you know what, it won't be that expensive!' And they say, 'Zero.'"   **BILLY CRUDUP**

"'One for the meal, one for the reel.' You know, you can say that but it's always a roll of the dice about whether people are going to see [your film] or not. There's no guarantees even if you say, 'Well I think maybe this movie feels more commercial/less commercial.' Who knows? It's the same thing with the small movies. Sometimes they break out and based on how much they cost, they have a tremendous upside that you don't really expect. So it's not so much the reason to do [a film]."

KEVIN BACON

★ ★ ★

When asked what troubles him most about Hollywood:

"There's a stronger drive than I can ever recall [now] toward pre-packaging films and reducing the risk to zero. You have a pre-sold director and actor. The thrust has been to disregard the nature of the film itself. That cuts off the creativity of young talent, the talent that needs to explore. The studios' idea is that you need such and such a name to generate capital. My contention is the project needs to be done right to generate capital. . . . The problem is, too much money is spent on individual films, $70 million, $100 million, $200 million. Everyone is always looking for that blockbuster hit. Somehow in there, they believe, is their identity. 'Wow, my film made $200 million. What did your film make, a lousy $10 million? You're a bum.'"

HARVEY KEITEL

★ ★ ★

"I've had better experiences making smaller movies than bigger studio films. Factor out the layer of executives, and then you can concentrate on what really matters."

MANDY MOORE

"Equity rules stated that if you were fired before five days of rehearsal, you would be paid only for the days you rehearsed. After the five-day period, you were entitled to at least two weeks' pay.

"There's an old apocryphal theater story about an actor who is handed a telegram after the fifth day of rehearsal. 'The bastards don't even have the courage to tell me to my face; they have to send me a wire,' the actor says as he opens the telegram. But then, as he reads the telegram, his facial expression turns calmer. 'It's okay,' he says. 'My mother just died.'"   ELI WALLACH

★   ★   ★

On the critics' response to her performance in The School for Scandal *on Broadway:*

"All my reviews were good except one. Walter Kerr still refused me a nod of approval. I was once told it was because I was a lot like his wife. I wonder."   PATRICIA NEAL

★   ★   ★

On making his Broadway debut in Tennessee Williams' Out Cry:

"I saw my name up in lights . . . on Broadway's Lyceum Theater. I arranged my things in my 'travesty of a dressing room.' The backstage, too, was tatty and the theater itself in a less than salubrious part of town. Only at night, when hundreds of billboards lit up the buildings, banishing the filth and tawdriness, did Broadway's sobriquet, 'the Great White Way' and its pretensions toward any sort of glamour have the remotest validity."   MICHAEL YORK

"Sidney Poitier gave me a piece of advice years ago: If they see you for free all week, they won't pay to see you on the weekend.' . . . I think a lot of the young kids today should take that and learn from it. If you're interested in the marathon and not a sprint, then you have to keep some mystery. Quite frankly, I'm not that interested in publicity. I do it because it's a part of my job, promoting the movie. I'm not interested in promoting myself. That's not what I do for a living. I'm an actor, and learning to be a director. That's what I do."
                                          DENZEL WASHINGTON

★   ★   ★

"You know, it's weird. . . . When I did *Donnie Brasco*, people within the industry said, 'He finally played a man.' And I didn't particularly get it. It's like, why was I a man? Because I punched a couple of guys? Because I kissed a girl, had sex? I guess that's it. I was sort of fascinated by that."
                                                JOHNNY DEPP

★   ★   ★

"I find it absolutely bizarre, this whole sort of entrance round [of applause] that people do [in the U.S.]. You spend however long rehearsing a play and working out exactly what the beats and rhythms are and what you want the focus to be, and then you walk out onstage and people clap. . . . People here clap at the end of a speech [even] before the scene is over. I find that extraordinary!"

When asked by the interviewer if this really isn't done in Britain, Sheen responded:

"Never! We've moved out of the 18th century."
                                                MICHAEL SHEEN

"Don't ever humiliate a man. If you're gonna have to dress
him out, you take him aside and do it that way. That's the
one thing I don't like about Hollywood: They go in for
public humiliation. You shouldn't do that to a man."

RIP TORN

★   ★   ★

"Actors want to book commercials because they want the
residuals, but they don't care if they sell much product or
if people fast-forward through the programming to get to
the next commercial so they can hear the dulcet tones of
William H. Macy. When I lived in New York I supported
myself by doing commercials. Mostly I auditioned. Once in
a blue moon I would actually book one. I have great respect
for commercials that can accomplish more in 30 seconds
than some films do in two hours. On the other hand, those
are the exceptions."   **WILLIAM H. MACY**

★   ★   ★

"Movie critics are not movie fans anymore. They're fans
of being clever and being read and being popular, and
particularly being quoted."   **BRUCE DERN**

★   ★   ★

"There's nothing for me to do in L.A. when I get up in the
morning except sit by the pool and shop."   **HARRISON FORD**

★   ★   ★

"Show me a bad script, and I will show you a big payday.
Conversely, show me a really great script and forget it.
You're lucky if you don't have to pay for it."   **AL PACINO**

"Broadway doesn't make stars anymore. The shows are the stars—*Cats, Les Miserables, Starlight Express,* and the whole Cameron Mackintosh/Andrew Lloyd Webber onslaught. There were no stars in those shows."   **TERRENCE MANN**

★ ★ ★

"When you're reading scripts, you want them to be *Three Days of the Condor.* But you know when they suck. If you can make $5 million doing a shitty movie, and if you can sit at home afterward and be okay with that, you should do it. But people will bring that movie up for the rest of your life, and for me, it hurts too much."   **AARON ECKHART**

★ ★ ★

"Broadway producers are happy to have a big Hollywood name they can post on the marquee, but most of them assume that television and film stars really can't handle stage work. Too often, they're right."   **RUE MCCLANAHAN**

★ ★ ★

"Just because someone can get [a project] done, that doesn't mean it should be done. Sure, I could go into a studio and say, 'I'd like to make a movie about coal miners,' and someone will produce a story about coal miners, and someone will direct it and we'll make a movie about coal miners. And no one will care. . . . The responsibility is to go into whatever it is full-bore. You can't have a passing interest. Because once I give them a yes, the trucks start pulling up and it starts costing money."   **TOM HANKS**

★ ★ ★

"I like to get up early and work in the morning and afternoon. I like to sleep at night. But to build my career I would force myself to do a play. Night work. Then to keep it interesting I would take [the show] on tour the minute the gross dipped below a certain figure."

KATHARINE HEPBURN

★   ★   ★

"I did one play [in Los Angeles], and that's the last one I'll do. I worked at the Pasadena Playhouse. . . . The businesspeople out there don't go to plays. To them, plays are a sign of weakness and are a distraction. The feeling is, actors are doing a play because they can't get a film."   **DYLAN BAKER**

★   ★   ★

"There is a natural tendency in this business to think that once a show ends, you'll never work again. Worse, when you're fired . . . you start to doubt your own talent. When I finally convinced myself I had nothing to feel guilty about [over losing my show], the anger set in. I wanted to hit someone. I wanted to hurt them like they had hurt me. I felt like another who'd had her child taken away. I wanted to part put my [show's] logo on a milk carton with the following caption: 'Have you seen this show?'"

VICKI LAWRENCE

★   ★   ★

"I've been in show business all my life. All my references, all my moves, my mind, the way I express myself, it is very reminiscent of the past. I am a foreigner in my own country because I come from another country, the country of show business. I speak that language and I have that way of dressing, of combing my hair, of moving my face. It makes me different. I am a foreigner." **Christopher Walken**

★ ★ ★

"[I recall] a quote from Gary Cooper: 'I need one movie out of three to be a hit.'" **Gene Wilder**

★ ★ ★

"Once a show goes into a tailspin . . . it's best to bail out." **Michael York**

★ ★ ★

On whether he prefers working in big budget Hollywood films or indies:

"They're all a machine. It's all a big machine. Isn't it depressing? I'm exaggerating the point but I also mean that in a way meaning that whether you're working in an independent film world or the big budget film world, all the same problems arise. All the same stuff happens. One you don't have as much money, as much time and just not as many frills or whatever extras. Craft service might not be as good but ultimately, you're under the gun like anything. There's something that needs to be made, needs to be made in a certain amount of time and somebody spent a lot of money." **Philip Seymour Hoffman**

★ ★ ★

On remakes:

In 2003, Michael Douglas and Albert Brooks did a remake of a classic comedy, The In-Laws *(1979), with Alan Arkin and Peter Falk. When the remake opened, Arkin called his former co-star. The following is a snippet of their conversation:*

ALAN ARKIN: (*chuckling*) "It's a turkey—the whole movie— in the toilet."

PETER FALK: (*big grin*) "No kidding."

ALAN ARKIN: (*now laughing*) "And you and I—we got raves—better reviews for the remake than for the original."

PETER FALK: (*full-out delight*) "No kidding. Better than the orig—" (*Can't finish—laughing too hard.*)

★   ★   ★

"If a play runs for a long time, particularly a musical, some participants get bored and think up amusing little surprises to maintain the enthusiasm.

"At the one-hundred-and-fiftieth performance of [*I Remember*] *Mama* a gigantic gorilla lopes into the wings just as I'm supposed to make my entrance. I fall on the floor with a scream of terror. Stagehands quickly pick me up and push me on stage. I am on Broadway singing "Every Day Comes Something Beautiful" and my body is frozen with fear, when I hear a discreet coughing in the wings. Out of the corner of my eye I see the propman take off his gorilla outfit."   LIV ULLMANN

On Gender Differences and Aging in the Biz

"It's different for women. Men really have a much longer shelf life than we do."
LORRAINE TOUSSAINT

★ ★ ★

"As I get older I see all the things I don't need. I don't need a great amount of preparation time, and I don't need to go into strange places, and I don't need to slavishly work on subtext. When you're young you want people to know you're acting. But when you get older you don't want people to know you're acting, you don't want them to catch you at it. . . . I wash my face, I brush my teeth, I put on the costume, and maybe 30 seconds before my first entrance I sort of take a moment to get into it, and then I do it. I wear no makeup. I haven't done makeup in years, unless it's something like *Cyrano*, where I have to wear a prosthetic."
FRANK LANGELLA

"I have noticed increasingly through the years, that when a man speaks his mind it is accepted as charming, interesting, sexy, but when a woman speaks hers she is aggressive, unattractive, pushy—some might even say a bitch."

LAUREN BACALL

★　★　★

"As you get older, you essentially try to do less—[your craft] goes deeper, and it becomes more fermented."

PENELOPE WILTON

★　★　★

"I'm speaking for women right now, because I don't know what men experience, but if you focus on your talent and on playing a wide range of roles rather than having your career hooked up on your looks, you have a better shot at a long, enduring career. . . . I feel very at home and relaxed with my abilities as an actor. There's not a lot that intimidates me, and I'm not afraid of failure. I know I'm doing what I love to do and it wasn't a mistake—and I feel like I can ride out the wave of my 40s."

ALLY SHEEDY

★　★　★

"The creative impulses of women are different from those of men. They are more fluid, more flexible, more tentative, sometimes more difficult to understand and more in need of clarification. But women take the journey of depth and tend to do it together. Men tend to take the journey of efficiency and tend to accomplish it separately."   SHIRLEY MacLAINE

★　★　★

"You know the five stages of an actor? 'Who's Doris Roberts?,'
'Get me Doris Roberts,' 'Get me a young Doris Roberts,'
'Get me an old Doris Roberts,' and 'Who's Doris Roberts?'"

DORIS ROBERTS

★   ★   ★

"Once women pass a certain age, you're invisible. Nobody
looks at you anymore."   **ANGELA LANSBURY**

★   ★   ★

"I don't know why women do Botox. It doesn't make them
look younger, it just makes them look like they had work
done."   **JULIANNE MOORE**

★   ★   ★

"[The funniest thing about being an actor is] the feeling that
one is still not a grown-up at 50. I'm reasonably intelligent,
I work hard, and if I'd been 35 years in the shoe business,
I'd be the president of the corporation or chairman of the
board and making my own decisions. As an actor, I'm still
waiting for phone calls."   **JERRY ORBACH**

★   ★   ★

"Many of the circles I move in are very male-oriented.
Take the movies, for example. All the big male movie stars
are making millions and millions of dollars while we're
scrounging around for the scraps. . . . Who made us not
equal to them? This kind of disparity helps ensure that we
[women] are kept out of the real positions of control in all
kinds of industries."   **LORRAINE BRACCO**

On the changes he noticed working with the Royal Shakespeare Company after an approximately 20-year hiatus:

"There is now much greater liberty and freedom felt by every member of the company. There has been a leveling out of that old hierarchical structure. Before, the younger actors wouldn't dare address the leading actors of the company without being invited to, or make suggestions or proposals. ... [During a run of *Antony and Cleopatra*] I was waiting to go on for one of those big battle entrances, and one of the actors playing a small role said: 'My armor has come undone, Patrick—can you do it up for me?' We managed to do every buckle just before the cue came. ... Afterwards, I realized that he had paid me a huge compliment. During my days at the RSC, if I had dared to turn to, say, Brewster Mason, playing Claudius when I was the First Player, and asked him if he'd adjust my costume, I'd have had my head knocked off!"
PATRICK STEWART

★   ★   ★

"The age of sophistication is getting younger and younger."
EDWARD NORTON

★   ★   ★

"I think it's easier to be an actress than an actor. I think that acting goes with femininity in many ways. Women are natural actors."
MONICA BELLUCCI

★   ★   ★

"An actress is slightly more than a woman, an actor is slightly less than a man."
Anonymous, though often attributed to **SIR RICHARD BURTON**

"When you're 20, you think, 'Well I can kind of sing, maybe I'll cut an album. Or, romantic comedies, I like those!' But as you get older you realize that you're only interested in certain things. And you're okay with saying, 'No, I'm not going to do that. That's out of my range.'"   **JODIE FOSTER**

★   ★   ★

"Wanted—employment. Mother of three. Divorced. Thirty years experience. Reasonably mobile. More affable than rumored."

Ad taken out in the trade papers by **BETTE DAVIS,** *who became frustrated by the lack of parts being offered to her.*

★   ★   ★

"Aging actors remember the old joke—I always open the paper to the obituary page and if I'm not listed, I feel better for the whole day."   **ELI WALLACH**

★   ★   ★

"Being an actor is such a humiliating experience, because you are selling yourself to the public, your face, your personality, and that is humiliating. As you get older, it becomes more humiliating because you've got less to sell."

KATHARINE HEPBURN

★   ★   ★

"I certainly intend to be acting as long as I can remember the lines. Things get very interesting in all sorts of ways when you're over 60. . . . When you ask me what I want to do in the fifth act, I just want to stay creative and experimental."

JOHN LITHGOW

"For an actress to be a success, she must have the face of
Venus, the brains of Minerva, the grace of Terpsichore, the
memory of Macaulay, the figure of Juno, and the hide of a
rhinoceros."　　　　　　　　　　　　　　**ETHEL BARRYMORE**

★　★　★

On The Subject Was Roses, *the first film she undertook after
suffering a stroke:*

"I had never once during my illness believed that the stroke
had affected my talent. Memory and movement, yes, but
my brain never stopped understanding how people think
and feel. I did limp and my right hand felt awkward, which
bothered me . . . but it was not all that noticeable to others.
At the beginning I struggled with every single line, and by
the time the production ended I could master five pages
without the help of a monitor."　　　　　**PATRICIA NEAL**

★　★　★

"The older one gets in this profession, the more people there
are with whom one would never work again."

LIV ULLMANN

★　★　★

"You're always going to think, 'Should I have done every
single thing I was offered?' 'Should I maybe have taken more
familiar kinds of roles?' But too much familiarity doesn't
help your work as an actress. Neither does too much of your
face or too many interviews. In the end, the whole thing will
just start to wear on the audience."

MARY ELIZABETH MASTRANTONIO

"A young actress once said to me, 'Miss Davis, back in your era, what was it really like in Hollywood?'

"I answered a bit testily: 'I have no era. I was acting *back then* and I am still acting. My era will end the day they put me in my grave.' On my tombstone should be written: 'She did it the hard way.' That is an accurate description of my life and my career. I have loved it all and would relish living *almost* all of it over again."

BETTE DAVIS

★   ★   ★

"One day, while we were shooting *Shattered*, I was lying under Tom Berenger in the missionary position and I thought, 'This is the third actor I've had on top of me within the last six months and it is really boring.' . . . I knew then that Hollywood wasn't for me. But I was much younger, with no children and very few commitments, so I could afford to pick and choose."

GRETA SCACCHI

★   ★   ★

"The strange thing is that as you grow older, along with knowledge, the pain of losses, the changes in your life, in your work, even the physical changes we all unhappily must experience—the thickening of the waist, the lines, the sags—even with all that and more, you don't stop wanting and needing to recapture the feelings you had when you began. I haven't stopped: that's the great surprise of life."

LAUREN BACALL

★   ★   ★

On turning 50:

"I'm a much more relaxed person [now]. I'm a lot looser and more confident than I was in my twenties. . . . When I was younger, my friends were always complaining about how uptight and tense I used to be and in a way they were right. I took things very seriously. . . . But when you're raising children, you have to learn to be able to play with your kids, relax and not worry about life too much. My children have taught me to have some fun."   **DENZEL WASHINGTON**

★ ★ ★

"Actors change every 10 years, or should. How many people my age are still acting? Not that I'm shocking the world, but instinctively I make the world aware of something."

ANTHONY QUINN

★ ★ ★

"It's no fun becoming old, but it can be fun for an actress because it's a nice feeling to command the respect that comes with age, wisdom, and experience. Older actors become a kind of royalty. When we were young, it was obvious what we didn't know. With age we are a mystery. When we were young, people wanted to know us from the outside in. With age they want to know us from the inside out. In youth people wanted to know us in bed. In age they simply want to know us. Our interior gold attracts many 'minors.'"

SHIRLEY MACLAINE

★ ★ ★

"The thing that suddenly disappears when you turn 40 is sensuality and sexuality. If you're playing an older woman,

God forbid you have sex and enjoy it, you're supposed to be matronly. They truly don't know what to do with you."

LORRAINE TOUSSAINT

★   ★   ★

"I work very hard to banish the fear of getting old. . . . My father was very ill a couple of years ago and his body gave out on him for a while. When they wheeled him out of heart surgery I thought, my body works. My skin may have wrinkles but it's because I'm smiling so much. That might sound like some terrible American Greetings card, but I feel it's immoral for me to castigate my body for getting older, when it does everything I ask of it."   **OLIVIA WILLIAMS**

★   ★   ★

"The peak of your career is in those moments when everything seems to come easy—the work, the imagination. You are aware of that artistic power. All artists have a fear of losing that. When I was unaffected by experience, when I was young and there was an idealism to it, I wasn't as fearful. Growing older, fear can creep in. And if you lose the thing that keeps your heart pumping, you lose the will to wake up in the mornings."   **PHILIP SEYMOUR HOFFMAN**

★   ★   ★

"People in Hollywood . . . thought I was making a mistake by letting my career stall in order to raise my daughter. . . . I certainly could have let myself feel torn between what people said and what I knew was right for me. But I made a choice. I ignored my agent. I didn't pay attention to the decreasing number of party lists I was on, how quickly the phone stopped ringing with job opportunities, or how the

free stuff that celebrities get stopped arriving in the mail.
I didn't want to go back to that insecure hell of being an
actress. Especially not now that I was a mom."

TERI HATCHER

★ ★ ★

"The great thing about getting older and having a long
history is that you finally feel you've got nothing to lose.
When you're younger, you feel like you have everything to
lose. And then you get to a point where you feel, 'What the
hell? I'm still here after the ups and downs that I've had. Just
go for it.' The thing that actually has helped me the most is
my bout with cancer. I know how lucky I am, first to still be
here and then to still be working, cancer or no cancer. So I
work with far more freedom than I did and far less angst,
and it takes some of the anxiety away. And the wonderful
thing about the theater is that the great roles can go on for
many years."

LYNN REDGRAVE

★ ★ ★

On death:

"When I played Richard Feynman on the stage, Feynman,
who was dying of cancer, told his doctor he didn't want an
anesthetic at the end, because 'if I'm going to die, I want to
be there when I do.' Even in this last moment, there will be
something to notice."

ALAN ALDA

On Awards and
Awards Ceremonies

"One of my favorite Emmy moments ever was in 1974
when . . . Tim [Conway] and Harvey [Korman] were both
up. They had worked out something they would do if one
of them won. Harvey won this time and he went up, and
Tim followed him up onstage. Harvey acted as if he didn't
know Tim was behind him, and was giving his speech. And
Tim—well, his little head would come out behind Harvey's
shoulder and look longingly at the Emmy that Harvey was
holding. He'd go back behind Harvey, then come around
the other side and give another look of pure longing. The
audience was screaming, tears and mascara were rolling
down. . . . Because you always wanted someone who didn't
win to show how he really felt!"   CAROL BURNETT

★　　★　　★

On winning an Oscar for Best Performance by an Actor in a Supporting Role:

"Well, it didn't suck. It's great to celebrate with your friends. But that lasts about a day. You can't carry it with you into a meeting with the studios. Really, they don't care at all."

GEORGE CLOONEY

★ ★ ★

"[Oscar celebrations are] not new to me. I've been here before. But I never tire of it. I love it. I look at my Oscar in my living room. Stare at it. Let people finger it. It's a holy relic. As I am myself."

PETER O'TOOLE

★ ★ ★

While examining the statuette in his hands:

"I don't know how you calibrate acting. I can't define for myself how you do it or how it turns out . . . [but] I love that he's called 'the Actor,' and he's not 'the Talent' or 'the Celebrity' or 'the Sound Byter' or 'the Whore,' or all of the things that we sometimes, you know, have to succumb to."

GEOFFREY RUSH,
accepting the SAG Award for Outstanding Performance by a Male Actor in a Television Movie or Miniseries

★ ★ ★

"I was born and raised in Hollywood, so I grew up thinking the Oscars were a national holiday."

RITA WILSON

★ ★ ★

"I have nothing against L.A. or parties or awards ceremonies, but that's not how I choose to spend my time. I have children, and I lived on a farm away from everywhere else."

JOHN MALKOVICH

★ ★ ★

"Early on they said I'd get only fat girl roles. I've since had five [Oscar] nominations."

KATE WINSLET

★ ★ ★

"Of course I want to win Oscars. Every actor wants to win Oscars. But then it sunk in: If I don't take something like this when it comes along and have a go at it, then what? Yeah, there's gonna be negatives, but I've got to try to accentuate the—ah, fuck, it sounds like I'm going to break into song any minute now. I figured, 'Fuck it, it's *Bond*. Enjoy it!'"

DANIEL CRAIG

★ ★ ★

"There seems to be this strange concept that if you get nominated for an Oscar, you become a Hollywood star. I've always made choices based on the challenge that something gives me. Even in my life, I don't like doing something I did the day before. I like to try things out, private things that may or may not work. It's important to find that out as an actress. All the other stuff is a by-product and I can't help but find it hilarious."

CATE BLANCHETT

★ ★ ★

Accepting her Tony Award for Best Actress in a Musical at the 61st Tony Awards ceremony in 2007:

"I left Hollywood when they told me I was over the hill. And now I'm standing here with this most distinguished award for what I consider to be the role of a lifetime. I'm over the hill in the role of a lifetime! This is so encouraging."

CHRISTINE EBERSOLE

★   ★   ★

"Well, [if] you've been to my house [then] you know where all of my awards are—nobody ever sees them unless they're trying to find something behind the couch." **DON CHEADLE**

★   ★   ★

During the 2008 Emmy season:

"I have never had an Emmy nomination before and now I have two. They are sort of like busses: You spend your whole life waiting for one to come and then two come at the same time."

TOM WILKINSON

★   ★   ★

"To be honest, when you're younger and cooler, you say these [awards] don't mean anything, but on the day when they pat you on the back and say, 'Look, mate, we're noticing what you're doing—thanks very much,' you think of the people who spent a life in the cinema and didn't receive that kind of accolade, and it's sort of a humbling experience. And it's very nice and all that. But it doesn't change the way I do things."

RUSSELL CROWE

"I keep my Oscar in a tiny room, a library. It has a bunch of books by people I like, and it has a couple of Golden Globes and SAG Awards. It's not a place where people really go. I'm proud of [my Oscar], but it's not something you go in and polish every day."   **GEORGE CLOONEY**

★   ★   ★

"I've never been nominated [for an Oscar], so what the fuck would I go [to the ceremony] for? Anyone with a brain knows that so many worthy things get left out. Awards are on one level a history of injustice—but if you want to have a sense of humor about it, you could say they're also a history of funny outfits and inappropriate speeches."   **VIGGO MORTENSEN**

★   ★   ★

"My father just didn't accept the idea of my being an actor. ... He kept the hardware store in operation, because I think he was pretty sure that I was going to be found out sooner or later, and he wanted to have a job for me to come back to. ... The night that I won the Oscar, he called me very late and said that he thought it was fine and that I should send it back to the hardware store and he'd put it on the knife counter. That's what I did, and it stayed there 20 years under a cheese bell."   **JIMMY STEWART**

★   ★   ★

"I wouldn't describe [winning] the Oscar as a peak, although for a while it's probably made it easier for people to hire me."   **PHILIP SEYMOUR HOFFMAN**

On Getting Typecast

"I was always a character actor. I just looked like Little Red Riding Hood."
PAUL NEWMAN

★   ★   ★

"People always say that they see me as the laid-back, surfer, stoner type. . . . I guess it's just being from Texas, and talking in a deliberate—I would say thoughtful—way, but other people would say it's slow. . . . Maybe I'm the victim of my hair color."
OWEN WILSON

★   ★   ★

"I've made so many movies playing a hooker that they don't pay me in the regular way any more. They leave [the money] on the dresser."
SHIRLEY MACLAINE

"There are many times that being Latin has actually helped me, being a Cuban-American has helped me . . . because whether you like this next statement or not, we are the future. . . . I don't mean Latinos, I just mean ethnic diversity. I speak English without an accent, and I speak Spanish without an accent. I really do have the best of both worlds. What makes it frustrating is when a director or a studio head doesn't see me for the same part that they'll see, let's say, Drew Barrymore for. Drew's a great friend of mine. But it's like, 'No, we want more of an American type of girl.' And it's like, American has opened up. I'm an American girl, born and raised. . . . People ask me if it's difficult being Cuban-American in this industry. I say, 'You know what? Not so difficult as it is being an Asian girl.'"   **Eva Mendes**

★   ★   ★

"I was never accepted in Mexico as part of their culture, and neither was my father, who fought in the Mexican revolution for Pancho Villa. I was never accepted as an American here. That was the time during the war when Van Johnson was the hero type, the blond boys were the heroes. So I played the villains. I always gave them a background, a pride so they would be full-bodied and -souled."

Anthony Quinn

★   ★   ★

"Listen, if you take interesting roles and you've got cheekbones, everybody thinks you kill people."

William Fichtner

★   ★   ★

"I left the screen because I didn't want what happened to Chaplin to happen to me. When he discarded the little tramp, the little tramp turned around and killed him."

MARY PICKFORD

★ ★ ★

"With a lot of comedians, one of their major attributes is that they look comedic, with a certain hangdog or manic expression. I look like the neighborhood bully. That doesn't elicit laughter."

SYLVESTER STALLONE

★ ★ ★

"Once you've appeared in *Playboy*, you can't ever work for Procter & Gamble."

JAIME PRESSLY

★ ★ ★

"I come off as psychotic. . . . I'm misrepresented as a scary person. I'm not. It's all about my size and my eyebrows."

LIEV SCHREIBER

★ ★ ★

"My great film role is yet to come. I've always been out of epoch in Hollywood, or sans epoque, as they say in France. I would have been right in the '30s. But when I started doing movies in the '50s, Leslie Howard types and romance were going out and the Angry Young Men—John Osborne and the boys—were coming in. I was caught in the middle. For today's films my face is all wrong. You can't cast me as a beach boy."

CHRISTOPHER PLUMMER

"Sometimes I feel limited by people's perceptions of what I can and cannot do, or what I do or don't look like. I always feel I can play a role—just give me the time to do the preparation and I'll be it. I hate it when somebody says, for example, 'Oh, we saw *Quiz Show* and she's not right for this.' I'm, like, give me a break. My whole thing is characterization. I like playing separate people; it's never about one quality." **MIRA SORVINO**

★   ★   ★

"I remember when I was 26. I was doing an interview and this guy said, 'Don't you feel that lesser actors are passing you by? Are you avoiding success, are you afraid of success? What's wrong with you?' And I thought, 'My God, I've just worked with John Sayles, Woody Allen and Stephen Frears!' He wanted to know why I wasn't Tom Cruise. Well, because I don't really wanna be. This journalist was a smart guy writing for a good magazine, but he was so indoctrinated. I thought I was winning, y'know? I don't have anything against Tom Cruise—he's made great films and worked with great people—but he wants to produce *Mission: Impossible* 2 and 3. That's his deal, what he gets off on." **JOHN CUSACK**

★   ★   ★

"My dad had some wonderful success in the late '50s with a TV show called *Sea Hunt*. Too much success, perhaps: people actually thought he was the skin diver of the show, so instead of it being a great acting job, to the public he was that character. In actuality, he was a very versatile actor. Growing up, I could see how frustrated he got out of developing such a strong persona. So I've gone about trying to make as many 180-degree turns as far as character choices go to keep it fun but also to not develop a persona.

That way, it's easier for the audience to imagine me as a character, rather than a type." **JEFF BRIDGES**

★   ★   ★

"My agent and I would joke that they're always calling me to play the guy that walks in the room and straightens everybody out. And I'd say, 'I don't want to play that guy anymore.' I want to be Michael Landon in *Little House on the Prairie*." **ALEC BALDWIN**

★   ★   ★

"In Hollywood, they only gave me parts where I was an old maid or some lost soul with a clubfoot. When I inspect old photographs, I now think, what were they talking about? I was fine. But it was in my head that I wasn't pretty, so that's the way my career went. I was someone useful, not special." **JESSICA TANDY**

★   ★   ★

"I picture my epitaph: Here lies Paul Newman, who died a failure because his eyes turned brown." **PAUL NEWMAN**

★   ★   ★

"Pretty runs out."
JAIME PRESSLY

★   ★   ★

"[The Industry] give[s] you a huge tank of gas. But even that tank runs out, and then you're done. And then you go and you star in independent films, and you do supporting roles

in studio films. And you never star in studio films again.
Ever."   ALEC BALDWIN

★   ★   ★

"I'm not comfortable with gratuitous nudity although I have
done an awful lot of it in my career."   SIENNA MILLER

★   ★   ★

"If they want someone who's going to roar and shout, they're
generally going to get someone else. If they want someone
who's going to be bemused and lost, well, they might think
of me."   BILL NIGHY

★   ★   ★

"It's been such a wonderful surprise when a script comes
[my] way where it's a great character and not specifically
Asian."   LUCY LIU

★   ★   ★

"I never look at [Woody Allen] movies. Why would I?
What am I gonna do, look back?"   DIANE KEATON

★   ★   ★

"People say, 'But I wrote this with you in mind.' I don't know
what they think I am. Maybe they think, 'He'll bring it to
life.' Well, I can't. I only know one person who can, and that's
Dom DeLuise. You could give him a dictionary to read, and
he'll make you laugh. I'm not like that. When the fire is lit,
then I can do it, but not just reading anything."
                                            GENE WILDER

"I was always cast as an artistic homicidal maniac. But at least I was artistic!" **DONALD SUTHERLAND**

★ ★ ★

"I was trying different agents, trying to figure out different ways to push [myself]. And people just weren't interested. You knew the career was dead as soon as you show[ed] up on both *Love Boat* and *Murder, She Wrote.*"

JACKIE EARLE HALEY,
who experienced great success as a teen actor, but barely worked for the next 30 years until his 2007 Oscar nomination for Best Performance by an Actor in a Supporting Role.

★ ★ ★

"Movies are expensive to make. And if you've demonstrated you can do something, they'll keep wanting you to do it. I was in a movie a while back with a guy who's always the hero. We were getting ready to film the scene I get killed in, and he said, 'Do you always die?' And I said, 'Pretty much.' He said, sort of wistfully, 'I've never died.' You could tell he wanted to, sometime." **CHRISTOPHER WALKEN**

★ ★ ★

"Because I started acting so young, I figured one of the ways to try to aspire to longevity in this profession was to try to be in as many different genres of movies as I could. Because if you start doing too much work in one genre, an audience really kind of latches on to it—you start having this sort of cinema personality that people identify with and grow accustomed to. You know, Clint Eastwood does westerns. So when he's playing Dirty Harry, it's kind of like a western Dirty Harry in your mind. And if you do too many romantic comedies, you're the romantic comedy guy; or too much sci-fi, and you're the sci-fi guy. So I've really tried to spin that around." **ETHAN HAWKE**

★   ★   ★

"For years, people would say, 'Hey, Welcome Back Kotter,' like I was an Indian with three names." **GABE KAPLAN**

★   ★   ★

"I'm not a leading man. I'm a character actor and the character actors are always working. . . . If you're alive and breathing and a character actor, you're always working. But if you're that good-looking type, you only last about seven to ten years at the most, maybe a little longer. But then the looks start to go and . . . they say, 'Who is that old man over there?'" **ERNEST BORGNINE**

★   ★   ★

"Almost anyone can give a good or representative performance when you're unknown. It's just easier. The real pro game of acting is after you're known to "Un-Jack" the character in my case and to get the audience to re-invest in a new and specific fictional person. In that sense I do take it into account. The early middle part, directors a little bit feared "Jackisms" and they wanted to make sure I didn't do this and that. It was an unnecessary fear but I did understand it. It's part of the craft. You really have to, in order to keep growing as an actor, you have to learn the devices that keep you from just relying on what works for you. At a press conference it's alright if I get nervous and I might know where there's a laugh or an easy answer that's going to be entertaining. In the job you've got to be that

person in that situation and get to the conflict."
                                        JACK NICHOLSON

★   ★   ★

"Some people find their shtick. . . . I've never figured out who 'Heath Ledger' is on film: 'This is what you expect when you hire me, and it will be recognizable.' . . . People always feel compelled to sum you up, to presume that they have you and can describe you. That's fine. But there are many stories inside of me and a lot I want to achieve outside of one flat note."
                                        HEATH LEDGER

★   ★   ★

"I never get the girl. . . . I wind up with a country instead."
                                        ANTHONY QUINN

★   ★   ★

"People ask me a lot, 'What's it feel like to be a character actor?' I say that when I work, I always see my character as the main character in his life story, even if it's a small part or a cameo."
                                        JOHN C. REILLY

★   ★   ★

"The one advantage that I have is that if you're looking for a Chris Walken type, you have got to get Chris Walken. There are not many people that can mess with me. I have a place. I own it. This means that I can work—and work for a long time."
                                        CHRISTOPHER WALKEN

★   ★   ★

"[Doing my TV show] was a hard decision to make. A lot of people at the time said I shouldn't do it, that the series would typecast me, and to a degree I think that did happen. . . . On the other hand, I wasn't getting a lot of wonderful offers. I'd get scripts from agents who would say a producer specifically wanted me for a role, thought I'd be perfect. I'd read it, and not know whether to be offended by it or laugh!"

VICKI LAWRENCE

★　★　★

"It's true that I'm not Gary Cooper, but there have always been two traditions in the American cinema. One of which is John Wayne and Gary Cooper. And the other is Jimmy Cagney, Edward G. Robinson, and Spencer Tracy. And that's who I am. And so is Dustin [Hoffman]. There will always be Robert Redford and Kevin Costner, which is a classic American thing, and there will always be guys like me and Dustin. . . . American movies are a broad spectrum of mythology. You can get everybody. You can get Arnold Schwarzenegger and Danny DeVito, and you figure it out. They're both movie stars. Categorize them. I can't. Nor should you have to."

RICHARD DREYFUSS

On the Importance of Keeping It Real and Having a Life

"Now I'm managing to carry performing power into my personal life and taking some personal life things onstage. The lives are starting to feed each other." ROBIN WILLIAMS

★   ★   ★

"The first thing I read in the morning is *The New York Times*. Always. I start with the front page and go right to the op-ed." GEORGE CLOONEY

★   ★   ★

"The oldest form of theater is the dinner table. The same people every night with a new script." MICHAEL J. FOX

★   ★   ★

"It is the simplest things in life that hold the most wonder;
the color of the sea, the sand between your toes, the laughter
of a child."   **GOLDIE HAWN**

★   ★   ★

"You can become a better actor by becoming a more
complete human being and you can become a more
complete human being by becoming a better actor."

TED DANSON

★   ★   ★

"You can write a book, you can make a movie, you can paint
a painting, but having kids is really the most extraordinary
thing I've ever taken on."   **BRAD PITT**

★   ★   ★

"I look at it like this: Either the man makes a success or the
success makes a man. If you're already a man, then success
is just the cherry on top."   **JAMIE FOXX**

★   ★   ★

"Once the kids were born, I decided to give up movies with
out-of-town locations."   **HARRY HAMLIN**

★   ★   ★

"My work is just another expression of my growth as a
person."   **FOREST WHITAKER**

★   ★   ★

"Let your abilities and your limitations shape your career. When you look in the mirror, know who is looking back at you. When you know your strengths and you recognize your weaknesses, then you can create art."   **DEBBIE ALLEN**

★   ★   ★

"Buddhists say you need three things in life: something to do, something to love, and something to hope for. Isn't that great?"   **DICK VAN DYKE**

★   ★   ★

"Great acting is being able to create a character. Great character is being able to be yourself."   **JOHN LEGUIZAMO**

★   ★   ★

"I'll drive in Ireland and park my car and run out into the field and rip all my clothes off and just run in the wheat fields naked. That's for no one to see. That's to have that freedom of feeling, like, at one with nature. So I am completely unguarded still."   **DREW BARRYMORE**

★   ★   ★

"My daughter used to sit and watch *Murder, She Wrote.* I tried to watch with her, but I fell asleep."

ANGELA LANSBURY

★   ★   ★

"It's a dangerous position to think, as an actor, that your opinion matters [in world affairs]. You're out there dressing up, pretending to be someone for others' entertainment. You're an entertainer. Actors were the fools in the old days. Like the jester in Shakespeare, you could affect people. . . . Ultimately, great actors are conduits for great scripts and great stories. They're not the center of the world."

HUGH JACKMAN

★   ★   ★

"I am a strong advocate of monogamy—sequentially, that is."

JOAN COLLINS

★   ★   ★

While filming Capote, *for which he won the Oscar for Best Performance by an Actor in a Leading Role in 2006:*

"I was a bit all over the place. My life was changing so rapidly on a personal level. I was exhausted. I wasn't on solid ground. And that's not a bad thing! What I'm saying is that I didn't know what change was coming, but I knew it was happening and I was hopeful that I could accept it without imploding."   **PHILIP SEYMOUR HOFFMAN**

★   ★   ★

"If you're fortunate enough to get work like I am, you can end up working and forget that that should enable you to do other things that you want to do."   **EWAN MCGREGOR**

★   ★   ★

"You have to live in order to act and what you put into your performance is what you've learned from life."

PEGGY ASHCROFT

"If you don't lead a real life and use it, you lose truth in
your work."   MEL GIBSON

★   ★   ★

"In defining the difference between reality in life and reality
in art, Tolstoy said, 'Something is added to nature which
wasn't there before.' That 'something' is the artist's point of
view and his power of selection, which comes *from* life,
and makes for *new* life."   UTA HAGEN

★   ★   ★

"I suppose it's true that no woman finds complete fulfillment
until she has a child. I feel that to be a really good actress,
equipped to play the widest variety of roles open to me
at my age, it is essential to have experienced childbirth."
                                              AUDREY HEPBURN

★   ★   ★

"I always found that dealing with personal problems was
far easier when I was working on a project I liked."
                                                BEN GAZZARA

★   ★   ★

"[My husband] Kevin [Bacon] is seven years older than me,
and he's a lot wiser than me in a lot of ways. For instance,
I can remember struggling in my 30s, work-wise, and he
said to me, 'We are workhorse actors and we will always be
workhorse actors.' It really resonated with me. I thought,
'Okay, I'm not going to get that mercurial rise. I'm not going

to have that thing that's going to make me the "star," but I'm going to work consistently.' And we both have."

KYRA SEDGWICK

★   ★   ★

"I definitely take everything with a pinch of salt, and I have a very healthy skepticism about everything, not just Hollywood, not just the film industry, but in life, and that's not a bad thing. . . . You can't get carried away with it. I'm a little bit of an old man before my time in that I don't really like to live the high life just because it's happening for two minutes."

JAMES MCAVOY

★   ★   ★

"My work should be the way I live. Thus my life is my work."

LIV ULLMANN

★   ★   ★

"Your joy can be measured only by the depth of your sorrow."

GOLDIE HAWN

★   ★   ★

"I was in makeup one day, and [my brother, who flew Tornado fighter-bombers in the Iraq War] was flying down in the Persian Gulf at the time. And a bunch of actors were standing around having coffee, and my phone buzzed, and I had a text from him. It said, *'Emergency landed into Basra last night, had to sleep under canvas at the side of the runway, got mortared all night and small-arms fire around the perimeter, have a nice day.'* And I said, 'Guys, we've got to stop moaning about the fucking coffee right now.'"

EWAN MCGREGOR

★ ★ ★

"Offscreen, I'm ordinary, predictable and very conservative.
I have two houses, a station wagon, cats, the same wife of
28 years, and I like to save money." CHRISTOPHER WALKEN

★ ★ ★

"People should fight for their privacy the way you should
fight to save a drowning child." FRANK LANGELLA

★ ★ ★

"There are many different kinds of success. If you are a
compassionate human being who can relate to a lot of
different kinds of people and cares about your world outside
of [your] own sphere, then that's a tremendous success."

KEVIN BACON

★ ★ ★

"As we act our lives, we have to make up our dialogue and
create ourselves as we go along." SIR MICHAEL CAINE

★ ★ ★

"You know, it's all just humor. Don't take life so seriously.
Don't take fashion so seriously. Don't take the movie
industry so seriously. Don't take love and your relationship
so goddamned heavy all the time. Laugh, laugh, laugh.
Life is high school and it's small and everybody talks about
everybody, so just laugh your ass off." DREW BARRYMORE

"When I started having kids, I thought, I don't want to do anything they can't watch." **DICK VAN DYKE**

★   ★   ★

"People who live in glass houses need ear plugs and a sense of humor." **HUMPHREY BOGART**

★   ★   ★

"Death frightens me. Being eaten by a shark would be scary. The thing about being scared is that sometimes you flip it in your head, and you can be inspired by it. When you confront your fears, you actually learn more than if you accept your fears." **JEREMY SISTO**

★   ★   ★

"[As I got older] everything changed, in terms of looking at the dreams that I had as a younger woman, and realizing that they no longer were really applicable to the life I was living. Once I junked them, I felt a lot better. You find yourself more in the moment. It's like an old acting tip from Sandy Meisner—he always said that acting was about living truthfully in the given imaginary circumstances. Well, you want to be in the moment, living your life in every moment. Not living your life based on what you hope for, some abstract idea of what your life is going to be. It doesn't work to your advantage if you're there a little too much, if you're parked in that zone, the zone of expectations. There's no parking there." **DIANE KEATON**

★   ★   ★

"My father was a garbage man in Brooklyn, and I always thought he had a noble job. No matter how cold or rainy, I'd hang onto his garbage truck right next to him, and he'd drop me off at Blessed Sacrament School every morning. My first day at high school he let me ride inside and drove me right to the door. I was bursting with pride." TONY DANZA

★   ★   ★

"I just want a really simple life. I want sim-pli-ci-ty. And a simple life is expensive, in my situation. I don't want to be stared at while I'm mowing my lawn. I want to wake up and have coffee and wander in my yard nude, or dressed as Abe Lincoln if I feel like it." JOHNNY DEPP

★   ★   ★

"I think part of being an actor is staying private. I do think it's (an) important part of doing my job—is that [the audience can] believe I'm someone else. You know, that's part of my job. And if they start watching me and thinking about the fact that I got a divorce or something in my real life. Or these things, I don't think I'm doing my job."
PHILIP SEYMOUR HOFFMAN

★   ★   ★

"Harvey [Keitel] had once asked me if I had that fire in the belly, the burning desire to achieve real artistry as an actor, and I said yes. . . . But I think we were talking about two different things. I wasn't willing to be consumed by the fire. I don't have that kind of ambition. You can't have peace and the flame. One is antithetical to the other."
LORRAINE BRACCO

"I always draw the line when I'm talking to the press. I will not tell you about my private life. My private life is private, so nobody knows who I'm attracted to or go to bed with or what sort of food I eat or the decoration of my house. I don't make comments on that sort of thing. If you get into the world where you invite the press to think of you as a person beyond your particular expertise as a singer or an actor, then you're likely to get into problems, and you're likely to be asked awkward questions and you're not prepared for them, and you give replies that only apply to you. It's very hard and I don't think we should expect people to do anything other than what they can do."   SIR IAN MCKELLEN

★   ★   ★

"When I was born [my father] quit acting because he couldn't make any money. We were very poor. I slept in a drawer. My parents couldn't afford a cradle. We moved from New York to New Jersey eventually, and he went back to acting. I really respect him for that. He took such a chance."

MIRA SORVINO

★   ★   ★

"I don't have a publicist. Never had one. I don't go to premieres. I don't go to parties. I don't covet the Oscar. I don't want any of that. I don't go out. I just have dinner at home every night with my kids. Being famous, that's a whole other career. And I haven't got the energy for it."

GARY OLDMAN

★   ★   ★

"You know, I've been asked if I'd ever direct, but me, I'd rather build [houses]. It's very similar to directing, because you get to walk among this piece of art, to live in it, be surrounded by it, which is just thrilling."   **BRAD PITT**

★   ★   ★

On her skyrocket to success at the age of 12 after starring in films like Little Miss Sunshine *and* Nim's Island:

"Nothing is that different. . . . I mean, I still have the same cat."
                                    ABIGAIL BRESLIN

★   ★   ★

On his long hiatus from doing films:

"What I've learned over the last years that I haven't done movies is that I've forgotten all the habits that you build up when you've made 35 or whatever movies—certain mugging habits, or certain things that work—and that I'm a better actor [because of it]."   **CHEVY CHASE**

★   ★   ★

On watching the birth of his daughter:

"Labor's a very strange thing. . . . You learn a lot in a very short period of time. Minutes. The first thing you learn is that women are far superior to men. The amount of work, the amount of determination required—a man could not do it. A man would fold."   **JOHNNY DEPP**

★   ★   ★

"What did Flaubert say? 'Be ordinary in your life so that you can be violent and original in your work!' I believe that. For me, that's how it is. I have a very, very normal life. I really do, with the exception of being very lucky and privileged. . . . I have a nice life. I have two children, a dog, a husband. We live in New York, the kids go to school. . . . I like that. That's what I want."   **JULIANNE MOORE**

★   ★   ★

"I have the great fortune of being able to have a fun job. It's a job that allows me to travel and that allows me, sometimes, to get out of myself. So that's my job. But it's not at all my life. Every day when I wake up in the morning, I've been studying international law. I try to make sure that each of my children has enough of my attention to feel equal. I try to make sure that my relationship with the man in my life is solid and complete and we're very connected and having a great life together and enjoying our children and being part of the world. . . . I have no animosity toward Hollywood or the demands of the red carpet, all that silliness. That's my job, and I'm happy to have it. But when I die, do I want to be remembered as an actress? No. I recently had an op-ed published in a newspaper. And at the end, it didn't say I was an actress. It said that I was a UN goodwill ambassador— that's all. And I was really proud."   **ANGELINA JOLIE**

★   ★   ★

On how she and husband Louis Zorich eventually left New York and bought a house in Montclair, New Jersey:

"Once we had signed the deed and the last page of the mortgage papers and shook hands with the banker, I promptly excused myself, went into the bathroom, and threw up. Then we went back into the city, packed up our belongings and our kids, and moved to New Jersey. Actors with a mortgage: inconceivable."   **OLYMPIA DUKAKIS**

Shakespeare on Acting

HAMLET. Speak the speech, I pray you, as I pronounced
it to you, trippingly on the tongue: but if
you mouth it, as many of your players do,
I had as lief the town-crier spoke my lines.
Nor do not saw the air too much with your
hand, thus, but use all gently; for in the
very torrent, tempest, and, as I may say, the
whirlwind of passion, you must acquire
and beget a temperance that may give it
smoothness. O, it offends me to the soul to
hear a robustious periwig-pated fellow tear
a passion to tatters, to very rags, to split the
ears of the groundlings, who for the most
part are capable of nothing but inexplicable
dumbshows and noise: I would have such a
fellow whipped for o'erdoing Termagant; it
out-herods Herod: pray you, avoid it.

FIRST PLAYER. I warrant your honour.

HAMLET.   Be not too tame neither, but let your own
               discretion be your tutor: suit the action to
               the word, the word to the action; with this
               special observance, that you o'erstep not the
               modesty of nature: for any thing so overdone
               is from the purpose of playing, whose end,
               both at the first and now, was and is, to hold,
               as 'twere, the mirror up to nature; to show
               virtue her own feature, scorn her own image,
               and the very age and body of the time his
               form and pressure. Now this overdone, or
               come tardy off, though it make the unskillful
               laugh, cannot but make the judicious grieve;
               the censure of the which one must in your
               allowance o'erweigh a whole theatre of others.
               O, there be players that I have seen play,
               and heard others praise, and that highly, not
               to speak it profanely, that, neither having
               the accent of Christians nor the gait of
               Christian, pagan, nor man, have so strutted
               and bellowed that I have thought some of
               nature's journeymen had made men and not
               made them well, they imitated humanity so
               abominably.

FIRST PLAYER. I hope we have reformed that indifferently
               with us, sir.

HAMLET.   O, reform it altogether. And let those that
               play your clowns speak no more than is set
               down for them; for there be of them that will
               themselves laugh, to set on some quantity of
               barren spectators to laugh too; though, in the
               mean time, some necessary question of the

play be then to be considered: that's villainous,
and shows a most pitiful ambition in the fool that
uses it. Go, make you ready."

> **HAMLET,** *act 3, scene 2, lines 1–41*

★   ★   ★

JAQUES. All the world's a stage,
    And all the men and women merely players.
    They have their exits and their entrances,
    And one man in his time plays many parts,
    His acts being seven ages.

> **AS YOU LIKE IT,** *act 2, scene 7, lines 139–143*

★   ★   ★

HAMLET. The play's the thing
    Wherein I'll catch the conscience of the King.

> **HAMLET,** *act 2, scene 2, lines 586–587*

★   ★   ★

VOLUMNIA. Action is eloquence.

> **CORIOLANUS,** *act 3, scene 2, line 76*

★   ★   ★

CASSIUS. How many ages hence
    Shall this our lofty scene be acted over
    In states unborn and accents yet unknown!

> **JULIUS CAESAR,** *act 3, scene 1, lines 111–113*

★   ★   ★

ROSALINE. A jest's prosperity lies in the ear
        Of him that hears it, never in the tongue
        Of him that makes it.
          LOVE'S LABOUR'S LOST, *act 5, scene 2, lines 871–873*

★ ★ ★

ISABELLA. Truth is truth
        To the end of reckoning.
          MEASURE FOR MEASURE, *act 5, scene 1, lines 45–46*

★ ★ ★

DESDEMONA. I understand a fury in your words,
        But not the words.
          OTHELLO, *act 4, scene 2, lines 29–30*

★ ★ ★

FABIAN. If this were played upon a stage now,
        I could condemn it as an improbable fiction.
          TWELFTH NIGHT, *act 3, scene 4, lines 140–141*

★ ★ ★

HAMLET. Is it not monstrous that this player here,
        But in a fiction, in a dream of passion,
        Could force his soul so to his own conceit
        That from her working all his visage wann'd,
        Tears in his eyes, distraction in's aspect,
        A broken voice, and his whole function suiting
        With forms to his conceit? and all for nothing!
        For Hecuba!
          HAMLET, *act 2, scene 2, lines 531–538*

Farewell

PROSPERO. Our revels now are ended. These our actors,
As I foretold you, were all spirits, and
Are melted into air, into thin air:
And, like the baseless fabric of this vision,
The cloud-capp'd towers, the gorgeous palaces,
The solemn temples, the great globe itself,
Yea, all which it inherit, shall dissolve,
And, like this insubstantial pageant faded,
Leave not a rack behind. We are such stuff
As dreams are made on; and our little life
Is rounded with a sleep.

THE TEMPEST, *act 4, scene 1, lines 148–158*

Acknowledgments

Like any production in which actors appear, books are a collaborative art form. They cannot be made without participation from many talented people whose names don't appear on the cover or title page.

Thanks must go to Martha Kaplan, whose patience, wisdom, and taste continue to amaze me.

To Jeffrey Goldman for seeing how this project might become a decent book.

To Brittany Yudkowsky for her exceptional editorial eye.

To Bill Esper and the late Joe Patenaude: this book is dedicated to them, but they deserve mention again.

To the many source publications that were cited to compile these pearls.

To the actors (of course!) who offered such remarkable insights into our craft.

To you, the reader, for wanting to know more.

And—last but not least—to Jessica, for her constant support, which is often unspoken, but never unnoticed.

Sources

ON WHAT ACTING IS

Chiu, Alexis. "Strange Bedfellows." *People*, October 17, 2005.

Gam, Rita. *Actors: A Celebration.* New York: St. Martin's Press, 1988.

Esper, William, and Damon DiMarco. *Actor's Art and Craft: William Esper Teaches the Meisner Technique.* New York: Random House, 2008.

Bankhead, Tallulah. *Tallulah: My Autobiography.* New York: Harper & Brothers, 1952.

Rockwell, Sam. "Sam Rockwell Interview, Star of Joshua." By Sheila Roberts. Moviesonline. http://www.moviesonline.ca/movienews_12358.html.

Gielgud, John. *Early Stages.* New York: Macmillan, 1939.

Ullmann, Liv. *Choices.* New York: Knopf, 1984.

Bates, Brian. *The Way of the Actor: A Path to Knowledge & Power.* Boston: Shambhala Publications, 1988.

"All Grown Up and Everywhere to Go." Special issue, *People*, Spring 1991.

Darrah, Brad. "Enchanting Manipulative Meryl." *Life*, December 1987.

Staats, Kenneth. "Aspiring to Greatness." *Century*, November 1980.

Dutka, Elaine. "Talking with Meryl Streep." *Redbook*, September 1982.

Brussell, Eugene E. *Webster's New World Dictionary of Quotable Definitions.* New York: Prentice Hall, 1970.

Cottrell, John. *Laurence Olivier.* New York: Prentice Hall, 1975.

Wallace, Terry. "Want to be a Force of Healing?" *Parade*, November 25, 1990.

Brussell, Eugene E. *Webster's New World Dictionary of Quotable Definitions.* New York: Prentice Hall, 1970.

Bankhead, Tallulah. *Tallulah: My Autobiography.* New York: Harper & Brothers, 1952.

"The 128 Best Things Anyone Ever Said in *People*." *People*, March 6, 1989.

Corsello, Andrew. "Christopher Walken Must Die." *Gentleman's Quarterly*, March 2000.

De Havilland, Olivia. "The Last Belle of the Cinema." Academy of Achievement interview, conducted on October 5, 2006 in Washington, D.C.

Strasberg, Lee. *A Dream of Passion.* New York: Penguin, 1987.

De Niro, Robert. "Robert De Niro: The (Non)Interview." By Lori Silverbush. Downtown Express. http://www.downtownexpress.com/de_207/robertdeniro.html.

Schatz, Howard, and Beverly J. Ornstein. *In Character: Actors Acting.* New York: Bulfinch, 2006.

Ullmann, Liv. *Choices.* New York: Knopf, 1984.

Gam, Rita. *Actors: A Celebration.* New York: St. Martin's Press, 1988.

Cusack, John. "The Total Film Interview—John Cusack." By Jamie Graham. Total Film. http://www.totalfilm.com/features/the-total-film-interview-john-cusack.

Fishburne, Laurence. "The Mentor." By Nell Minow. Beliefnet. http://www.beliefnet.com/Entertainment/Movies/2006/04/The-Mentor.aspx.

Rockwell, Sam. "Sam Rockwell Interview, Star of Joshua." By Sheila Roberts. MoviesOnline. http://www.moviesonline.ca/movienews_12358.html.

Smith, Anna Deavere. "Voice of America." By Carol Lloyd. Salon.com. http://www.salon.com/people/bc/1998/12/08/deaveresmith/index.html.

Brando, Marlon, and Robert Lindsey. *Songs My Mother Taught Me*. New York: Random House, 1994.

Hirschberg, Lynn. "Buttoned Up." *New York Times Magazine*, January 15, 2006.

Rose, Cynthia. "John Malkovich: Profile." *Arena* (UK), 1990.

ON WHAT ACTORS ARE

Rosenbaum, Ron. "Acting: The Creative Mind of Jack Nicholson." *New York Times Magazine*, July 13, 1986.

Zucker, Carole. *In the Company of Actors*. New York: Theatre Arts Books, 2001.

Yakir, Dan. "The Future is Now." *Cabletime*, April 1987.

Baker, Fred, and Ross Firestone. *Movie People: At Work in the Business of Film*. New York: Lancer Books, 1973.

Saturday Evening Post, May 22, 1943.

Brussell, Eugene E. *Webster's New World Dictionary of Quotable Definitions*. New York: Prentice Hall, 1970.

Brussell, Eugene E. *Webster's New World Dictionary of Quotable Definitions*. New York: Prentice Hall, 1970.

Brady, Shaun. "Looking for Inspiration." *Metro*, March 23–25, 2007.

Adler, Stella. *The Art of Acting*. Compiled and edited by Howard Kissel. New York: Applause Books, 2000.

Bogart, Stephen Humphrey. *Bogart: In Search of My Father*. New York: Penguin, 1995.

Hagen, Uta. *A Challenge for the Actor*. New York: Scribner, 1991.

Dominus, Susan. "Rip Torn Won't Go Gentle Into That Good Night." *New York Times*, May 7, 2006.

Washington, Denzel. "Interview: Denzel Washington's Difference of Opinion with Harvey Weinstein on 'The Great Debaters.'" By Adam Feldman. HollywoodChicago.com. http://www.hollywoodchicago.com/2007/12/interview-denzel-washingtons-difference.html.

Langella, Frank. "The Demon Seesaw Actor's Ride." *New York Times*, 1989.

Artaud, Antonin. *The Theatre and Its Double*. Translated by Mary Caroline Richards. New York: Grove Press, 1958.

Matthews, Brander, and Laurence Hutton, eds. *Actors and Actresses of Great Britain and the United States: From the Days of David Garrick to the Present Time*. New York: Cassell and Company, Ltd., 1886.

Blanks, Tim. "Monica Bellucci." *Interview*, September 2007.

Adler, Stella. *The Art of Acting*. Compiled and edited by Howard Kissel. New York: Applause Books, 2000.

Chekhov, Michael. *To the Actor*. New York: Harper & Row, 1953.

Hepburn, Katharine. *Me: Stories of My Life*. New York: Random House, 1991.

Douglas, Kirk. *Let's Face It: 90 Years of Living, Loving, and Learning*. Hoboken, NJ: John Wiley & Sons, 2007.

Penn, Sean. "The Total Film Interview—Sean Penn." By Hilary Morgan. Total Film. http://www.totalfilm.com/features/the-total-film-interview-sean-penn.

Baker, Fred, and Ross Firestone. *Movie People: At Work in the Business of Film*. New York: Lancer Books, 1973.

Artaud, Antonin. *The Theatre and Its Double*. Translated by Mary Caroline Richards. New York: Grove Press, 1958.

Malden, Karl, and Carla Malden. *When Do I Start?* New York: Simon & Schuster, 1997.

ON ACTORS AND SOCIETY

Grodin, Charles. *I Like It Better When You're Funny: Working in Television and Other Precarious Adventures*. New York: Random House, 2002.

Burns, Khephra. "A Love Supreme." *Essence*, December 1994.

Fischoff, Stuart. "Clint Eastwood." *Psychology Today*, January/February 1993.

Raab, Scott. "Penn." *Esquire*, September 2007.

Alda, Alan. *Things I Overheard While Talking to Myself*. New York: Random House, 2007.

Rose, Cynthia. "Jimmy Smits: Law and Ardor." *British Vogue*, 1991.

Cheadle, Don. "Don Cheadle Talks About 'Hotel Rwanda.'" By Rebecca Murray. About.com. http://movies.about.com/od/hotelrwanda/a/rwanda121704.htm.

Cumming, Alan. "The 5-minute Interview: Alan Cumming, Actor." By Sara Newman. *The Independent* (London), July 5, 2007.

Jenkins, Garry. *Harrison Ford: Imperfect Hero*. New York: Birch Lane Press, 1998.

Rose, Cynthia. "John Malkovich: Profile." *Arena* (UK), 1990.

Washington, Denzel. "The Total Film Interview—Denzel Washington." By Jan Janssen. Total Film. http://www.totalfilm.com/features/the-total-film-interview-denzel-washington.

Raab, Scott. "Penn." *Esquire*, September 2007.

Moir, Jan. "'Beautiful? I'm Usually Just a Scruff.'" *The Telegraph* (London), February 14, 2005.

Shewey, Don. "The Secret Life of Wally Shawn." *Esquire*, 1983.

Seymour, Gene. "Shades of Fishburne." *Los Angeles Times*, August 25, 1997.

Cusack, John. "Was Hitler Human?" By David Talbot. Salon.com. http://dir.salon.com/story/ent/movies/int/2002/09/09/cusack/index.html.

Dreifus, Claudia. "The Progressive." *Interview*, May 1993.

Horowitz, Simi. "Cinema 'Paraiso.'" *Back Stage East*, April 30, 2008.

ON WHY WE ACT

Raab, Scott. "What I've Learned: Rip Torn." *Esquire*, May 1, 2001.

Adams, Cindy. "Here Comes Cindy Claus . . ." *New York Post*, December 14, 2006.

Heath, Chris. "And Now, 972 Words from Robert De Niro." *Gentleman's Quarterly*, January 2007.

"A Misery-able Trip from Stage to Screen." Special issue, *People*, Spring 1991.

Boleslavsky, Richard. *Acting: The First Six Lessons*. New York: Theatre Arts Books, 1933.

Ansen, David. "Fabulous Pfeiffer." *Newsweek*, November 6, 1989.

York, Michael. *Accidentally On Purpose: An Autobiography*. New York: Simon & Schuster, 1991.

Verini, Bob. "Latenight Killed the Vaudeo Star." *Daily Variety*, May 30, 2007.

Ullmann, Liv. *Changing*. New York: Knopf, 1977.

"Thesps Speak for Themselves." *Daily Variety*, January 26, 2007.

Mansfield, Stephanie. "Andy Garcia Keeps His Shirt On." *Gentleman's Quarterly*, December 1990.

Ninth Annual Screen Actors' Guild Awards, originally broadcast on March 9, 2003, by TNT.

"Shirley MacLaine Goes Out on a Limb." *TV Guide*, January 17, 1987.

Poitier, Sidney. *The Measure of a Man: A Spiritual Autobiography*. New York: HarperCollins, 2000.

"Kevin Costner." *People*, November 19, 1991.

Cahill, Tim. "Mel Gibson—Back from the Edge." *Premiere*, December 1988.

Meisner, Sanford, and Dennis Longwell. *Sanford Meisner: On Acting*. New York: Vintage Books, 1987.

Darrah, Brad. "Enchanting Manipulative Meryl." *Life*, December 1987.

Leigh, Danny. "Desert Island Risks." *The Guardian,* January 12, 2001.

Corliss, Richard. "Bette Steals Hollywood." *Time*, March 3, 1987.

Dukakis, Olympia, and Emily Heckman. *Ask Me Again Tomorrow*. New York: Perennial, 2003.

Demaris, Ovid. "First Make Peace with Yourself." *Parade*, March 22, 1992.

Young, Josh. "Renee Revealed." *Life: America's Weekend Magazine*. January 5, 2007.

Iley, Chrissy. "Red Alert." *The Observer* (UK), July 6, 2008.

Cage, Nicolas. "Acting Weird: Nicolas Cage Talks About Selling Imperfection." By Elgy Gillespie. Salon.com. http://www.salon.com/ent/movies/int/1998/08/cov_07int.html.

Senior, Jennifer. "Lions in Spring." *New York Times*, April 16, 2007.

Gurerwitsch, Matthew. "Risk Taker Supreme." *Connoisseur*, December 1989.

"10 Questions for Al Pacino." *Time*, June 25, 2007.

Fussman, Cal. "What I've Learned: Leslie Nielsen." *Esquire*, March, 2008.

Hoffman, Barbara. "Great Brit." *New York Post*, January 14, 2007.

Greene, Bob. "Jessica Lange Speaks for Herself." *Esquire*, December 1985.

A Tribute to Cary Grant. Originally broadcast on November 1990 by PBS.

Mansfield, Stephanie. "Andy Garcia Keeps His Shirt On." *Gentleman's Quarterly*, December 1990.

Friedman, Devin. "Metaphorically Speaking." *Gentleman's Quarterly*, February 2007.

Twelfth Annual Screen Actors' Guild Awards, originally broadcast on January 29, 2007, by TNT.

Schatz, Howard, and Beverly J. Ornstein. *In Character: Actors Acting*. New York: Bulfinch, 2006.

Raab, Scott. "The Quiet One." *Esquire*, March 2007.

Willis, Bruce. "Bruce Willis Interview: His Way." By Elvis Mitchell. ReadersDigest.com. http://www.rd.com/bruce-willis-interview/article26494.html.

Brando, Marlon, and Robert Lindsey. *Songs My Mother Taught Me.* New York: Random House, 1994.

Malden, Karl, and Carla Malden. *When Do I Start?* New York: Simon & Schuster, 1997.

Blanks, Tim. "Monica Bellucci." *Interview*, September 2007.

Nicholson, Jack. "Jack Nicholson—Something's Gotta Give." By Nev Pierce. BBC. http://www.bbc.co.uk/films/2004/02/05/jack_nicholson_somethings_gotta_give_interview.shtml.

Logan, Brian. "I Can Do Anything." *The Guardian*, January 2, 2001.

Bates, Kathy. "Kathy Bates Talks About 'About Schmidt.'" By Rebecca Murray and Fred Toppel. About.com. http://movies.about.com/library/weekly/aaaboutschmidtintb.htm.

Kline, Kevin. "Kevin Kline Interview." By Dotson Rader. *Parade*, October 16, 1994.

Brady, Shaun. "Looking for Inspiration." Weekend issue, *Metro*, March 23–25, 2007.

Wood, Mark Dundas. "Some Kisser." *Back Stage East*, March 22–28, 2007.

Hofler, Robert. "Employed, Happy and Laffing All the Way to ShoWest." *Variety*, March 15, 2007.

Grodin, Charles. *If I Only Knew Then . . .: Learning from Our Mistakes.* New York: Springboard Press, 2007.

Sorvino, Mira. "Mira Sorvino." By Graham Fuller. BNET. http://findarticles.com/p/articles/mi_m1285/is_n11_v25/ai_17632992/.

Ansen, David. "Fabulous Pfeiffer." *Newsweek*, November 6, 1989.

Cooper, Chet. "Jack Lemmon Interview." *Ability Magazine*.

Wood, Sam Taylor. "Daniel Craig." *Interview*, July 2007.

Mitchell, Elvis. "Brad Pitt." *Interview*, March 2007.

Ullmann, Liv. *Changing.* New York: Knopf, 1977.

Willis, Bruce. "Bruce Willis Interview: His Way." By Elvis Mitchell. ReadersDigest.com. http://www.rd.com/bruce-willis-interview/article26494.html.

Redgrave, Michael. *In My Mind's I: An Actor's Autobiography.* New York: Viking, 1983.

Barbara Walters Special. Originally broadcast on March 24, 1991, by CBS.

ON CONQUERING STAGE FRIGHT AND DEVELOPING CONFIDENCE IN YOUR TALENT

Ferrell, Will. "Will Ferrell . . . Answers Your Questions." People.com. http://www.people.com/people/article/0,,1556740,00.html.

Demaris, Ovid. "Finally He Can Play the Bad Guy." *Parade*, February 14, 1990.

Hagen, Uta, and Haskel Frankel. *Respect for Acting.* Hoboken, NJ: Wiley Publishing, 1973.

Boleslavsky, Richard. *Acting: The First Six Lessons.* New York: Theatre Arts Books, 1933.

Beale, Lewis. "Swank Makes the Grade." *amNewYork*, January 4, 2007.

Walker, Alexander. *Audrey: Her Real Story.* New York: St. Martin's Press, 1994.

Burstyn, Ellen. *Lessons in Becoming Myself.* New York: Riverhead Books, 2006.

Hawn, Goldie, and Wendy Holden. *Goldie: A Lotus Grows in the Mud.* New York: The Berkley Publishing Group, 2005.

Adler, Stella. *The Art of Acting.* Compiled and edited by Howard Kissel. New York: Applause Books, 2000.

Irons, Jeremy. "Actor/Risk-taker." Academy of Achievement interview, conducted on October 27, 2000, in London, England.

Hackman, Gene. "Two Old Friends Talk About 'Runaway Jury.'" By Rebecca Murray. About.com. http://movies.about.com/cs/therunawayjury/a/runawayintgh.htm.

Johnson, Richard. "I'm Not Scary." New York Post, January 8, 2007.

Jolie, Angelina. "Brad Pitt and Angelina Jolie Talk About Mr. and Mrs. Smith." By Rebecca Murray. About.com. http://movies.about.com/od/mrandmrssmith/a/joliepitt060805.htm.

Fussman, Cal. "What I've Learned: Dick Van Dyke." Esquire, February 2007.

Baker, Fred, and Ross Firestone. Movie People: At Work in the Business of Film. New York: Lancer Books, 1973.

Associated Press. "From the Contenders' Mouths." Buzz Section, amNewYork, January 24, 2007.

"It's Not Easy Being a Star, Says Sophia Loren." AFP News Service, June 1, 2007.

Ninth Annual Screen Actors' Guild Awards, originally broadcast on March 9, 2003, by TNT.

Nicholson, Jack. "Jack Nicholson—Something's Gotta Give." By Nev Pierce. BBC. http://www.bbc.co.uk/films/2004/02/05/jack_nicholson_somethings_gotta_give_interview.shtml.

Cohen, David S. "AFI Honoree Arrives with Desire Intact." Daily Variety, June 7, 2007.

Norton, Edward. "Jonah Hill." Interview, September 2007.

Andrews, Julie. "Julie Andrews Interview: Legend of Stage and Screen." Academy of Achievement interview, conducted on June 10, 2004, in Chicago, Illinois.

De Havilland, Olivia. "The Last Belle of the Cinema." Academy of Achievement interview, conducted on October 5, 2006, in Washington, D.C.

Riley, Jenelle. "Do Not Disturb." Back Stage East, June 21–27, 2007.

Cooper, Chet. "Jack Lemmon Interview." Ability Magazine.

Horowitz, Simi. "Crashing the Gates." Back Stage East, June 21–27, 2007.

Portman, Natalie. "What I've Learned (So Far)." Parade, October 28, 2007.

Emer, David. "Angela's Assets." The Guardian, September 29, 2001.

Jones, James Earl. "The Voice of Triumph." Academy of Achievement interview, conducted on June 29, 1996, in Sun Valley, Idaho.

"It's Not Easy Being a Star, Says Sophia Loren." AFP News Service, June 1, 2007.

Wienir, David, and Jodie Langel. Making It on Broadway: Actors' Tales of Climbing to the Top. New York: Allworth Press, 2004.

Hepburn, Katharine. Me: Stories of My Life. New York: Random House, 1991.

Davis, Bette, and Michael Herskowitz. This 'N That. New York: Putnam, 1987.

Lyall, Sarah. "To Boldly Go Where Shakespeare Calls." New York Times, January 27, 2008.

Sager, Mike. "What I've Learned: Faye Dunaway." Esquire, August 1999.

Brooks, Albert. "Wise Guy: Albert Brooks." By Steve Kurutz. Details.com. http://men.style.com/details/wiseguy/landing?&id=content_4706.

Grodin, Charles. I Like It Better When You're Funny: Working in Television and Other Precarious Adventures. New York: Random House, 2002

Zucker, Carole. In the Company of Actors: Reflections on the Craft of Acting. New York: Routledge, 1999.

Litwak, Mark. Reel Power. New York: Morrow, 1986.

Taylor, Susan L. "Heart Stuff with Ruby Dee." Essence, October 2005.

Zucker, Carole. *In the Company of Actors: Reflections on the Craft of Acting.* New York: Routledge, 1999.

Alda, Alan. *Never Have Your Dog Stuffed and Other Things I've Learned.* New York: Random House, 2006.

Rader, Dotson. "I Found Purpose." *Parade,* July 7, 2002.

Gazzara, Ben. *In the Moment: My Life as an Actor.* New York: Carroll & Graf Publishers, 2004.

Goldstein, Toby. *William Hurt: The Actor and His Work.* New York: St. Martin's Press, 1987.

Salvini, Tommaso. *Leaves from the Autobiography of Tommaso Salvini.* New York: The Century Company, 1893.

Isenberg, Barbara. "Frank Gets Really Frank." *Los Angeles Times,* May 9, 1993.

Riley, Jenelle. "Master Class." *Back Stage East,* June 13, 2008.

Garfield, Simon. "Oscar Knight." *The Observer* (UK), February 26, 2006.

Hirschberg, Lynn. "The Empathist." *New York Times,* November 13, 2005.

Steinberg, Jacques. "An Unmistakable Face, and a Name You Can't Quite Place." *New York Times,* July 23, 2006.

ON THE ACTOR'S LIFE

Douglas, Kirk. *Let's Face It: 90 Years of Living, Loving, and Learning.* New York: John Wiley & Sons, 2007.

Heath, Chris. "And Now, 972 Words from Robert De Niro." *Gentleman's Quarterly,* January 2007.

Heath, Chris. "The Hardass." *Gentleman's Quarterly,* March 2005.

Alterman, Glenn. *An Actor's Guide—Making It in New York City.* New York: Allworth Press, 2002.

Penn, Nate. "Christian Rocks!" *Gentleman's Quarterly,* March 2007.

Adams, Cindy. "One Lady Who's Not Invisible." *New York Post,* March 15, 2007.

Young, Josh. "Renee Revealed." *Life: America's Weekend Magazine,* January 5, 2007.

Johnson, Richard. "Rough Business." Page Six, *New York Post,* January 13, 2007.

Bankhead, Tallulah. *Tallulah: My Autobiography.* New York: Harper & Brothers, 1952.

Bussel, Rachel Kramer. "Hot Seat: Gene Wilder." *New York Post,* February 25, 2007.

Reagan, Ronald. *Where's the Rest of Me? The Autobiography of Ronald Reagan.* New York: Karz Pubs, 1981.

Hayes, Helen. *A Gift of Joy.* Philadelphia, PA: J.B. Lippincott & Co., 1965.

Goldstein, Toby. *William Hurt: The Actor and His Work.* New York: St. Martin's Press, 1987.

Riedel, Michael. "Dennehy . . . neat." *New York Post,* April 13, 2007.

Heath, Chris. "The Hardass." *Gentleman's Quarterly,* March 2005.

Duvall, Robert. "Robert Duvall Uncut." By Ian Daly. Details.com. http://men.style.com/details/features/landing?id=content_5485.

Grammer, Kelsey. *So Far . . .* New York: Dutton, 1995.

Fox, Michael J. *Lucky Man: A Memoir*. New York: Hyperion, 2002.

Daly, John. "60 Seconds: Philip Seymour Hoffman." *Metro UK,* March 2, 2006.

Wilk, Max. *The Wit and Wisdom of Hollywood*. New York: Atheneum, 1971.

Douglas, Kirk. *Let's Face It: 90 Years of Living, Loving, and Learning*. Hoboken, NJ: John Wiley & Sons, 2007.

Caine, Michael. *Acting in Film: An Actor's Take on Movie Making*. New York: Applause, 1990.

Chambers, Andrea. "Bio—Christopher Plummer." *People*, March 15, 1982.

Wienir, David, and Jodie Langel. *Making It on Broadway: Actor's Tales of Climbing to the Top*. New York: Allworth Press, 2004.

Wallach, Eli. *The Good, the Bad, and Me: In My Anecdotage*. Orlando, FL: Harcourt, 2005.

Irons, Jeremy. "Actor/Risk-taker." *Academy of Achievement* interview, conducted on October 27, 2000, in London, England.

Raab, Scott. "What I've Learned: Rip Torn." *Esquire*, May 1, 2001.

Gam, Rita. *Actors: A Celebration*. New York: St. Martin's Press, 1988.

Pierce, David Hyde. "David Hyde Pierce." By Beth Stevens. Broadway.com. http://www.broadway.com/David-Hyde-Pierce/broadway_news/548527.

Bankhead, Tallulah. *Tallulah: My Autobiography*. New York: Harper & Brothers, 1952.

Redgrave, Michael. *In My Mind's I: An Actor's Autobiography*. New York: Viking Press, 1983.

Smith, Anna Deavere. *Letters to a Young Artist*. New York: Anchor Books, 2006.

Hepburn, Katharine. *Me: Stories of My Life*. New York: Random House, 1991.

Snyder, Gabriel. "What, Me Worry?" *W*, August 2007.

Apatow, Judd. "Paul Rudd." *Interview*, August 2007.

Wood, Sam Taylor. "Daniel Craig." *Interview*, July 2007.

Cohen, David S. "AFI Honoree Arrives with Desire Intact." *Daily Variety*, June 7, 2007.

Pruzan, Todd. "Wiseguy." *Details*, December 2006.

Smith, Anna Deavere. *Letters to a Young Artist*. New York: Anchor Books, 2006.

Riedel, Michael. "Dennehy . . . neat." *New York Post*, April 13, 2007.

Hoffman, Barbara. "Great Brit." *New York Post*, January 14, 2007.

Freeman, Morgan. "Morgan Freeman Discusses Lucky Number Slevin." By Rebecca Murray. About.com. http://movies.about.com/od/luckynumberslevin/a/slevin033106.htm.

Bardin, Brantley. "Idol Chatter." *Premiere*, January 2007.

Dench, Judy. "Show Stoppers: Premiere Salutes the Finest Performances of 2006." Interviews conducted by various. *Premiere*, January 2007.

Callon, Michael Feeney. *Anthony Hopkins: A Three Act Life*. London: Robson Books, 2005.

Friedman, Devin. "Metaphorically Speaking." *Gentleman's Quarterly*, February 2007.

Grodin, Charles. *I Like It Better When You're Funny: Working in Television and Other Precarious Adventures*. New York: Random House, 2002.

Twelfth Annual Screen Actors' Guild Awards, originally broadcast on January 29, 2006, by TNT.

Norton, Edward. "Jonah Hill." *Interview*, September 2007.

Penn, Nate. "Christian Rocks!" *Gentleman's Quarterly*, March 2007.

"Acting Is a challenge." *Maclean's*, February 11, 2002.

Stanislavski, Constantin. *Building a Character*. New York: Routledge, 1989.

Logan, Brian. "I Can Do Anything." *The Guardian*, January 2, 2001.

Hoffman, Philip Seymour. "Philip Seymour Hoffman Gets Candid" By Steve Kroft CBSNews.com http://www.cbsnews.com/stories/2006/02/16/60minutes/main1323924.shtml.

Zucker, Carole. *In the Company of Actors: Reflections on the Craft of Acting*. New York: Routledge, 1999.

Tucker, Reed. "Hot Seat: John Malkovich." *New York Post*, March 18, 2007.

Borgnine, Ernest. "Ernest Borgnine." By Clyde Jeavons. BFI. http://www.bfi.org.uk/features/interviews/borgnine.html.

Chaplin, Charles. *My Autobiography*. New York: Simon & Schuster, 1964.

Brady, Shaun. "Looking for Inspiration." Weekend issue, *Metro*, March 23–25, 2007.

Allen, Woody. *Mere Anarchy*. New York: Random House, 2007.

Caine, Michael. "Wiseguy: Michael Caine." By Mickey Rapkin. Details.com. http://men.style.com/details/wiseguy/landing?&id=content_4710.

Olivier, Laurence. *Confessions of an Actor*. Philadelphia, PA: Coronet Books, 1982.

Jenkins, Garry. *Harrison Ford: Imperfect Hero*. New York: Birch Lane Press, 1998.

Green, Jesse. "She Sings! She Acts! She Prays!" *New York Times*, December 3, 2006.

Burdette, Nicole. "Hail Mary" *Interview*, May 1993.

Adams, Cindy. "He loves theater—but 'it's no life.'" *New York Post*, March 20, 2007.

Tichler, Rosemarie, and Barry Jay Kaplan. *Actors at Work*. New York: Faber and Faber, 2007.

Ross, Lillian, and Helen Ross. *The Player*. New York: Simon & Schuster, 1961.

Fussman, Cal. "What I've Learned: Dick Van Dyke." *Esquire*, February 2007.

ON AUDITIONING

Schruers, Fred. "Vince Vaughn." *Rolling Stone*, June 12, 1997.

Zorich, Louis, ed. *What Have You Done?: The Inside Stories of Auditioning from the Ridiculous to the Sublime*. USA: Louis Zorich, 2005.

Alterman, Glenn. *An Actor's Guide—Making It in New York City*. New York: Allworth Press, 2002.

Grodin, Charles. *It Would Be So Nice if You Weren't Here*. New York: Morrow, 1989.

Miller, Penelope Ann. "No Longer an Armpiece, But Still a Chameleon." Special issue, *People*, Spring 1991.

Cahill, Tim. "Mel Gibson—Back from the Edge." *Premiere*, December 1988.

Hunt, Gordon. *How to Audition*. New York: Harper & Row, 1979.

Poitier, Sidney. *The Measure of a Man: A Spiritual Autobiography*. New York: HarperCollins, 2000.

Garr, Teri, and Henriette Mantel. *Speedbumps: Flooring It Through Hollywood*. New York: Penguin, 2005.

Olyphant, Timothy. "Interview: Timothy Olyphant for 'Catch and Release.'" By Paul Fischer. Dark Horizons. http://www.darkhorizons.com/interviews/831/timothy-olyphant-for-catch-and-release-.

Horowitz, Simi. "Crashing the Gates." *Back Stage East*, June 21–27, 2007.

Dern, Bruce, Christopher Fryer, and Robert Crane. *Things I've Said, But Probably Shouldn't Have*. Hoboken, NJ: John Wiley & Sons, 2007.

Riley, Jenelle. "Declaration of Independence." *Back Stage East*, May 28, 2008.

Fox, Michael J. *Lucky Man: A Memoir*. New York: Hyperion, 2002.

Tichler, Rosemarie, and Barry Jay Kaplan. *Actors at Work*. New York: Faber and Faber, 2007.

Grodin, Charles. *It Would Be So Nice if You Weren't Here*. New York: Morrow, 1989.

Dern, Bruce, Christopher Fryer, and Robert Crane. *Things I've Said, But Probably Shouldn't Have*. Hoboken, NJ: John Wiley & Sons, 2007.

Bracco, Lorraine. *On the Couch*. New York: Berkley Books, 2007.

Walken, Christopher. "Christopher Walken Uncut." By Jeffrey Gordinier. Details.com. http://men.style.com/details/features/landing?id=content_5751.

Dukakis, Olympia, and Emily Heckman. *Ask Me Again Tomorrow*. New York: HarperCollins, 2003.

ON STRUGGLING AND BUILDING A CAREER

Bradlee, Ben, Jr. "The Enigma Next Door." *Vanity Fair*, February 1989.

Heath, Chris. "And Now, 972 Words from Robert De Niro." *Gentleman's Quarterly*, January 2007.

Griffin, Nancy. "Lethal Charm." *US*, December 12, 1989.

Stein, Joel. "Can Jim Carrey Turn It Around?" *Time*, February 26, 2007.

Smith, Anna Deavere. *Letters to a Young Artist*. New York: Anchor Books, 2006.

Lamb, Rose Marie. "Nathan the Crazy Man, Otto the Wild Man, Hamlet the Brooding Man. Kevin Kline, Hell of an Actor, Man!" *Arts & Entertainment*, April 1993.

Schnabel, Julian. "Jack Nicholson—Interview." *Interview,* April 1, 2003.

Richardson, John H. "The Unprocessed Johnny Depp." *Esquire*, May 2004.

Pacino, Al. "Pacino's Way." By Simon Hattenstone. Salon.com. http://dir.salon.com/story/ent/feature/2004/12/03/pacino/print.html.

O'Toole, Peter. "What I've Learned: Peter O'Toole." By Stephen Garrett. *Esquire*, January 2007.

West, Kevin. "Stayin' Alive." *W*, July 2007.

Alterman, Glenn. *An Actor's Guide—Making It in New York City*. New York: Allworth Press, 2002.

Horowitz, Simi. "Crashing the Gates." *Back Stage East*, June 21–27, 2007.

Jenkins, Garry. *Harrison Ford: Imperfect Hero*. New York: Birch Lane Press, 1998.

Leguizamo, John. *Pimps, Hos, Playa Hatas, and All the Rest of My Hollywood Friends*. New York: HarperCollins, 2006.

Dukakis, Olympia. "An Interview with Olympia Dukakis." By Jan Nargi. Broadwayworld.com. http://broadwayworld.com/article/An_Interview_with_Olympia_Dukakis_20070110.

"10 Questions for Sir Ben Kingsley." *Time*, August 13, 2007.

Smith, Liz. "'Honey' the Movie." *New York Post*, July 17, 2007.

Reeve, Christopher. *Still Me*. New York: Random House, 1998.

Smith, Anna Deavere. *Letters to a Young Artist*. New York: Anchor Books, 2006.

Caine, Michael. "Wiseguy: Michael Caine." By Mickey Rapkin. Details.com. http://men.style.com/details/wiseguy/landing?&id=content_4710.

Garr, Teri, and Henriette Mantel. *Speedbumps: Flooring It Through Hollywood*. New York: Penguin, 2005.

Walker, Alexander. *Audrey: Her Real Story*. New York: St. Martin's Press, 1994.

Alda, Alan. *Never Have Your Dog Stuffed and Other Things I've Learned*. New York: Random House, 2006.

Turturro, John. "The Good Shepherd, John Turturro." London.net. http://www.londonnet.co.uk/ln/out/ent/cinema_thegoodshepherd_turturro.php.

Goldfarb, Brad. "Amy Adams." *Interview*, February 2008.

Shewey, Don. "Willem Dafoe." *In Fashion*, May/June 1987.

Meisner, Sanford. *Sanford Meisner Master Class*. DVD. Los Angeles, CA: Open Road Films, 2006.

"Outtakes." *Theatre Week*, August 12, 1991.

Friedman, Devin. "Metaphorically Speaking." *Gentleman's Quarterly*, February 2007.

Pacino, Al, and Lawrence Grobel. *Al Pacino: In Conversations with Lawrence Grobel*. New York: Simon Spotlight Entertainment, 2006.

Guzman, Sandra. "La Dolce 'Rita.'" *New York Post*, January 10, 2007.

Reeve, Christopher. *Still Me*. New York: Random House, 1998.

Callon, Michael Feeney. *Anthony Hopkins: A Three Act Life*. London: Robson Books, 2005.

Falk, Peter. *Just One More Thing: Stories from My Life*. New York: Carroll & Graf, 2006.

Neal, Patricia. *As I Am: An Autobiography*. New York: Simon & Schuster, 1988.

Benson, Sheila. "Laurence Fishburne: the Actor who puts Risk before Reputation—and Proves why that Matters so Much." *Interview*, January 1995.

Garfield, Simon. "Oscar Knight." *The Observer* (UK), February 26, 2006.

Wilder, Gene. *Kiss Me Like A Stranger: My Search for Love and Art*. New York: St. Martin's Press, 2005.

Meisner, Sanford. *Sanford Meisner Master Class*. DVD. Los Angeles, CA: Open Road Films, 2006.

Bogart, Stephen Humphrey. *Bogart: In Search of My Father*. New York: Penguin, 1995.

Emer, David. "Angela's Assets." *The Guardian*, September 29, 2001.

Newhart, Bob. *I Shouldn't Even Be Doing This and Other Things That Strike Me as Funny*. New York: Hyperion, 2006.

Walken, Christopher. "Christopher Walken Uncut" By Jeffrey Gordinier. Details.com. http://men.style.com/details/features/landing?id=content_5751.

Duffy, Karen. "Genius—Walter Matthau." *Interview*, December 1994.

"Was There Ever a Time You Thought About Quitting?" *Back Stage East*, June 21–27, 2007.

Jefferson, Joseph. *The Autobiography of Joseph Jefferson*. New York: The Century Company, 1889.

Jenkins, Garry. *Harrison Ford: Imperfect Hero*. New York: Birch Lane Press, 1998.

Sella, Marshall. "The Two Jakes." *Gentleman's Quarterly*, February 2007.

Bogart, Stephen Humphrey. *Bogart: In Search of My Father*. New York: Penguin, 1995.

Thirteenth Annual Screen Actors' Guild Awards, originally broadcast on January 28, 2007, by TNT.

Penn, Nate. "Christian Rocks!" *Gentleman's Quarterly*, March 2007.

Adams, Cindy. "Cindy Adams at the Oscars." *New York Post*, February 26, 2007.

Benfer, Amy. "The Internationalist." Weekend issue, *Metro*, January 26–28, 2007.

Foxx, Jamie. "Interview: Jamie Foxx for Dreamgirls." By Garth Franklin. Dark Horizons. http://www.darkhorizons.com/news/6301/interview-jamie-foxx-for-dreamgirls.

Stewart, Sara. "Hot Seat: Diane Keaton." *New York Post*, January 28, 2007.

Ninth Annual Screen Actors' Guild Awards, originally broadcast on March 9, 2003, by TNT.

Washington, Denzel. "Interview: Denzel Washington's Difference of Opinion with Harvey Weinstein on 'The Great Debaters.'" By Adam Feldman. HollywoodChicago.com. http://www.hollywoodchicago.com/2007/12/interview-denzel-washingtons-difference.html.

Stein, Joel. "Can Jim Carrey Turn It Around?" *Time*, February 26, 2007.

Bogart, Stephen Humphrey. *Bogart: In Search of My Father*. New York: Penguin, 1995.

Goldstein, Toby. *William Hurt: The Actor and His Work*. New York: St. Martin's Press, 1987.

Tichler, Rosemarie, and Barry Jay Kaplan. *Actors at Work*. New York: Faber and Faber, 2007.

Gazzara, Ben. *In the Moment: My Life as an Actor*. New York: Carroll & Graf Publishers, 2004.

Dench, Judi. "Judy Dench" By Philipp Hoschka. Film Scouts. http://www.filmscouts.com/scripts/interview.cfm?File=3065.

McKellen, Ian. Interview by Lizo. *Newsround*, CBBC, May 1, 2003.

Bogart, Stephen Humphrey. *Bogart: In Search of My Father*. New York: Penguin, 1995.

Hofler, Robert. "Employed, Happy and Laffing All the Way to ShoWest." *Variety*, March 15, 2007.

Barker, Andrew. "The Hired Gun Now Does the Hiring." *Variety*, March 15, 2007.

Jones, James Earl. "The Voice of Triumph." Academy of Achievement interview, conducted on June 29, 1996, in Sun Valley, Idaho.

Gibson, Mel. "Interview: Mel Gibson." By Todd Gilchrist. IGN.com. http://movies.ign.com/articles/751/751225p1.html.

Zahn, Steve. "Q&A: Steve Zahn." *Esquire*, July 2007.

Patterson, John. "Total Recall." *The Guardian*, September 3, 2005.

Harris, Kate, and Ewan Jeffrey. "Interview with Peter Bartlett." *The Theatre Archive Project*, October 20, 2005.

Ford, Harrison. "Harrison Ford—Interview." By Calista Flockhart. *Interview*, June 2003.

Snyder, Gabriel. "What, Me Worry?" *W*, August 2007.

Riley, Jenelle. "Do Not Disturb." *Back Stage East*, June 21–27, 2007.

"Was There Ever a Time You Thought About Quitting?" *Back Stage East*, June 21–27, 2007.

Douglas, Kirk. *Let's Face It: 90 Years of Living, Loving, and Learning*. Hoboken, NJ: John Wiley & Sons, 2007.

Cohen, David S. "AFI Honoree Arrives with Desire Intact." *Daily Variety*, June 7, 2007.

Cooper, Chris. "Chris Cooper Interview, BREACH." By Sheila Roberts. MoviesOnline. http://www.moviesonline.ca/movienews_11257.html.

Lyman, Rick. "So, as Paul Said to Tom . . ." *The Observer* (UK), September 15, 2002.

Grodin, Charles. *I Like It Better When You're Funny: Working in Television and Other Precarious Adventures.* New York: Random House, 2002.

ON THE IMPORTANCE OF TECHNIQUE AND TRAINING

Moore, Sonia. *The Stanislavski System.* New York: Viking Press, 1965.

Boleslavsky, Richard. *Acting: The First Six Lessons.* New York: Theatre Arts Books, 1933.

Sager, Mike. "What I've Learned: Alan Arkin." *Esquire,* January 2007.

Jefferson, Joseph. *The Autobiography of Joseph Jefferson.* New York: The Century Company, 1889.

Yakir, Dan. "Surprise, Surprise." *Cabletime,* November 1987.

Marill, Alvin H. *Katharine Hepburn.* New York: Galahad Books, 1973.

Brady, James. "In Step with Glenn Close." *Parade,* August 27, 2007.

Warner, Kara. "Shy Guy Stiller." Weekend issue, *amNewYork,* December 8–10, 2006.

Malden, Karl, and Carla Malden. *When Do I Start?* New York: Simon & Schuster, 1997.

Belasco, David. "About Acting." *The Saturday Evening Post,* September 24, 1921.

Burton, Hal. *Great Acting.* New York: Bonanza Books, 1967.

"The 128 Best Things Anyone Ever Said in *People.*" *People,* March 6, 1989.

Connell, Kathy. "Q & A with Julie Andrews." *Screen Actor,* Winter 2006.

Widmark, Richard. "Richard Widmark." By Adrian Wooton. BFI. http://www.bfi.org.uk/features/interviews/widmark.html.

Meisner, Sanford. *Sanford Meisner Master Class.* DVD. Los Angeles, CA: Open Road Films, 2006.

Alterman, Glenn. *An Actor's Guide—Making It in New York City.* New York: Allworth Press, 2002.

Debruge, Peter. "Q&A: Martin Landau—Training Never Ends for the Serious Actor." *Variety,* April 25, 2007.

Strasberg, Lee, and Robert H. Hethmon. *Strasberg at the Actors Studio.* New York: Theater Communications Group, 1965.

Dench, Judi. "Judi Dench on National Public Radio." By Susan Stamberg. National Public Radio, June 17, 2004.

Kalbacker, Warren. "20 Questions with Hugh Jackman." *Playboy,* February 2002.

Brady, James. "In Step with Sigourney Weaver." *Parade,* April 1, 2007.

Alda, Alan. *Things I Overheard While Talking to Myself.* New York: Random House, 2007.

Boleslavsky, Richard. *Acting: The First Six Lessons.* New York: Theatre Arts Books, 1933.

Burstyn, Ellen. *Lessons in Becoming Myself.* New York: Riverhead Books, 2006.

Lyman, Rick. "So, as Paul Said to Tom . . ." *The Observer* (UK), September 15, 2002.

Rockwell, Sam. "Sam Rockwell Interview, Star of Joshua." By Sheila Roberts. MoviesOnline. http://www.moviesonline.ca/movienews_12358.html.

Hawke, Ethan. "Paul Dano." *Interview,* December/January 2008.

Hattenstone, Simon. "How to Be Charming." *The Guardian,* February 2, 2008.

Goldfarb, Brad. "Amy Adams." *Interview,* February 2008.

Getlen, Larry. "Hot Seat: James Lipton." *New York Post*, December 31, 2006.

Hill, Harry. *A Voice for the Theatre*. New York: Holt, Rinehart and Winston, 1985.

Meisner, Sanford. *Sanford Meisner Master Class*. DVD. Los Angeles, CA: Open Road Films, 2006.

Morris, Eric, and Joan Hotchkis. *No Acting Please*. Los Angeles, CA: Ermor Enterprises, 1977.

Burstyn, Ellen. *Lessons in Becoming Myself*. New York: Riverhead Books, 2006.

Debruge, Peter. "Q&A: Martin Landau—Training Never Ends for the Serious Actor." *Variety*, April 25, 2007.

Wilder, Gene. *Kiss Me Like A Stranger: My Search for Love and Art*. New York: St. Martin's Press, 2005.

Christon, Lawrence. "Art of Deception." *Daily Variety*, November 1, 2007.

Blanks, Tim. "Keira Knightley." *Interview*, December/January 2008.

Meisner, Sanford, and Dennis Longwell. *Sanford Meisner: On Acting*. New York: Vintage Books, 1987.

Baker, Fred, and Ross Firestone. *Movie People: At Work in the Business of Film*. New York: Lancer Books, 1973.

Leguizamo, John. *Pimps, Hos, Playa Hatas, and All the Rest of My Hollywood Friends*. New York: HarperCollins, 2006.

Bardin, Brantley. "Idol Chatter." *Premiere*, January 2007.

Newhart, Bob. *I Shouldn't Even Be Doing This and Other Things That Strike Me as Funny*. New York: Hyperion, 2006.

Raab, Scott. "The Quiet One." *Esquire*, March 2007.

Arkin, Alan. "Futurist Radio Hour." By Stephen Capen. KUSF-FM, October 10, 1995.

Riley, Jenelle. "Breaking & Entering." *Back Stage East*, March 8–14, 2007.

Ford, Harrison. "Harrison Ford—Interview." By Calista Flockhart. *Interview*, June 2003.

Wood, Mark Dundas. "Some Kisser." *Back Stage East*, March 22–28, 2007.

Debruge, Peter. "Q&A: Martin Landau—Training Never Ends for the Serious Actor." *Variety*, April 25, 2007.

Morris, Eric, and Joan Hotchkis. *No Acting Please*. Los Angeles, CA: Ermor Enterprises, 1977.

Riley, Jenelle. "Master Class." *Back Stage East*, June 13, 2008.

Stanislavski, Constantin. *Creating a Role*. New York: Routledge, 1961.

Rose, Cynthia. "John Malkovich: Profile." *Arena* (UK), 1990.

Stewart, Jimmy. "Jimmy Stewart." By Joan Bakewell. BFI. http://www.bfi.org.uk/features/interviews/stewart.html.

Corsello, Andrew. "Christopher Walken Must Die." *Gentleman's Quarterly*, March 2000.

Jones, Tommy Lee. "Interview with American Actor Tommy Lee Jones." By Elmer Kelton. BNET. http://findarticles.com/p/articles/mi_m1285/is_n6_v25/ai_17231480/.

Morris, Eric, and Joan Hotchkis. *No Acting Please*. Los Angeles, CA: Ermor Enterprises, 1977.

Dukakis, Olympia, and Emily Heckman. *Ask Me Again Tomorrow*. New York: Perennial, 2003.

Burdette, Nicole. "Hail Mary." *Interview*, May 1993.

Gam, Rita. *Actors: A Celebration*. New York: St. Martin's Press, 1988.

Wilder, Gene. *Kiss Me Like A Stranger: My Search for Love and Art*. New York: St. Martin's Press, 2005.

Goldblum, Jeff. "Jeff Goldblum, Raines Interview." By Kyle Braun. UGO. http://www.ugo.com/ugo/html/article/?id=16941.

ON THE IMPORTANCE OF MAINTAINING A HEALTHY AND EXPRESSIVE INSTRUMENT

Stanislavski, Constantin. *Building a Character*. New York: Routledge, 1989.

Chekhov, Michael. *To the Actor*. New York: Harper & Row, 1953.

Edwards, Gavin. "The Two Faces of Aaron Eckhart." *Men's Journal,* August 2007.

Hunt, Gordon. *How to Audition*. New York: Harper & Row, 1979.

Rand, Ronald, and Luigi Scorcia. *Acting Teacher of America: A Vital Tradition*. New York: Allworth Press, 2007.

Adams, Cindy. "One Lady Who's Not Invisible." *New York Post*, March 15, 2007.

Stewart, Patrick. "Patrick Stewart." By Kathy Henderson. Broadway.com. http://www.broadway.com/Patrick-Stewart/broadway_news/564809.

Artaud, Antonin. *The Theatre and Its Double*. Translated by Mary Caroline Richards. New York: Grove Press, 1958.

Gam, Rita. *Actors: A Celebration*. New York: St. Martin's Press, 1988.

Rovin, J. "Shirley!" *Ladies' Home Journal*, August 1985.

Bridges, Jeff. "The Total Film Interview—Jeff Bridges" By Simon Crook. Total Film. http://www.totalfilm.com/features/the-total-film-interview-jeff-bridges.

Redgrave, Michael. *In My Mind's I: An Actor's Autobiography*. New York: Viking, 1983.

Wheatley, Jane. "Patrick Stewart: From Captain to Hamlet." *The (London) Times,* July 14, 2008.

Artaud, Antonin. *The Theatre and Its Double*. Translated by Mary Caroline Richards. New York: Grove Press, 1958.

Garfield, Simon. "Daniel Radcliffe." *Details*, August 2007.

Stanislavski, Constantin. *Creating a Role*. New York: Routledge, 1961.

Taylor, Laurette. "The Quality You Need Most." *The Green Book Magazine*, April 1914.

Pacino, Al. "Pacino's Way." By Simon Hattenstone. Salon.com. http://dir.salon.com/story/ent/feature/2004/12/03/pacino/print.html.

Zucker, Carole. *In the Company of Actors: Reflections on the Craft of Acting*. New York: Routledge, 1999

Schatz, Howard, and Beverly J. Ornstein. *In Character: Actors Acting*. New York: Bulfinch, 2006.

Tucker, Reed. "Hot Seat: Aaron Eckhart." *New York Post*, July 22, 2007.

Gielgud, John. *Early Stages*. New York: Macmillan, 1939.

Artaud, Antonin. *The Theatre and Its Double*. Translated by Mary Caroline Richards. New York: Grove Press, 1958.

Grodin, Charles. *If I Only Knew Then . . .: Learning from Our Mistakes*. New York: Springboard Press, 2007.

Arnest, Mark. "Redgrave's Curtain Call." *The (Colorado Springs) Gazette,* July 21, 2006.

ON THE IMPORTANCE OF IMAGINATION, INSPIRATION, FANTASY, AND STORYTELLING

Stanislavski, Constantin. *An Actor Prepares*. New York: Theatre Arts Books, 1936.

Alexander, Jane. *New York Theatre Review*, March 1979.

Adler, Stella. *The Art of Acting*. Compiled and edited by Howard Kissel. New York: Applause Books, 2000.

Hawn, Goldie, and Wendy Holden. *Goldie: A Lotus Grows in the Mud*. New York: The Berkley Publishing Group, 2005.

Hochberg, Mena. "Favorite Flicks." *amNewYork*, January 8, 2007.

Hedegaard, Erik. "Jack Nicholson: A Singular Guy." *Rolling Stone*, October 5, 2006.

Pollock, Sir Frederick, ed. *Macready's Reminiscences, and Selections from His Diaries and Letters*. New York: Macmillan and Co., 1875.

Bussel, Rachel Kramer. "Hot Seat: Gene Wilder." *New York Post*, February 25, 2007.

Eighth Annual Screen Actors' Guild Awards, originally broadcast on March 10, 2002, by TNT.

Norton, Edward. "Interview: Edward Norton for 'The Painted Veil.'" By Garth Franklin. Dark Horizons. http://www.darkhorizons.com/interviews/820/edward-norton-for-the-painted-veil-.

Sella, Marshall. "The Two Jakes." *Gentleman's Quarterly*, February 2007.

Mackenzie, Suzie. "You Have to Laugh." *The Guardian*, November 20, 2004.

Rockwell, Sam. "Sam Rockwell Interview, Star of Joshua." By Sheila Roberts. MoviesOnline. http://www.moviesonline.ca/movienews_12358.html.

McKellen, Ian. Interview by Lizo. *Newsround*, CBBC, May 1, 2003.

Jones, Tommy Lee. "Interview with American Actor Tommy Lee Jones." By Elmer Kelton. BNET. http://findarticles.com/p/articles/mi_m1285/is_n6_v25/ai_17231480/.

Hoffman, Philip Seymour. "Philip Seymour Hoffman Gets Candid" By Steve Kroft. CBSNews.com. http://www.cbsnews.com/stories/2006/02/16/60minutes/main1323924.shtml.

Stanislavski, Constantin. *An Actor Prepares*. New York: Theatre Arts Books, 1936.

Rader, Dotson. "Kevin Kline Interview." *Parade*, October16, 1994.

Sutherland, Donald. "Interview: Donald Sutherland (Pride & Prejudice)." By Deven Faraci. CHUD.com. http://chud.com/articles/articles/4997/1/INTERVIEW-DONALD-SUTHERLAND-PRIDE--PREJUDICE/Page1.html.

Blanks, Tim. "Keira Knightley." *Interview*, December/January 2008.

Sinise, Gary. "Of Mars and Men: Gary Sinise Goes on a Mission to Mars." By Ray Greene. Reel.com. http://www.reel.com/reel.asp?node=features/interviews/sinise.

Sorvino, Mira. "Mira Sorvino." By Graham Fuller. BNET. http://findarticles.com/p/articles/mi_m1285/is_n11_v25/ai_17632992/.

Mitchell, Elvis. "Brad Pitt." *Interview*, March 2007.

Stanislavski, Constantin. *An Actor Prepares*. New York: Theatre Arts Books, 1936.

Taylor, Laurette. "The Quality You Need Most." *The Green Book Magazine*, April 1914.

Olivier, Laurence. *Confessions of an Actor*. Philadelphia, PA: Coronet Books, 1982.

Grammer, Kelsey. *So Far . . .* New York: Dutton, 1995.

Stanislavski, Constantin. *Building a Character*. New York: Routledge, 1989.

Goldstein, Toby. *William Hurt: The Actor and His Work.* New York: St. Martin's Press, 1987.

Blanchett, Cate. "Cate Blanchett." By Kitty Bowe Hearty. BNET. http://findarticles.com/p/articles/mi_m1285/is_n1_v28/ai_20208954/?tag=content;col1.

Adler, Stella. *The Art of Acting.* Compiled and edited by Howard Kissel. New York: Applause Books, 2000.

Fischoff, Stuart. "Clint Eastwood." *Psychology Today,* January/February 1993.

ON BUILDING A CHARACTER

Greene, Bob. "Streep." *Esquire,* December 1984.

Hochberg, Mina. "Call Him Jack the Quipper." *amNewYork,* October 2, 2006.

Ninth Annual Screen Actors' Guild Awards, originally broadcast on March 9, 2003, by TNT.

Burton, Hal. *Great Acting.* New York: Bonanza Books, 1967.

Heath, Chris. "The Hardass." *Gentleman's Quarterly,* March 2005.

Rovin, J. "Shirley!" *Ladies' Home Journal,* August 1985.

Irons, Jeremy. "Actor/Risk-taker." Academy of Achievement interview, conducted on October 27, 2000, in London, England.

Salvini, Tommaso. *Leaves from the Autobiography of Tommaso Salvini.* New York: The Century Company, 1893.

Hagen, Uta with Frankel, Haskel. *Respect for Acting.* Hoboken, NJ: Wiley Publishing, 1973.

Skow, John. "What Makes Meryl Magic." *Time,* September 7, 1981.

Yakir, Dan. "Surprise, Surprise." *Cabletime,* November 1987.

Wheelock, Katherine. "Clive." *Details,* September 2007.

Chen, Sandie Angulo. "Thesps Not Caught in Method's Stranglehold." *Daily Variety,* January 4, 2008.

Robins, Cynthia. "Final Curtain." *San Francisco Examiner,* November 10, 1991, Image section.

Rosenbaum, Ron. "Acting: The Creative Mind of Jack Nicholson." *New York Times Magazine,* July 13, 1986.

Levine, Stuart. "Searching for the Next Gandolfini." *Daily Variety,* June 8, 2007.

Shewey, Don. "Rock-and-Roll Jesus with a Cowboy Mouth (Revisited)." *American Theatre,* April 2004.

Blanks, Tim. "Maggie Gyllenhaal." *Interview,* May 2008.

Pepper, Curtis Bill. "Still Mastroianni." *New York Times Magazine,* September 20, 1987.

Stanwyck, Barbara. Interview with Hedda Hopper, 1953.

Fonseca, Nicholas. "The Truman Show." *Entertainment Weekly,* October 7, 2005.

Blanks, Tim. "Monica Bellucci." *Interview,* September 2007.

Boleslavsky, Richard. *Acting: The First Six Lessons.* New York: Theatre Arts Books, 1933.

Hoskings, Bob. "Bob Hoskins." *People,* January 5, 1986.

Brode, Douglas. *The Films of Dustin Hoffman.* Secaucus, NJ: Citadel Press, 1983.

Riedel, Michael. "Great Scott." *Theatre Week,* October 14, 1991.

Cottrell, John. *Laurence Olivier.* New York: Prentice Hall, 1975.

Burton, Hal. *Great Acting.* New York: Bonanza Books, 1967.

Jonze, Spike. "Chris Cooper." *Interview,* August 2003.

Hagen, Uta. *A Challenge for the Actor.* New York: Scribner, 1991.

Cusack, John. "Interview & Profile: John Cusack." By Carlo Cavagna. AboutFilm. http://www.aboutfilm.com/movies/i/iceharvest/cusack.htm.

Brock, Pope. "Jeff Daniels Up in Michigan." *Gentleman's Quarterly,* October 1987.

Washington, Denzel. "Interview: Denzel Washington's Difference of Opinion with Harvey Weinstein on 'The Great Debaters.'" By Adam Feldman. HollywoodChicago.com. http://www.hollywoodchicago.com/2007/12/interview-denzel-washingtons-difference.html.

Beale, Lewis. "Swank Makes the Grade." *amNewYork,* January 4, 2007.

Hunt, Gordon. *How to Audition.* New York: Harper & Row, 1979.

Getlen, Larry. "Hot Seat: Chris Meloni." *New York Post,* January 14, 2007.

Gyllenhaal, Jake. "Jake Gyllenhaal Talks About Brokeback Mountain." By Rebecca Murray. About.com. http://movies.about.com/od/brokebackmountain/a/brokeback112905.htm.

Hackman, Gene. "Two Old Friends Talk About 'Runaway Jury.'" By Rebecca Murray. About.com. http://movies.about.com/cs/therunawayjury/a/runawayintgh.htm.

Pacino, Al, and Lawrence Grobel. *Al Pacino: In Conversations with Lawrence Grobel.* New York: Simon Spotlight Entertainment, 2006.

Hoffman, Barbara. "Scripts, not names, add Sheen to roles." *New York Post,* April 23, 2007.

Mermelstein, David. "Drama's New Law." *Variety,* March 2, 2007.

Penn, Nate. "Christian Rocks!" *Gentleman's Quarterly,* March 2007.

Heath, Chris. "Johnny Depp's Savage Journey." *Rolling Stone,* June 11, 1998.

Mermelstein, David. "Drama's New Law." *Variety,* March 2, 2007.

Baldwin, Alec. "Interview: Alec Baldwin for 'The Last Shot.'" By Paul Fischer. Dark Horizons. http://www.darkhorizons.com/interviews/70/alec-baldwin-for-the-last-shot-.

Edwards, Gavin. "The Two Faces of Aaron Eckhart." *Men's Journal,* August 2007.

Riley, Jenelle. "Breaking & Entering." *Back Stage East,* March 8–14, 2007.

Hoffman, Philip Seymour. "Philip Seymour Hoffman." By Meghan O'Rourke. Slate.com. http://www.slate.com/id/2135151/.

Penn, Sean. "The Total Film Interview—Sean Penn." By Hilary Morgan. Total Film. http://www.totalfilm.com/features/the-total-film-interview-sean-penn.

Hawke, Ethan. "Ethan Hawke." By Robert Elms. BFI. http://www.bfi.org.uk/features/interviews/hawke.html.

McDowell, Malcolm. "Malcolm McDowell." By Paul Ryan. BFI. http://www.bfi.org.uk/features/interviews/mcdowell.html.

Duvall, Robert. "Robert Duvall Uncut." By Ian Daly. Details.com. http://men.style.com/details/features/landing?id=content_5485.

Stanislavski, Constantin. *Creating a Role.* New York: Routledge, 1961.

Strasberg, Lee. *A Dream of Passion.* New York: Penguin, 1987.

Iley, Chrissy. "Red Alert." *The Observer* (UK), July 6, 2008.

Fein, Esther B. "Role Call: Waif, Wife, Drummer Girl." *New York Times,* April 26, 1987.

MacLaine, Shirley. *My Lucky Stars: A Hollywood Memoir.* New York: Bantam, 1995.

Taylor, Laurette. "The Quality You Need Most." *The Green Book Magazine,* April 1914.

Jones, Cherry. "Cherry Jones Part Three." By Douglas Anderson. And Another Thing . . . http://idigdoug.blogspot.com/2005_07_01_archive.html.

Caine, Sir Michael. "Cockney Rebel." By Amy Reiter. Salon.com. http://dir.salon.com/story/ent/movies/int/2003/12/15/caine/index.html.

Salvini, Tommaso. *Leaves from the Autobiography of Tommaso Salvini*. New York: The Century Company, 1893.

Ullmann, Liv. *Choices*. New York: Knopf, 1984.

ON REHEARSALS AND THE ACTING PROCESS

Hagen, Uta, and Haskel Frankel. *Respect for Acting*. Hoboken, NJ: Wiley Publishing, 1973.

Stanislavski, Constantin. *Building a Character*. New York: Routledge, 1989.

Grotowski, Jerzy. *Theatre Laboratorie*. Translated by Helen Krich Chinoy. Wroclaw, 1967.

Burstyn, Ellen. *Lessons in Becoming Myself*. New York: Riverhead Books, 2006.

Rapp, Anthony. *Without You: A Memoir of Love, Loss, and the Musical Rent*. New York: Simon & Schuster, 2006.

Cottrell, John. *Laurence Olivier*. New York: Prentice Hall, 1975.

Duvall, Robert. "Robert Duvall Uncut." By Ian Daly. Details.com. http://men.style.com/details/features/landing?id=content_5485.

Bettany, Paul. "Paul Bettany Sets Sail in 'Master and Commander.'" By Rebecca Murray. About.com. http://movies.about.com/cs/mastercommander/a/mcpaulbettany.htm.

Grodin, Charles. *If I Only Knew Then . . .: Learning from Our Mistakes*. New York: Springboard Press, 2007.

Barker, Andrew. "The Hired Gun Now Does the Hiring." *Variety*, March 15, 2007.

Foster, Jodie. "Jodie Foster: Panic Room." By Paul Webber. BBC. http://www.bbc.co.uk/films/2002/03/28/jodie_foster_panic_room_interview.shtml.

Jenkins, Garry. *Harrison Ford: Imperfect Hero*. New York: Birch Lane Press, 1998.

Ross, Lillian, and Helen Ross. *The Player*. New York: Simon & Schuster, 1961.

Ansen, David. "Five Foot Two, How She Grew." *Newsweek*, December 28, 1989.

Mortimer, Emily. "Michael Sheen." *Interview*, July 2007.

Hauer, Rutger, and Patrick Quinlan. *All These Moments*. New York: HarperCollins, 2007.

Mitchell, Elvis. "Brad Pitt." *Interview*, March 2007.

Grodin, Charles. *If I Only Knew Then . . .: Learning from Our Mistakes*. New York: Springboard Press, 2007.

Loren, Sophia. "Interview with Sophia Loren." By Larry King. *Larry King Live*, CNN, December 2, 2004.

Verini, Bob. "Latenight Killed the Vaudeo Star." *Daily Variety*, May 30, 2007.

Rossellini, Isabella. *Some of Me*. New York: Random House, 1997.

Roddick, Nick. "Robert De Niro Doesn't Want a Strike." *Evening Standard* (London), July 10, 2008.

Rose, Cynthia. "Maid in Heaven: Mary Elizabeth Mastrantonio." *Entertainment Weekly*, 1991.

Isenberg, Barbara. "Frank Gets Really Frank." *Los Angeles Times*, May 9, 1993.

Hagen, Uta, and Haskel Frankel. *Respect for Acting*. Hoboken, NJ: Wiley Publishing, 1973.

Duffy, Karen. "Genius—Walter Matthau." *Interview*, December 1994.

Rand, Ronald, and Luigi Scorcia. *Acting Teacher of America: A Vital Tradition*. New York: Allworth Press, 2007.

Reeve, Christopher. *Still Me*. New York: Random House, 1998.

Deneuve, Catherine. *Close Up and Personal: The Private Diaries of Catherine Deneuve*. Translated by Polly McLean. New York: Pegasus Books, 2005.

Foster, Jodie. "Jodie Foster: Panic Room." By Paul Webber. BBC. http://www.bbc.co.uk/films/2002/03/28/jodie_foster_panic_room_interview.shtml.

Redgrave, Michael. *In My Mind's I: An Actor's Autobiography*. New York: Viking, 1983.

Stanislavski, Constantin. *My Life in Art*. Translated by J.J. Robbins. New York: Theatre Arts Books, 1948.

Bettany, Paul. "Paul Bettany Sets Sail in 'Master and Commander.'" By Rebecca Murray. About.com. http://movies.about.com/cs/mastercommander/a/mcpaulbettany.htm.

Hoffman, Barbara. "Great Brit." *New York Post*, January 14, 2007.

Hackman, Gene. "Two Old Friends Talk About 'Runaway Jury.'" By Rebecca Murray. About.com. http://movies.about.com/cs/therunawayjury/a/runawayintgh.htm.

Nicholson, Jack. "Show Stoppers: Premiere Salutes the Finest Performances of 2006." Interviews conducted by various. *Premiere*, January 2007.

Pacino, Al, and Lawrence Grobel. *Al Pacino: In Conversations with Lawrence Grobel*. New York: Simon Spotlight Entertainment, 2006.

Olyphant, Timothy. "Interview: Timothy Olyphant for 'Catch and Release.'" By Paul Fischer. Dark Horizons. http://www.darkhorizons.com/interviews/831/timothy-olyphant-for-catch-and-release-.

Streep, Meryl. "Show Stoppers: Premiere Salutes the Finest Performances of 2006." Interviews conducted by various. *Premiere*, January 2007.

Corsello, Andrew. "Christopher Walken Must Die." *Gentleman's Quarterly*, March 2000.

Twelfth Annual Screen Actors' Guild Awards, originally broadcast on January 29, 2006, by TNT.

Hagen, Uta. *A Challenge for the Actor*. New York: Scribner, 1991.

Macy, William H. "Interview: William H. Macy for Everyone's Hero and Bobby." By Paul Fischer. Dark Horizons. http://www.darkhorizons.com/news/6363/interview-william-h-macy-for-everyone-s-hero-and-bobby.

Falk, Peter. *Just One More Thing: Stories from My Life*. New York: Carroll & Graf, 2006.

Gazzara, Ben. *In the Moment: My Life as an Actor*. New York: Carroll & Graf Publishers, 2004.

Wallach, Eli. "Eli Wallach in conversation with Niall Macpherson." By Niall Macpherson. BFI. http://www.bfi.org.uk/features/interviews/wallach.html.

Stanislavski, Constantin. *Building a Character*. New York: Routledge, 1989.

Jonze, Spike. "Chris Cooper." *Interview*, August 2003.

Chaplin, Charles. *My Autobiography*. New York: Simon & Schuster, 1964.

Callow, Simon. *Being an Actor*. New York: Penguin Books, 1984.

Jefferson, Joseph. *The Autobiography of Joseph Jefferson*. New York: The Century Company, 1889.

Polanyi, Margaret. "Christopher Plummer: Behind the Many Faces." *Readers Digest* (Canada), August 2002.

Riedel, Michael. "Dennehy . . . neat." *New York Post*, April 13, 2007.

McDowell, Malcolm. "Malcolm McDowell." By Paul Ryan. BFI. http://www.bfi.org.uk/features/interviews/mcdowell.html.

Wallach, Eli. "Eli Wallach in conversation with Niall Macpherson." By Niall Macpherson. BFI. http://www.bfi.org.uk/features/interviews/wallach.html.

Ford, Harrison. "Harrison Ford—Interview." By Calista Flockhart. *Interview*, June 2003.

Duffy, Karen. "Genius—Walter Matthau." *Interview*, December 1994.

Belasco, David. "About Acting." *The Saturday Evening Post,* September 24, 1921.

Rand, Ronald, and Luigi Scorcia. *Acting Teacher of America: A Vital Tradition.* New York: Allworth Press, 2007.

Stewart, Jimmy. "Jimmy Stewart." Interviewed by Joan Bakewell. BFI. http://www.bfi.org.uk/features/interviews/stewart.html.

Ricci, Christina. "Christina Ricci." By Stephen Lemons. Salon.com. http://archive.salon.com/people/conv/2001/06/01/ricci/index.html.

Wheelock, Katherine. "Clive." *Details*, September 2007.

Alda, Alan. *Never Have Your Dog Stuffed and Other Things I've Learned.* New York: Random House, 2006.

Stanislavski, Constantin. *An Actor Prepares.* New York: Theatre Arts Books, 1936.

ON COLLABORATING WITH DIRECTORS, WRITERS, PRODUCERS, DESIGNERS, AND OTHER INDUSTRY PROFESSIONALS

Brode, Douglas. *The Films of Dustin Hoffman.* Secaucus, NJ: Citadel Press, 1983.

Andrews, Julie. "Q & A with Julie Andrews." By Kathy Connell. *Screen Actor,* Winter 2006.

Heath, Chris. "The Hardass." *Gentleman's Quarterly*, March 2005.

Wilder, Gene. *Kiss Me Like A Stranger: My Search for Love and Art.* New York: St. Martin's Press, 2005.

Goldstein, Toby. *William Hurt: The Actor and His Work.* New York: St. Martin's Press, 1987.

Katkov, Norman. *The Fabulous Fanny.* New York: Alfred A. Knopf, 1952.

White, Nicholas. "Viggo Mortensen Talks About Sex." *People,* October 10, 2005.

Caine, Michael. *Acting in Film: An Actor's Take on Movie Making.* New York: Applause, 1990.

Hagen, Uta. *A Challenge for the Actor.* New York: Scribner, 1991.

Kingsley, Ben. "Interview with Ben Kingsley." By Ray Pride. Movie City News. http://www.moviecitynews.com/Interviews/kingsley.html.

Chekhov, Michael. *To the Actor.* New York: Harper & Row, 1953.

Wood, Mark Dundas. "Some Kisser." *Back Stage East*, March 22–28, 2007.

Widmark, Richard. "Richard Widmark." By Adrian Wooton. BFI. http://www.bfi.org.uk/features/interviews/widmark.html.

Strasberg, Lee, and Robert H. Hethmon. *Strasberg at the Actors Studio.* New York: Theater Communications Group, 1965.

Short, Martin. Presenting at the 58th Annual Tony Awards, originally broadcast on June 6, 2004, by CBS.

Leguizamo, John. *Pimps, Hos, Playa Hatas, and All the Rest of My Hollywood Friends.* New York: HarperCollins, 2006.

Caine, Michael. *Acting in Film: An Actor's Take on Movie Making*. New York: Applause, 1990.

Clooney, George. "George Clooney and Catherine Zeta-Jones Discuss *Intolerable Cruelty*." By Rebecca Murray. About.com. http://movies.about.com/cs/intolerablecruelty/a/intcrueltyint.htm.

Baker, Fred, and Ross Firestone. *Movie People: At Work in the Business of Film*. New York: Lancer Books, 1973.

Getlen, Larry. "Hot Seat: Chris Meloni." *New York Post*, January 14, 2007.

Olyphant, Timothy. "Interview: Timothy Olyphant for 'Catch and Release.'" By Paul Fischer. Dark Horizons. http://www.darkhorizons.com/interviews/831/timothy-olyphant-for-catch-and-release-.

Sella, Marshall. "The Two Jakes." *Gentleman's Quarterly*, February 2007.

Grodin, Charles. *I Like It Better When You're Funny: Working in Television and Other Precarious Adventures*. New York: Random House, 2002.

Falk, Peter. *Just One More Thing: Stories from My Life*. New York: Carroll & Graf, 2006.

Stewart, Sara. "Hot Seat: John Leguizamo." *New York Post*, December 3, 2006.

Gam, Rita. *Actors: A Celebration*. New York: St. Martin's Press, 1988.

Affleck, Ben. "Smokin' Affleck." *People*, February 12, 2007.

Brando, Marlon, and Robert Lindsey. *Songs My Mother Taught Me*. New York: Random House, 1994.

Wood, Sam Taylor. "Daniel Craig." *Interview*, July 2007.

Hauer, Rutger, and Patrick Quinlan. *All These Moments*. New York: HarperCollins, 2007.

Zucker, Carole. *In the Company of Actors*. New York: Theatre Arts Books, 2001.

Sella, Marshall. "The Two Jakes." *Gentleman's Quarterly*, February 2007.

Sutherland, Donald. "Interview: Donald Sutherland (Pride & Prejudice)." By Deven Faraci. CHUD.com. http://chud.com/articles/articles/4997/1/INTERVIEW-DONALD-SUTHERLAND-PRIDE--PREJUDICE/Page1.html.

Zucker, Carole. *In the Company of Actors*. New York: Theatre Arts Books, 2001.

Jenkins, Garry. *Harrison Ford: Imperfect Hero*. New York: Birch Lane Press, 1998.

Farrow, Mia. *What Falls Away: A Memoir*. New York: Nan A. Talese, Doubleday, 1997.

Malden, Karl, and Carla Malden. *When Do I Start?* New York: Simon & Schuster, 1997.

Obst, Lynda. "Kate Winslet—Interview." *Interview*, November 2000.

Berenger, Tom. "Tom Berenger Interview." By Staci Wilson. About.com.

"Acting is a challenge." *Maclean's*, February 11, 2002.

Deneuve, Catherine. *Close Up and Personal: The Private Diaries of Catherine Deneuve*. Translated by Polly McLean. New York: Pegasus Books, 2005.

Hirschberg, Lynn. "The Empathist." *New York Times*, November 13, 2005.

Granville-Barker, Harley. "The Heritage of the Actor." *The Quarterly Review*, July 1923.

Keegan, Rebecca Winters. "From Real Life with Love." *Time*, August 13, 2007.

Garr, Teri, and Henriette Mantel. *Speedbumps: Flooring It Through Hollywood*. New York: Penguin, 2005.

Bacall, Lauren. *Now*. New York: Alfred A. Knopf, 1994.

Stewart, Patrick. "Patrick Stewart" By Kathy Henderson. Broadway.com. http://www.broadway.com/Patrick-Stewart/broadway_news/564809.

Jenkins, Garry. *Harrison Ford: Imperfect Hero*. New York: Birch Lane Press, 1998.

Widmark, Richard. "Richard Widmark." By Adrian Wooton. BFI. http://www.bfi.org.uk/features/interviews/widmark.html.

Malden, Karl, and Carla Malden. *When Do I Start?* New York: Simon & Schuster, 1997.

Penn, Sean. "The Total Film Interview—Sean Penn." By Hilary Morgan. Total Film. http://www.totalfilm.com/features/the-total-film-interview-sean-penn.

Grodin, Charles. *It Would Be So Nice if You Weren't Here*. New York: Morrow, 1989.

Walken, Christopher. "Christopher Walken Uncut." By Jeffrey Gordinier. Details.com. http://men.style.com/details/features/landing?id=content_5751.

Collins, Joan. *Past Imperfect*. New York: Simon & Schuster, 1984.

Jenkins, Garry. *Harrison Ford: Imperfect Hero*. New York: Birch Lane Press, 1998.

Farrell, Mike. *Just Call Me Mike: A Journey to Actor and Activist*. New York: Akashic Books/RDV Books, 2007.

Patterson, John. "Total Recall." *The Guardian*, September 3, 2005.

Kingsley, Ben. "Interview with Ben Kingsley." By Ray Pride. Movie City News. http://www.moviecitynews.com/Interviews/kingsley.html.

Garner, Jack. "Steven Spielberg and Tom Hanks." *Rochester Democrat and Chronicle*, July 24, 1998.

Grodin, Charles. *If I Only Knew Then . . .: Learning from Our Mistakes*. New York: Springboard Press, 2007.

Christon, Lawrence. "Art of Deception." *Daily Variety*, November 1, 2007.

ON THE STAGE AND THE SCREEN

Andrews, Julie. "Q & A with Julie Andrews." By Kathy Connell. *Screen Actor*, Winter 2006.

Wallach, Eli. *The Good, the Bad, and Me: In My Anecdotage*. Orlando: Harcourt, 2005.

Martin, Guy. "Harrison Ford and the Jungle of Gloom." *Esquire*, October 1986.

Leguizamo, John. *Pimps, Hos, Playa Hatas, and All the Rest of My Hollywood Friends*. New York: HarperCollins, 2006.

Douglas, Kirk. *Parade*, December 30, 1990.

Gordon, Lois, and Alan Gordon. *American Chronicle*. New York: Atheneum, 1987.

Lawrence, Vicki, and Marc Eliot. *Vicki!: The True-Life Adventures of Miss Fireball*. New York: Simon & Schuster, 1995.

Alterman, Glenn. *An Actor's Guide—Making It in New York City*. New York: Allworth Press, 2002.

Raab, Scott. "What I've Learned: Christopher Walken." *Esquire*, June 2009.

Schatz, Howard, and Beverly J. Ornstein. *In Character: Actors Acting*. New York: Bulfinch, 2006.

Schatz, Howard, and Beverly J. Ornstein. *In Character: Actors Acting*. New York: Bulfinch, 2006.

Deneuve, Catherine. *Close Up and Personal: The Private Diaries of Catherine Deneuve*. Translated by Polly McLean. New York: Pegasus Books, 2005.

Turner, Kathleen. "Two Summer Shoot-outs." *Life*, June 1985.

Hill, Harry. *A Voice for the Theatre*. New York: Holt, Rinehart and Winston, 1985.

Benson, Sheila. "Laurence Fishburne: the Actor who puts Risk before Reputation—and Proves why that Matters so Much." *Interview*, January 1995.

Rogers, Will. *The Autobiography of Will Rogers*. New York: Lancer Books, 1963.

York, Michael. *Accidentally On Purpose: An Autobiography*. New York: Simon & Schuster, 1991.

Lee, Marc. "Patrick Stewart, Captain of His Own Destiny." *The Telegraph* (London), July 24, 2006.

Shewey, Don. "Patriot Acts." *Village Voice*, November 17, 2004.

Brussell, Eugene E. *Webster's New World Dictionary of Quotable Definitions*. New York: Prentice Hall, 1970.

Rossellini, Isabella. *Some of Me*. New York: Random House, 1997.

Leguizamo, John. *Pimps, Hos, Playa Hatas, and All the Rest of My Hollywood Friends*. New York: HarperCollins, 2006.

Raab, Scott. "Penn." *Esquire*, September 2007.

Clooney, George. "George Clooney and Catherine Zeta-Jones Discuss *Intolerable Cruelty*." By Rebecca Murray. About.com. http://movies.about.com/cs/intolerablecruelty/a/intcrueltyint.htm.

Zucker, Carole. *In the Company of Actors*. New York: Theatre Arts Books, 2001.

Jefferson, Joseph. *The Autobiography of Joseph Jefferson*. New York: The Century Company, 1889.

Baker, Fred, and Ross Firestone. *Movie People: At Work in the Business of Film*. New York: Lancer Books, 1973.

DiCaprio, Leonardo. "Show Stoppers: Premiere Salutes the Finest Performances of 2006." Interviews conducted by various. *Premiere*, January 2007.

Sella, Marshall. "The Two Jakes." *Gentleman's Quarterly*, February 2007.

Callon, Michael Feeney. *Anthony Hopkins: A Three Act Life*. London: Robson Books, 2005.

Jackson, Samuel L. "Samuel L. Jackson Interview." By Staci Wilson. About.com.

Grant, Hugh. "Hugh Grant Charms His Way Through 'Bridget Jones: The Edge of Reason.'" By Rebecca Murray. About.com. http://movies.about.com/od/bridgetjonesedgereason/a/bridgethg103004.htm.

Brando, Marlon, and Robert Lindsey. *Songs My Mother Taught Me*. New York: Random House, 1994.

Olivier, Laurence. *Confessions of an Actor*. Philadelphia, PA: Coronet Books, 1982.

Scacchi, Greta. "Greta Scacchi Interview." By Staci Wilson. About.com.

Goldstein, Toby. *William Hurt: The Actor and His Work*. New York: St. Martin's Press, 1987.

Macy, William H. "Interview: William H. Macy for Everyone's Hero and Bobby." By Paul Fischer. Dark Horizons. http://www.darkhorizons.com/news/6363/interview-william-h-macy-for-everyone-s-hero-and-bobby.

Lamb, Rose Marie. "Nathan the Crazy Man, Otto the Wild Man, Hamlet the Brooding Man. Kevin Kline, Hell of an Actor, Man!" *Arts & Entertainment*, April 1993.

Froelich, Paula, Bill Hoffman, and Corynne Steindler. Page Six, *New York Post*, February 18, 2007.

Dench, Judi. "Judy Dench" By Philipp Hoschka. Film Scouts. http://www.filmscouts.com/scripts/interview.cfm?File=3065.

McKellen, Ian. Interview by Lizo. *Newsround*, CBBC, May 1, 2003.

Adams, Cindy. "One Lady Who's Not Invisible." *New York Post*, March 15, 2007.

Kalbacker, Warren. "20 Questions with Hugh Jackman." *Playboy*, February 2002.

Arnest, Mark. "Redgrave's Curtain Call." *The (Colorado Springs) Gazette,* July 21, 2006.

Granger, Farley, and Robert Calhoun. *Include Me Out: My Life from Goldwyn to Broadway*. New York: St. Martin's Press, 2007.

Hauer, Rutger, and Patrick Quinlan. *All These Moments*. New York: HarperCollins, 2007.

Artaud, Antonin. *The Theatre and Its Double*. Translated by Mary Caroline Richards. New York: Grove Press, 1958.

Kalbacker, Warren. "20 Questions with William H. Macy." *Playboy*, December 2003.

Connell, Kathy. "Q & A with Julie Andrews." *Screen Actor*, Winter 2006.

Dukakis, Olympia. "An Interview with Olympia Dukakis" By Jan Nargi. Broadwayworld. com. http://broadwayworld.com/article/An_Interview_with_Olympia_ Dukakis_20070110.

Horowitz, Simi. "Crashing the Gates." *Back Stage East,* June 21–27, 2007.

Hirschberg, Lynn. "Buttoned Up." *New York Times Magazine*, January 15, 2006.

Rand, Ronald, and Luigi Scorcia. *Acting Teacher of America: A Vital Tradition*. New York: Allworth Press, 2007.

Mitchell, Elvis. "Brad Pitt." *Interview*, March 2007.

Shewey, Don. *Caught in the Act: New York Actors Face to Face*. New York: NAL Books, 1986.

Strasberg, Lee. *A Dream of Passion*. New York: Penguin, 1987.

Duffy, Karen. "Genius—Walter Matthau." *Interview*, December 1994.

Goldstein, Toby. *William Hurt: The Actor and His Work*. New York: St. Martin's Press, 1987.

Tennant, Laura. "Olivia Williams: Growing Up in Public." *The Independent* (London), April 25, 2003.

Caine, Sir Michael. "Cockney Rebel." By Amy Reiter. Salon.com. http://dir.salon.com/story/ent/movies/int/2003/12/15/caine/index.html.

ON DOING TELEVISION: SOAPS, SITCOMS, EPISODICS, AND LIVE BROADCASTS

Baker, Fred, and Ross Firestone. *Movie People: At Work in the Business of Film*. New York: Lancer Books, 1973.

Granger, Farley, and Robert Calhoun. *Include Me Out: My Life from Goldwyn to Broadway*. New York: St. Martin's Press, 2007.

Verini, Bob. "Latenight Killed the Vaudeo Star." *Daily Variety*, May 30, 2007.

Jones, Tommy Lee. "Interview with American Actor Tommy Lee Jones." By Elmer Kelton. BNET. http://findarticles.com/p/articles/mi_m1285/is_n6_v25/ai_17231480/.

Malden, Karl, and Carla Malden. *When Do I Start?* New York: Simon & Schuster, 1997.

Rorke, Robert. "Close Call." *New York Post*, July 22, 2007.

Brooks, Albert. "Wise Guy: Albert Brooks." By Steve Kurutz. Details.com. http://men.style.com/details/wiseguy/landing?&id=content_4706.

Stiller, Jerry. "Quotebook." *Variety*, April 9, 2007.

Bankhead, Tallulah. *Tallulah: My Autobiography*. New York: Harper & Brothers, 1952.

Campbell, Bruce. *If Chins Could Kill: Confessions of a B Movie Actor*. New York: LA Weekly Books, 2002.

Jones, Tommy Lee. "Interview with American Actor Tommy Lee Jones." By Elmer Kelton. BNET. http://findarticles.com/p/articles/mi_m1285/is_n6_v25/ai_17231480/.

Hart, Kitty Carlisle. "Thesp was a Gameshow Staple." By *Variety* staff, with contributions from the Associated Press. *Variety*, April 19, 2007.

Reeve, Christopher. *Still Me*. New York: Random House, 1998.

Granger, Farley, and Robert Calhoun. *Include Me Out: My Life from Goldwyn to Broadway*. New York: St. Martin's Press, 2007.

Grammer, Kelsey. *So Far . . .* New York: Dutton, 1995.

McClanahan, Rue. *My First Five Husbands . . . And the Ones that Got Away*. New York: Broadway Books, 2007.

Garr, Teri, and Henriette Mantel. *Speedbumps: Flooring it Through Hollywood*. New York: Penguin, 2005.

ON DEALING WITH THE UPS AND DOWNS OF FAME AND FORTUNE

Harmetz, Aljean. "On Screen, Winona Ryder Comes of Age." *New York Times*, December 9, 1990.

"They Had A Very Good Year." *People*, November 27, 2006.

Douglas, Kirk. *Let's Face It: 90 Years of Living, Loving, and Learning*. Hoboken, NJ: John Wiley & Sons, 2007.

Duvall, Robert. The Biography Channel, various air dates.

Goldman, Andrew. "Matt Damon." *Details*, December 2006.

Litwak, Mark. *Reel Power*. New York: Morrow, 1986.

Penn, Sean. "The Total Film Interview—Sean Penn." By Hilary Morgan. Total Film. http://www.totalfilm.com/features/the-total-film-interview-sean-penn.

West, Kevin. "Stayin' Alive." *W*, July 2007.

Junod, Tom. "Angelina Jolie Dies for Our Sins." *Esquire*, July 2007.

Tucker, Redd. "Hotseat: Matthew McConaughey." *New York Post*, December 17, 2006.

Tucker, Reed. "Hot Seat: John Malkovich." *New York Post*, March 18, 2007.

Baker, Fred, and Ross Firestone. *Movie People: At Work in the Business of Film*. New York: Lancer Books, 1973.

Walker, Alexander. *Audrey: Her Real Story*. New York: St. Martin's Press, 1994.

Young, Josh. "Renee Revealed." *Life: America's Weekend Magazine*. January 5, 2007.

Fonseca, Nicholas. "The Truman Show." *Entertainment Weekly*, October 7, 2005.

Hayes, Helen. *On Reflection: An Autobiography*. New York: M. Evans & Co., 1968.

Garfield, Simon. "Daniel Radcliffe." *Details*, August 2007.

Snyder, Gabriel. "What, Me Worry?" *W*, August 2007.

Brooks, Louise. *Lulu in Hollywood*. New York: Knopf, 1982.

Allen, Fred. *Much Ado About Me*. New York: Amereon, Ltd., 1956.

Edwards, Anne. *Judy Garland*. New York: Simon & Schuster, 1975.

Caine, Michael. *Acting in Film: An Actor's Take on Movie Making*. New York: Applause, 1990.

Crook, Marshall. "Buzzworthy: Eddie Admits Flops." *amNewYork*, December 14, 2006.

Lawrence, Vicki, and Marc Eliot. *Vicki!: The True-Life Adventures of Miss Fireball.* New York: Simon & Schuster, 1995.

Klein, Steven. "Brad Pitt." *Details*, October 2007.

Alda, Alan. *Things I Overheard While Talking to Myself.* New York: Random House, 2007.

Fox, Michael J. *Lucky Man: A Memoir.* New York: Hyperion, 2002.

Farrow, Mia. *What Falls Away: A Memoir.* New York: Nan A. Talese, 1997.

Curtis, Nick. "Philip Seymour Hoffman and His Band." *Evening Standard* (London), September 18, 2008.

Goldman, Andrew. "Matt Damon." *Details*, December 2006.

Katz, David. "Girl On Fire." *Esquire*, February 2007.

Hatcher, Teri. *Burnt Toast and Other Philosophies of Life.* New York: Hyperion, 2006.

Schneller, Johanna. "Julia Roberts." *Gentleman's Quarterly*, February 1991.

Marill, Alvin H. *Katharine Hepburn.* New York: Galahad Books, 1973.

Bardin, Brantley. "Idol Chatter." *Premiere*, January 2007.

Pacino, Al, and Lawrence Grobel. *Al Pacino: In Conversations with Lawrence Grobel.* New York: Simon Spotlight Entertainment, 2006.

Seventh Annual Screen Actors' Guild Awards, originally broadcast on March 11, 2001, by TNT.

Raab, Scott. "The Quiet One." *Esquire*, March 2007.

Brando, Marlon, and Robert Lindsey. *Songs My Mother Taught Me.* New York: Random House, 1994.

Turan, Kenneth. "Harrison Ford wants to be alone." *Gentleman's Quarterly*, November 1986.

Sager, Mike. "What I've Learned: Faye Dunaway." *Esquire*, August 1999.

Redgrave, Michael. *In My Mind's I: An Actor's Autobiography.* New York: Viking, 1983.

York, Michael. *Accidentally On Purpose: An Autobiography.* New York: Simon & Schuster, 1991.

Daly, John. "60 Seconds: Philip Seymour Hoffman." *Metro UK,* March 2, 2006.

Rose, Tiffany. "Q The Interview: John Cusack." *The Independent* (London), December 23, 2001.

Keegan, Rebecca Winters. "Q & A: Mark Wahlberg." *Time*, February 26, 2007.

Junod, Tom. "Angelina Jolie Dies for Our Sins." *Esquire*, July 2007.

Rawls, Eugenia. *Tallulah: A Memory.* Birmingham: University of Alabama, 1979.

"Acting is a challenge." *Maclean's*, February 11, 2002.

Logan, Brian. "I Can Do Anything." *The Guardian*, January 2, 2001.

Tucker, Reed. "Hot Seat: John Malkovich." *New York Post*, March 18, 2007.

Garfield, Simon. "Daniel Radcliffe." *Details*, August 2007.

Irons, Jeremy. "Actor/Risk-taker." Academy of Achievement interview, conducted on October 27, 2000, in London, England.

O'Toole, Lesley. "An Oscar? No thanks." *Daily Express* (UK), February 6, 2000.

Loren, Sophia. "Interview with Sophia Loren." By Larry King. *Larry King Live*, CNN, December 2, 2004.

Heath, Chris. "The Hardass." *Gentleman's Quarterly*, March 2005.

Fischoff, Stuart. "Clint Eastwood." *Psychology Today*, January/February 1993.

Penn, Sean. "The Total Film Interview—Sean Penn." By Hilary Morgan. Total Film. http://www.totalfilm.com/features/the-total-film-interview-sean-penn.

DePaulo, Lisa. "Intentional Man of Mystery."*Gentleman's Quarterly*, August 2007.

Martin, Steve. Interview by Terry Gross. *Fresh Air*, WHYY, October 21, 2005. Originally taken from the *New York Times*.

ON HOLLYWOOD, BROADWAY, AND SHOW BUSINESS

"Hepburn: She's the Best." *Los Angeles Times*, November 24, 1974.

Baldwin, Alec. "Interview: Alec Baldwin for 'The Last Shot.'" By Paul Fischer. Dark Horizons. http://www.darkhorizons.com/interviews/70/alec-baldwin-for-the-last-shot-.

Brussell, Eugene E. *Webster's New World Dictionary of Quotable Definitions*. New York: Prentice Hall, 1970.

Gordinier, Jeff. "Wiseguy: Christopher Walken." *Details*. August 2007.

"Dennis Hopper." Translated from the French. *Paris Match*, August 18, 1995.

Nicholson, Jack. "Jack Nicholson: Something's Gotta Give." By Nev Pierce. BBC. http://www.bbc.co.uk/films/2004/02/05/jack_nicholson_somethings_gotta_give_interview.shtml.

Arkin, Alan. Interview by Stephen Capen. *Futurist Radio Hour*, KUSF-FM, October 10, 1995.

Peterson, Mark. "Brooke Shields in Chicago." *Entertainment Weekly*, October 14, 2005.

Baker, Fred, and Ross Firestone. *Movie People: At Work in the Business of Film*. New York: Lancer Books, 1973.

Sessums, Kevin. "Johnny Be Good." *Vanity Fair*, February 1997.

Macy, William H. "Interview: William H. Macy for Everyone's Hero and Bobby." By Paul Fischer. Dark Horizons. http://www.darkhorizons.com/news/6363/interview-william-h-macy-for-everyone-s-hero-and-bobby.

Brussell, Eugene E. *Webster's New World Dictionary of Quotable Definitions*. New York: Prentice Hall, 1970.

McClanahan, Rue. *My First Five Husbands . . . And the Ones that Got Away*. New York: Broadway Books, 2007.

Clarkson, Wensley. *Mel Gibson: Living Dangerously*. New York: Thunder's Mouth Press, 1998.

Mortimer, Emily. "Michael Sheen." *Interview*, July 2007.

Barker, Andrew. "The Hired Gun Now Does the Hiring." *Variety*, March 15, 2007.

Widmark, Richard. "Richard Widmark." By Adrian Wooton. BFI. http://www.bfi.org.uk/features/interviews/widmark.html.

Mitchell, Elvis. "Brad Pitt." *Interview*, March 2007.

Littleton, Cynthia. "Manager Cast Wide Influence." *Daily Variety*, Monday, August 11, 2008.

MacLaine, Shirley. *My Lucky Stars: A Hollywood Memoir*. New York: Bantam, 1995.

Bonin, Liane. "Walken Talkin.'" EW Online, August 23, 1999. http://www.ew.com/ew/article/0,,84606,00.html

Artaud, Antonin. *The Theatre and Its Double*. Translated by Mary Caroline Richards. New York: Grove Press, 1958.

Viner, Brian. "The Thursday Interview; Olympian Ambition; Olympia Dukakis." *The Independent* (London), November 1, 2001.

Ford, Harrison. "Harrison Ford—Interview." By Calista Flockhart. *Interview*, June 2003.

Green, Jesse. "Billy Crudup: Almost Infamous." *New York Times*, October 10, 2004.

Bacon, Kevin. "Kevin Bacon Talks About Death Sentence." By Rebecca Murray. About. com. http://movies.about.com/od/deathsentence/a/deathkb072807.htm.

Keitel, Harvey. "Risky Business." By Ron Dicker. Salon.com. http://www.salon.com/05/features/keitel.html.

Yamagata, Rachael. "Mandy Moore." *Interview*, September 2007.

Wallach, Eli. *The Good, the Bad, and Me: In My Anecdotage*. Orlando: Harcourt, 2005.

Neal, Patricia. *As I Am: An Autobiography*. New York: Simon & Schuster, 1988.

York, Michael. *Accidentally On Purpose: An Autobiography*. New York: Simon & Schuster, 1991.

Cohen, David S. "Precision Performer." *Daily Variety,* November 1, 2007.

Schneller, Johanna. "Where's Johnny?" *Premiere*, December 1999.

Hoffman, Barbara. "Scripts, not names, add Sheen to roles." *New York Post*, April 23, 2007.

Raab, Scott. "What I've Learned: Rip Torn." *Esquire*, May 1, 2001.

Kalbacker, Warren. "20 Questions with William H. Macy." *Playboy*, December 2003.

Dern, Bruce, Christopher Fryer, and Robert Crane. *Things I've Said, But Probably Shouldn't Have*. Hoboken, NJ: John Wiley & Sons, 2007.

Jenkins, Garry. *Harrison Ford: Imperfect Hero*. New York: Birch Lane Press, 1998.

Cohen David S. "AFI Honoree Arrives with Desire Intact." *Daily Variety*, June 7, 2007.

Wienir, David, and Jodie Langel. *Making It on Broadway: Actor's Tales of Climbing to the Top*. New York: Allworth Press, 2004.

Edwards, Gavin. "The Two Faces of Aaron Eckhart." *Men's Journal*, August 2007.

McClanahan, Rue. *My First Five Husbands . . . And the Ones that Got Away*. New York: Broadway Books, 2007.

Leigh, Danny. "Desert Island Risks." *The Guardian,* January 12, 2001.

Hepburn, Katharine. *Me: Stories of My Life*. New York: Random House, 1991.

Alterman, Glenn. *An Actor's Guide—Making It in New York City*. New York: Allworth Press, 2002.

Lawrence, Vicki, and Marc Eliot. *Vicki!: The True-Life Adventures of Miss Fireball*. New York: Simon & Schuster, 1995.

Hedegaard, Erik. "The Devil Inside." *Details*, December 1993.

Wilder, Gene. *Kiss Me Like A Stranger: My Search for Love and Art*. New York: St. Martin's Press, 2005.

York, Michael. *Accidentally On Purpose: An Autobiography*. New York: Simon & Schuster, 1991.

Hoffman, Philip Seymour. "Philip Seymour Hoffman Interview—The Savages." Posted by Frosty. Interview based on a transcript of a roundtable interview. Collider.com. http://www.collider.com/entertainment/article.asp/aid/6189/cid/13/tcid/1.

Falk, Peter. *Just One More Thing: Stories from My Life*. New York: Carroll & Graf, 2006.

Ullmann, Liv. *Choices*. New York: Knopf, 1984.

ON GENDER DIFFERENCES AND AGING IN THE BIZ

Sobchack, Vivian. "Party of 5: Straight Talk on the Challenges and Triumphs of Aging in Hollywood." *Screen Actor,* Summer 2007.

Hodgins, Paul. "A Mature 'Father.'" *Orange County Register,* April 5, 1998.

Bacall, Lauren. *Now.* New York: Alfred A. Knopf, 1994.

Zucker, Carole. *In the Company of Actors.* New York: Theatre Arts Books, 2001.

"Are We Invisible?" *Screen Actor,* Summer 2007.

MacLaine, Shirley. *My Lucky Stars: A Hollywood Memoir.* New York: Bantam, 1995.

Sobchack, Vivian. "Party of 5: Straight Talk on the Challenges and Triumphs of Aging in Hollywood." *Screen Actor,* Summer 2007.

Adams, Cindy. "One Lady Who's Not Invisible." *New York Post,* March 15, 2007.

Iley, Chrissy. "Red Alert." *The Observer* (UK), July 6, 2008.

Shewey, Don. *Caught in the Act: New York Actors Face to Face.* New York: NAL Books, 1986.

Bracco, Lorraine. *On the Couch.* New York: Berkley Books, 2007.

Cavendish, Dominic. "Shakespeare is Coursing Through Me." *The Telegraph* (London), July 16, 2007.

Norton, Edward. "Jonah Hill." *Interview,* September 2007.

Blanks, Tim. "Monica Bellucci." *Interview,* September 2007.

Conita, Jenny. "Mind Game." *W,* September 2007.

Litwak, Mark. *Reel Power.* New York: Morrow, 1986.

Wallach, Eli. *The Good, the Bad, and Me: In My Anecdotage.* Orlando: Harcourt, 2005.

Edwards, Anne. *A Remarkable Woman: A Biography of Katharine Hepburn.* New York: William Morrow & Co., 1985.

Tichler, Rosemarie, and Barry Jay Kaplan. *Actors at Work.* New York: Faber and Faber, 2007.

Nathan, George Jean. *The Theatre in the Fifties.* New York: Knopf, 1953.

Neal, Patricia. *As I Am: An Autobiography.* New York: Simon & Schuster, 1988.

Ullmann, Liv. *Choices.* New York: Knopf, 1984.

Rose, Cynthia. "Maid in Heaven: Mary Elizabeth Mastrantonio." *Entertainment Weekly,* 1991.

Davis, Bette, and Michael Herskowitz. *This 'N That.* New York: Putnam, 1987.

Hellicar, Michael. "'Nobody asks me to strip anymore' says Scorchy Greta Scacchi." *Daily Mail,* August 1, 2008.

Bacall, Lauren. *Now.* New York: Alfred A. Knopf, 1994.

Washington, Denzel. "The Total Film Interview—Denzel Washington." By Jan Janssen. Total Film. http://www.totalfilm.com/features/the-total-film-interview-denzel-washington.

Witchel, Alex. "At Home with Anthony Quinn; the Number It Takes to Tango." *New York Times,* July 6, 1995.

MacLaine, Shirley. *My Lucky Stars: A Hollywood Memoir.* New York: Bantam, 1995.

Sobchack, Vivian. "Party of 5: Straight Talk on the Challenges and Triumphs of Aging in Hollywood." *Screen Actor,* Summer 2007.

Tennant, Laura. "Olivia Williams: Growing Up in Public." *The Independent* (London), April 25, 2003.

Curtis, Nick. "Philip Seymour Hoffman and His Band." *Evening Standard* (London), September 18, 2008.

Hatcher, Teri. *Burnt Toast and Other Philosophies of Life*. New York: Hyperion, 2006.

Redgrave, Lynn. "Lynn Redgrave." By Eric Grode. Broadway.com. http://www.broadway.com/Lynn-Redgrave/broadway_news/514904.

Alda, Alan. *Things I Overheard While Talking to Myself*. New York: Random House, 2007.

ON AWARDS AND AWARDS CEREMONIES

Verini, Bob. "Latenight Killed the Vaudeo Star." *Daily Variety*, May 30, 2007.

Benfer, Amy. "The Reluctant Matinee Idol." *Metro*, December 15–17, 2006.

Adams, Cindy. "Cindy Adams at the Oscars." *New York Post*, February 26, 2007.

Eleventh Annual Screen Actors' Guild Awards, originally broadcast on February 5, 2005, on TNT.

Wilson, Rita. "What Happened to Taking Fashion Risks?" *Harper's Bazaar*, February 2007.

Tucker, Reed. "Hot Seat: John Malkovich." *New York Post*, March 18, 2007.

Adams, Cindy. "Cindy Adams at the Oscars." *New York Post*, February 26, 2007.

Katz, David. "Bond is Dead." *Esquire*, September 2006.

O'Toole, Lesley. "An Oscar? No thanks." *Daily Express* (UK), February 6, 2000.

David Rooney. "'Spring' Awakens Tonys Love." *Daily Variety*, June 11, 2007.

Mortimer, Emily. "Don Cheadle." *Interview*, July 2007.

Levine, Stuart, and Mia McNiece. "Elated Nominees Toast Their Colleagues and Emmy Announcers." *Daily Variety*, July 18, 2008.

Heath, Chris. "The Hardass." *Gentleman's Quarterly*, March 2005.

Clooney, George. "George's World." *People*, November 27, 2006.

Sella, Marshall. "The Antihero." *Gentleman's Quarterly*, September 2007.

Stewart, Jimmy. "Jimmy Stewart." Interviewed by Joan Bakewell. BFI. http://www.bfi.org.uk/features/interviews/stewart.html.

Curtis, Nick. "Philip Seymour Hoffman and His Band." *Evening Standard* (London), September 18, 2008.

ON GETTING TYPECAST

Dowd, Maureen. "Testing Himself." *New York Times Magazine*, September 28, 1986.

"They Had A Very Good Year." *People*, November 27, 2006.

MacLaine, Shirley. *Out on a Limb*. New York: Bantam Books, 1983.

Colman, David. "Eva." *Interview*, August 2008.

Witchel, Alex. "At Home with Anthony Quinn; the Number It Takes to Tango." *New York Times*, July 6, 1995.

Rodriquez, Brenda. "Q&A with William Fichtner." *People*, November 27, 2006.

Harmetz, Aljean. "America's Sweetheart Lives." *New York Times*, March 28, 1971.

Pruzan, Todd. "Wiseguy." *Details*, December 2006.

Sager, Mike. "What I've Learned: Jaime Pressly." *Esquire*, January 2007.

Johnson, Richard. "I'm Not Scary." *New York Post*, January 8, 2007.

Chambers, Andrea. "Bio—Christopher Plummer." *People*, March 15, 1982.

Sorvino, Mira. "Mira Sorvino." By Graham Fuller. BNET. http://findarticles.com/p/articles/mi_m1285/is_n11_v25/ai_17632992/.

Cusack, John. "The Total Film Interview—John Cusack." By Jamie Graham. Total Film. http://www.totalfilm.com/features/the-total-film-interview-john-cusack.

Bridges, Jeff. "The Total Film Interview—Jeff Bridges" By Simon Crook. Total Film. http://www.totalfilm.com/features/the-total-film-interview-jeff-bridges.

Kaylin, Lucy. "Alec Baldwin's Blue Period." *Gentleman's Quarterly*, October 2006.

Adams, Cindy. "Jessica Tandy: The Classiest Star." *Ladies' Home Journal*, April 1991.

Dowd, Maureen. "Testing Himself." *New York Times Magazine*, September 28, 1986.

Sager, Mike. "What I've Learned: Jaime Pressley." *Esquire*, January 2007.

Kaylin, Lucy. "Alec Baldwin's Blue Period." *Gentleman's Quarterly*, October 2006.

Katz, David. "Girl On Fire." *Esquire*, February 2007.

Hoffman, Barbara. "Great Brit." *New York Post*, January 14, 2007.

Liu, Lucy. "Lucy Liu for 'Codename: The Cleaner.'" By Paul Fischer. Dark Horizons. http://www.darkhorizons.com/interviews/670/lucy-liu-for-codename-the-cleaner-.

Stewart, Sara. "Hot Seat: Diane Keaton." *New York Post*, January 28, 2007.

Bussel, Rachel Kramer. "Hot Seat: Gene Wilder." *New York Post*, February 25, 2007.

Patterson, John. "Total Recall." *The Guardian*, September 3, 2005.

Kane, Michael. "A Kid, Again." *New York Post*, February 25, 2007.

Corsello, Andrew. "Christopher Walken Must Die." *Gentleman's Quarterly*, March, 2000.

Hawke, Ethan. "Ethan Hawke." By Robert Elms. BFI. http://www.bfi.org.uk/features/interviews/hawke.html.

Georgiades, William. "The Class Clown." *New York Post*, July 15, 2007.

Borgnine, Ernest. "Ernest Borgnine." By Clyde Jeavons. BFI. http://www.bfi.org.uk/features/interviews/borgnine.html.

Nicholson, Jack. "Jack Nicholson Talks About 'About Schmidt.'" By Rebecca Murray and Fred Topel. About.com. http://movies.about.com/library/weekly/aaaboutschmidtinta.htm.

Lyall, Sarah. "In Stetson or Wig, He's Hard to Pin Down." *New York Times*, November 4, 2007.

Compiled from Times Wires, including the Associated Press. "Zorba the Greek star Anthony Quinn Dies." *St. Petersburg Times*, June 4, 2001.

Steinberg, Jacques. "An Unmistakable Face, And a Name You Can't Quite Place." *New York Times,* July 23, 2006.

Hedegaard, Erik. "The Devil Inside." *Details*, December 1993.

Lawrence, Vicki with Eliot, Marc. *Vicki!: The True-Life Adventures of Miss Fireball.* New York: Simon & Schuster, 1995.

Dreifus, Claudia. "The Progressive." *Interview*, May 1993.

ON THE IMPORTANCE OF KEEPING IT REAL AND HAVING A LIFE

Gruwald, Lisa. "Robin Williams Has a Big Premise." *Esquire*, June 1989.

Clooney, George. "George's World." *People*, November 27, 2006.

Buschel, Bruce. "The Rise and Rise of Michael J. Fox." *Gentleman's Quarterly*, December 1986.

Hawn, Goldie, and Wendy Holden. *Goldie: A Lotus Grows in the Mud*. New York: The Berkley Publishing Group, 2005.

Benedetti, Robert L. *The Actor At Work*. New York: Prentice Hall, 1986.

"They Had A Very Good Year." *People*, November 27, 2006.

"They Had A Very Good Year." *People*, November 27, 2006.

Siegel, Micki. "I Can't Do It Alone." *New York Post*, June 28, 2007.

Sager, Mike. "What I've Learned: Forest Whitaker." *Esquire*, January 2007.

Terry, Wallace. "Don't Be Afraid to Fail." *Parade*, November 17, 1991.

Fussman, Cal. "What I've Learned: Dick Van Dyke." *Esquire*, February 2007.

Leguizamo, John. Hennessy advertisement. *Gentleman's Quarterly*, January 2007.

Warner, Kara. "A Free Spirit in the Buff." *amNewYork*, January 16, 2007.

Adams, Cindy. "One Lady Who's Not Invisible." *New York Post*, March 15, 2007.

Kalbacker, Warren. "20 Questions with Hugh Jackman." *Playboy*, February 2002.

Collins, Joan. *Past Imperfect*. New York: Simon & Schuster, 1984.

Fonseca, Nicholas. "The Truman Show." *Entertainment Weekly*, October 7, 2005.

Power, Matthew. "Hollywood's Gentleman Explorer." *Men's Journal*, January 2007.

Burton, Hal. *Great Acting*. New York: Bonanza Books, 1967.

Yakir, Dan. "Mel's Flights of Fancy." *Entertainment Weekly*, August 17, 1990.

Hagen, Uta, and Haskel Frankel. *Respect for Acting*. Hoboken, NJ: Wiley Publishing, 1973.

Walker, Alexander. *Audrey: Her Real Story*. New York: St. Martin's Press, 1994.

Gazzara, Ben. *In the Moment: My Life as an Actor*. New York: Carroll & Graf Publishers, 2004.

Tulich, Katherine. "Kyra Sedgwick." *Redbook*, August 2008.

Fries, Laura. "Nervously Accepting Accolades." *Daily Variety*, January 4, 2008.

Ullmann, Liv. *Choices*. New York: Knopf, 1984.

Hawn, Goldie, and Wendy Holden. *Goldie: A Lotus Grows in the Mud*. New York: The Berkley Publishing Group, 2005.

Power, Matthew. "Hollywood's Gentleman Explorer." *Men's Journal*, January 2007.

Terry, Wallace. "It's Hard For Me To Play The Guy Next Door." *Parade*, September 21, 1997.

Smith, Dinitia. "A Very Private Actor On a Very Private Author." *New York Times*, December 2, 1996.

Tulich, Katherine. "Third Degree with Kevin Bacon." *Redbook*, August 2008.

Caine, Sir Michael. *A Tribute to Cary Grant*. PBS, November 1990.

Brown, Laura. "Drew Confessions." *Harper's Bazaar*, February 2007.

Fussman, Cal. "What I've Learned: Dick Van Dyke." *Esquire*, February 2007.

Bogart, Stephen Humphrey. *Bogart: In Search of My Father*. New York: Penguin, 1995.

Sisto, Jeremy. "Jeremy Sisto Interview." By Staci Wilson. About.com.

Stewart, Sara. "Hot Seat: Diane Keaton." *New York Post*, January 28, 2007.

Adams, Cindy. "Celebs Look Into Their Fathers' Eyes." *New York Post*, June 15, 2007.

Schneller, Johanna. "Where's Johnny?" *Premiere*, December 1999.

Hoffman, Philip Seymour. "Philip Seymour Hoffman Gets Candid" By Steve Kroft. CBS News. http://www.cbsnews.com/stories/2006/02/16/60minutes/main1323924.shtml.

Bracco, Lorraine. *On the Couch*. New York: Berkley Books, 2007.

McKellen, Sir Ian. "Interview With Sir Ian McKellen." By Michael Jensen. AfterElton. http://www.afterelton.com/archive/elton/people/2006/9/mckellen.html.

Adams, Cindy. "Celebs Look Into Their Fathers' Eyes." *New York Post*, June 15, 2007.

Johnson, Richard and staff. "No Help Needed." Page Six, *New York Post*, June 28, 2007.

Mitchell, Elvis. "Brad Pitt." *Interview*, March 2007.

Riley, Jenelle. "The Young Vet." *Back Stage East*, March 20, 2008.

Chase, Chevy. "Wise Guy: Chevy Chase." By Pete Wells. Details.com. http://men.style.com/details/wiseguy/landing?id=content_4628.

Schneller, Johanna. "Where's Johnny?" *Premiere*, December 1999.

Mottram, James. "Julianne Moore Interview." *Marie Claire*, July 14, 2008.

Junod, Tom. "Angelina Jolie Dies for Our Sins." *Esquire*, July 2007.

Dukakis, Olympia, and Emily Heckman. *Ask Me Again Tomorrow*. New York: Perennial, 2003.

Index